Other People's Blood

OTHER PEOPLE'S BLOOD

U.S. Immigration Prisons in the Reagan Decade

ROBERT S. KAHN

WestviewPress

A Division of HarperCollins*Publishers*

For Jennifer, Carlos, Alex, and Cecilia

Copyright © 1996 by Westview Press, A Division of HarperCollins Publishers, Inc.

Published in 1996 in the United States of America by Westview Press, 5500 Central Avenue, Boulder, Colorado, 80301-2877, and in the United Kingdom by Westview Press, 12 Hid's Copse Road, Cumnor Hill, Oxford OX2 9JJ.

Kahn, Robert S.
   Other people's blood : U.S. immigration prisons in the Reagan
decade / Robert S. Kahn
     p.   cm.
   Includes bibliographical references (p.) and index.
   ISBN 0-8133-2445-9 (alk. paper). — ISBN 0-8133-2446-7 (pbk.: alk.
paper)
     1. Refugees—Government policy—United States. 2. Immigrants—
Government policy—United States. 3. United States—Emigration and
immigration—Government policy. 4. Prisons—United States.
5. United States—Politics and government—1981–1989. I. Title.
JV6601.K35 1996
365'.4—dc20   96-9119
                                                   CIP

This book was typeset by Letra Libre, 1705 Fourteenth Street, Suite 391, Boulder, CO 80302.

10   9   8   7   6   5   4   3   2   1

CONTENTS

Researchers have already cast much darkness on the subject, and if they continue their investigations we shall soon know nothing at all about it.

—*Mark Twain*

Author's Note

There are no composite scenes, interviews, or characters in this book. Refugees who did not want to be identified have been given a name here that may or may not be their own. Thus, an interview with José in the Laredo immigration prison was conducted at the time and place cited, but the man's name may not have been José. All the refugees interviewed for this book knew that the author was writing a book and consented that their story be told. All people identified by full names have given permission for their use.

All articles cited from the *Brownsville Herald*, the *Boston Globe*, *National Catholic Reporter*, the *Baltimore Sun*, and *Newsday* are by the author unless noted otherwise.

The lawsuits *Orantes-Hernandez v. Smith*, *Orantes-Hernandez v. Meese*, and *Orantes-Hernandez v. Thornburgh* are one and the same case. The title of the suit was amended to substitute the name of the new defendant. This is also the case with *American Baptist Churches v. Meese* and *American Baptist Churches v. Thornburgh*.

ACKNOWLEDGMENTS

This book owes its existence to Barbara Ellington, my editor at Westview Press. Thanks also to her assistant, Patricia Heinicke, and to Jon Brooks, of Letra Libre.

Of the three thousand Salvadoran and Guatemalan refugees I met, I am reasonably certain I saved one man's life. The Salvadoran government would have killed him if he were deported, and the only reason he wasn't deported is that I helped him get out of an immigration prison. This book is also for him, and for others who must be nameless.

Throughout the 1980s, a tiny number of prison workers worked much harder than I did and saved many more lives. Among them are Lisa Brodyaga, Patrick Hughes, Clare Cherkasky, Jonathan T. Jones, Jonathan Moore, Jack Elder, Peter Upton, Salvador Colon, Niels Frenzen, Meg Burkhardt, Thelma Garcia and her family, Jonathan Fried, Nancy Kelly, Tracy Jones, Danny Katz, Mark Schneider, Dora Jones, Karen Pettit, Sheila Neville, Peter Schey, Lucas Guttentag, Sam Williamson, Jeff Larsen, and the late James Cushman.

INTRODUCTION

When California voters approved Proposition 187—the "Save Our State" initiative that would deny public education and health care to undocumented immigrants—they voted for a bill that even its authors acknowledged was unconstitutional. This state-rights initiative, approved by 59 percent of California voters in November 1994, came less than four years after the U.S. Department of Justice acknowledged in federal court that by denying fair trials to immigrants and by deporting refugees seeking political asylum to countries at war, it had violated its own laws and the Geneva Conventions more than 100,000 times.[1]

The very name of the group that sponsored Proposition 187—SOS—is a measure of the hysteria attendant upon the issue of immigration to the United States today. After voters approved Proposition 187, federal courts blocked it immediately.[2] The initiative will cost California millions of dollars to litigate, tens of millions of dollars to enforce, and billions in lost federal aid if the courts permit it—which they will not. And even if it were constitutional, it is difficult to see how denying education to children or health care to the sick would benefit the state or the nation.

For more than a decade, the debate about immigration to the United States has been framed in terms that are dishonest and willfully amnesiac. By one measure, the anti-immigration forces have already won. No politician in either party today is prepared to say a good word about immigration. Yet the recent history of immigration to the United States, and the U.S. role in it, are a blank page in our national memory.

The U.S. Immigration and Naturalization Service was the foremost promoter of undocumented immigration during the 1980s. INS officials, directed by the U.S. attorney general, encouraged Nicaraguans to settle here, issued them work permits, and protected them from deportation, regardless of the weakness of their claims to political asylum.[3] These same officials directed that Salvadoran and Guatemalan refugees with solid claims for asylum be imprisoned, denied asylum, and deported. It is no accident that the framers of Proposition 187—former INS Commissioner

Alan Nelson and former INS Western District Commissioner Harold Ezell—were also chief enforcers of the immigration policies that violated U.S. laws. The U.S. Justice Department conceded this in the federal lawsuits *American Baptist Churches v. Thornburgh* and *Orantes-Hernandez v. Thornburgh*. That these men led a voter initiative that is unconstitutional on its face, and that California's voters approved it overwhelmingly, is a sad measure of the misunderstanding of the nature of immigration, the misguided judgments about it, and the abuse and misconduct that have characterized U.S. immigration policy for more than a decade.

Issues related to human migration are virtually endless: economic growth and its limits, labor and workers' rights, language, culture, education, wars and civil wars, health, and the problems attendant upon each. But as immigration moves to the top of the national agenda, we should remember that most of us came here as immigrants. Blaming social and economic problems on immigrants may be convenient, but it doesn't explain anything, and it doesn't solve the problems.

Whether or not the impacts of illegal immigration are on balance negative, the fear of immigrants is useful to politicians. Proposition 187— the centerpiece of Republican Governor Pete Wilson's successful reelection campaign in 1994—would require public school teachers and health workers to denounce undocumented children and people seeking medical care to the INS, to be deported. Failure to report suspected undocumented people would be a violation of the law. Similar laws against the "failure to denounce" were the chief vehicle by which Joseph Stalin sent millions to the gulag. Yet liberal Democrats fear, rightly, that the remnants of their union constituency might resent lawmakers who are "soft on immigrants," whose cheap labor may hurt unions and depress wages. Thus the debate over immigration has been used to divide the body politic while it distorts national values. This noisy denunciation of immigration disguises a national ignorance of our calculated abuse of immigrants. "Fear, the worst of political counselors, has come to supersede thought."[4]

The United States did have an immigration crisis in the 1980s—a crisis partly of its own making. Civil wars raging in El Salvador and Guatemala, fueled largely by U.S. military assistance in training and arming dictatorships, drove 1 million refugees to the United States. The U.S.-sponsored Contra war in Nicaragua had the same effect. More than 1 million Central Americans fled their homelands to escape the first large-scale aerial warfare in this hemisphere.[5]

Federal courts responded to the crisis slowly, by judicial decrees. Congress responded with inadequate legislation, such as the Boland Amendments that putatively prohibited federal funding for the Contra war in

Nicaragua. But the brouhaha that spawned Proposition 187 was not a crisis. It was an artificial prolongation of it, by people who helped create it, in search of political gain. Proposition 187, and other repressive measures like it, are a belated response to a decade that has ended.

This book describes what happened to the Salvadoran and Guatemalan refugees who came to the United States in the 1980s, fleeing war. It is based on interviews with more than 3,000 Central American refugees in the United States and on the author's work as a legal assistant in four immigration prisons. I have omitted from it practically all of the tortures these people suffered in El Salvador and Guatemala: the Salvadoran math teacher who was raped and tortured so badly by police that she bled from her eyes; the veterinarian's assistant who was forced to watch as guards raped and tortured his wife in Mariona prison; the nurse who fled El Salvador when she saw two co-workers eviscerated in the street. I have concentrated instead on what happened to these people once they reached the United States.

Our country may be, as former President Reagan said, "the last, best hope for man on earth," or it may not. Undocumented immigrants may drain off citizens' tax dollars, or they may pay more in taxes than they receive in benefits—or perhaps U.S. citizens break even. A high rate of immigration may exacerbate divisions in U.S. society, or may strengthen it. A multilingual society may be more expensive to support, or multilingualism may be a normal part of the human condition. Controlling immigration may be vital to national security, or it may be insignificant. Most of this, however, is not susceptible to proof, and it is not my intention to take a position on any of it. What I do know is that reality cannot be wished away. The 1 million Central American immigrants about whom this book is written exist; they live here now. Their children will live here for generations. How they got here, why they came here, and what happened to them on the streets and in U.S. immigration prisons are a part of our history, whether we like it or not, and it is continuing, whether we admit it or not.

The destructive results of this decade of government misconduct on a generation of people, and especially the children of Central America, have not yet entered our national memory and may never enter it. But we must acknowledge it, and we must remember it. If Germany were to pass exclusionary race laws today, the world would be outraged. Yet U.S. lawmakers of both parties continue writing "tougher" immigration laws, fueling hatred and fear of immigrants, as though the lies, abuses, and murders of the 1980s had never happened and that the violence is not continuing, above all, on the U.S.-Mexican border.

Unpleasant as it is to learn that one's government has committed war crimes, it is shameful and dangerous to pretend it never happened.

Notes

1. *American Baptist Churches et al. v. Richard L. Thornburgh, Gene McNary, and James Baker III,* U.S. District Court, Northern District of California. Stipulated Settlement Agreement, December 14, 1990. Thornburgh was U.S. attorney general at the time; McNary was INS commissioner; Baker was secretary of state.

2. Backers of Proposition 187 acknowledged during the election campaign that sections of the law violated the U.S. Constitution and the 1982 U.S. Supreme Court order in *Plyler v. Doe,* which states that public schools must accept children regardless of their immigration status. In the final days of the campaign, a spokeswoman for the Save Our State committee told the author, "perhaps we could get a waiver" of certain sections of the U.S. Constitution, if the measure should pass.

In December 1995, U.S. District Judge Marianna Pfaelzer found major sections of Proposition 187 unconstitutional, including sections that forbade primary schooling for undocumented children. Pfaelzer also struck down the so-called squealer provisions requiring teachers to report students suspected of illegal immigration status, and she ruled that medical and social benefits can be withheld only if no federal money is involved in the program.

Pfaelzer wrote in a seventy-two-page ruling:

> The California voters' overwhelming approval of Proposition 187 reflects their justifiable frustration with the federal government's inability to enforce the immigration laws effectively. No matter how serious the problem may be, however, the authority to regulate immigration belongs exclusively to the federal government and state agencies are not permitted to assume authority. The state is powerless to enact its own scheme to regulate immigration or to devise immigration regulations which run parallel to or purport to supplement the federal immigration laws.

League of United Latin American Citizens v. Gov. Pete Wilson, CV 95-7569, U.S. District Court, Central District of California, Los Angeles.

3. On July 7, 1987, U.S. Attorney General Edwin Meese ordered the Immigration and Naturalization Service to stop deporting Nicaraguans and to grant work permits to all Nicaraguans who applied for political asylum in the United States. The INS announced the new policy in a press release on July 8, 1987. The *New York Times* reported the policy change on July 9, 1987, in an Associated Press dispatch, "Immigration Rules Are Eased for Nicaraguan Exiles in U.S." See "Brownsville," note 5.

4. This sentence is taken from Samuel Eliot Morison and Henry Steele Commager's *The Growth of the American Republic,* vol. I, p. 563; it describes the attitude of the Southern United States toward abolitionists, on the eve of the Civil War.

5. The U.S. Immigration and Naturalization Service reported that 501,299 Salvadorans and Guatemalans were admitted or apprehended between fiscal years 1981 and 1991; this number does not include apprehensions for fiscal year 1985. However, INS statistics are unreliable. On February 22, 1996, INS spokesman Daniel Kane in Washington, D.C., told the author that apprehensions by nationality were not recorded until 1987. Yet the author has INS statistics on apprehensions of Salvadorans and Guatemalans dating back to 1977.

In interviews with Border Patrol intelligence officials in all nine sectors on the U.S.-Mexican border in 1989, officers estimated the Border Patrol arrests from one-third to one-tenth of all undocumented entrants. Assuming, generously, that the INS managed to count 50 percent of all Salvadoran and Guatemalan immigrants in the 1980s, immigration from those two countries totalled one million during the decade.

The INS did not create a statistical category for apprehensions of Nicaraguans until 1987, by which time Nicaraguan immigration surpassed Guatemalan and equalled or exceeded immigration from El Salvador. Nicaraguans were grossly undercounted. The INS located 3,290 deportable Nicaraguans in fiscal year 1988; in that year the agency located 9,246 deportable Guatemalans and 14,322 deportable Salvadorans. Yet with the generous provisions offered to Nicaraguans, actual immigration from that country greatly exceeded immigration from Guatemala that year and probably exceeded immigration from El Salvador. The INS statistics on immigration from Nicaragua are skewed because most Nicaraguans were not formally arrested or formally admitted but were permitted to remain in the United States under terms of Attorney General Meese's July 1987 order.

The INS reported that 64,318 Nicaraguans were admitted between fiscal years 1980 and 1991; 15,016 Nicaraguans were apprehended between fiscal years 1987 and 1991; and 116,118 Nicaraguan asylum applications were filed with district directors between fiscal years 1981 and 1990. This partial total of 195,452 Nicaraguans counted by the INS during the decade represents a small fraction of total immigration from Nicaragua: Many political asylum applications are submitted for an entire family, so one application may represent husband, wife, and children; furthermore, most political asylum applications are not filed with an INS district director but before an immigration judge.

Most immigration prison workers agree that the number of Nicaraguans who entered the country between 1986 and 1990 equalled or exceeded the number of Salvadorans who entered the country between 1981 and 1985. These conservative estimates based on INS statistics yield a total of 1.5 million to 2 million Central American immigrants entering the United States during the 1980s. "Monthly Report of Deportable Aliens Found in U.S. by Nationality, Status at Entry," U.S. Immigration and Naturalization Service, fiscal years 1977–1984; "Immigrants Admitted by Region and Selected Country of Birth, Fiscal Years 1980–94," INS Office of Public Affairs, telefax communication to author, February 22, 1996; "Deportable Aliens Located by Status at Entry and Region and Selected Country of Nationality, Fiscal Years 1988–1989," U.S. Immigration and Naturalization Service; Harlingen INS District Director E. Michael Trominski to author, April 3, 1992, in response to author's request under the Freedom of Information Act; and author's handwritten notes from INS statistics compiled by the Refugee Policy Group in Washington, D.C., February 1985.

THE BORDER IS A THIRD COUNTRY

*The Lempa River had been turned into a ceme-
tery. It was full of bodies of students and murdered workers. They would tie heavy things to
the corpses to keep them from rising. In order
to eat fish, it was necessary to season them
with garlic, because of the stink of human
flesh. People would clean fish and find human
fingers in them, and in spite of this, they ate
them, because there was nothing else to eat.*

—Salvadoran refugee in Los Angeles, 1984

SALE OF HUMAN BEINGS is a multimillion-dollar industry on the U.S.-Mexican border. Veronica Coronado, a pretty nineteen-year-old Honduran traveling legally in Mexico, got half a block from the Matamoros bus station when she was abducted by city policemen at 4 A.M. on February 22, 1989. "We were looking for a place to stay, and the police were at the bus station, waiting," said her boyfriend Wendell, twenty-three, who was abducted with her.

Two squad cars followed Wendell and Veronica for half a block. "Then we were captured by the city police. They asked for money, for papers. They told us, 'Well, if you have money we can make an arrangement now. If you give us the money we can let you go, and we can help you cross the border.' That's what the police said."

They didn't have enough money. The police shook them down, then took them to a windowless wood and tar paper shack at 12 El Carmen Street in a poor neighborhood less than a mile from the Rio Grande. There the police sold them to an alien-smuggler, or *coyote*, for fifty dollars apiece. Raul Torres, the coyote, said he would hold them there until they each came up with $350. For $350, Torres said, he would take them to the United States.

There were twenty-four Central Americans crammed into the tiny shack when Torres bought Wendell and Veronica. Armed guards and Torres's M-16 discouraged thoughts of escape. Across the street was Police Station 25, a tiny white, concrete building with blue trim in front of a cemetery. At the north end of the cemetery was the Rio Grande. Torres told his hostages he paid the city police $1,000 a month for protection. He fed the hostages beans and bread twice a day.

All twenty-six people in the tiny shack on El Carmen Street had been robbed and sold to Torres by Mexican police or customs or immigration officers. They all wanted to go to the United States. Hostages with no money were put to forced labor, building a "magnificent" house for Torres at the end of a block in *Fraccionamiento Rio,* an exclusive section of new houses on an eight-block strip of land that juts into the Rio Grande one mile east of Gateway International Bridge to Brownsville. Many of Torres's neighbors in *Fraccionamiento Rio* were officers in the Mexican Judicial Police.

I met Wendell at Casa Oscar Romero, a refugee shelter run by the Catholic Diocese of Brownsville just outside the city limits. Torres had taken Wendell across the Rio Grande and told him to find $700 if he wanted to see Veronica again. Wendell crossed the river at 3 A.M. on an inner tube tied to a rope hauled by a man on the other side. Wendell didn't know where Torres's shack was. All he had was Torres's telephone number written on a tiny scrap of paper. He told me his story and asked me not to print it until he got Veronica out. He was afraid of what Torres might do to her. He didn't know where he would get the $700.

Nine other residents of Casa Romero had been held hostage by Torres. They had all been kidnapped by Mexican officials and sold for $50 apiece, U.S. currency. River Escoto, a seventeen-year-old Nicaraguan, said he was held in the shack for one month. "The Mexican police arrested me at three in the evening on the street," Escoto said. "They took me to the coyote." Escoto had no money and no relatives in the United States who could send him money, so Torres put him to work for fourteen days building the two-story gray concrete house, "making bricks, carrying sand, carrying concrete."

José, a thirty-six-year-old Nicaraguan from Masaya, said he was kidnapped by Mexican immigration officers who robbed him and sold him to Torres. He had been in the house for four days when Wendell and Veronica arrived. "There were twenty-three in the house with me," José said. "Some people said they had been there for three months because they did not have the money to pay."

Matamoros city police arrested and robbed Sandra and Roberto Nuñez, a married Honduran couple, and sold them to Torres for $100. The Nuñez family wired Torres $700 by Western Union to get them released. He took them in a blue van to his house by the river. At 3 A.M., another man took them to the Rio Grande. They crossed on the inner tube, walked for "fifty or sixty minutes" on the U.S. side, then Torres picked them up in the blue van and dropped them off three blocks from Casa Romero.

Torres was one of hundreds of coyotes who worked with Mexican police to smuggle Central Americans into the United States. Victor Clark Alfaro, a director of the Binational Center for Human Rights in Tijuana, interviewed smuggling bosses who worked the bus station there in early 1989. He reported that one gang paid Mexican police, immigration, and customs officers $100,000 a month for protection. Another gang coughed up $20,000 a month.[1]

Things didn't get much better for Central Americans when they reached the United States. Professional con men, unscrupulous attorneys, corrupt immigration agents, even high school students made thousands of dollars selling refugees phony documents. It's easy to steal from refugees: They are scared, they are carrying their life's savings, they don't know the law, they don't know the language, and because they are undocumented, they have no one to turn to after they've been cheated.

And there were thousands of them. Through the winter and spring of 1988–1989, more than 2,000 Central Americans entered the United States illegally each week near Brownsville.[2] The few roads north were watched by the Border Patrol. Because the Immigration and Naturalization Service (INS) prisons had long since run out of space for new arrivals, the INS arrested refugees, released them, and told them to stay in South Texas. If they tried to leave the Harlingen INS District—the four counties of southmost Texas, one of the poorest areas in the United States—they would be rearrested and put into an immigration prison somewhere with a $10,000 bond. So the refugees wandered the streets of Brownsville.

Two hundred slept at Casa Romero. More than 300 slept under cardboard boxes, plastic garbage bags, under bushes, and in holes in the ground in a field across a dirt road from the shelter. Another 350 had moved into the Amber Motel, an abandoned and condemned two-story building at the north end of a strip of hotels on Central Boulevard. As night fell, refugees filled the courtyards of other hotels on Central Boulevard. Those with money rented rooms. It was not unusual for the Border Patrol to arrest fifty or sixty refugees at a time—then release them to the streets. And across the river in Matamoros, a gang of drug dealers led by a charismatic homosexual named Adolfo de Jesus Constanzo was buying drugs from Mexican Judicial Police and torturing, sacrificing, and dismembering people in search of magical powers to protect their drug smuggling.[3] By the time I helped Veronica get out of the Port Isabel immigration prison twenty-five miles northeast of Brownsville, Constanzo's gang had been chased out of Matamoros to a hideout in Mexico City. "I'm glad I was held hostage and then put in prison," Veronica told me in a tiny interview room at the Port Isabel prison. "At least I wasn't out on the streets."

By March 1989, one-quarter of a million people had been killed in civil wars in Central America, most of them by their own governments, most of them by U.S.-supplied weapons: 70,000 dead in El Salvador, 140,000 dead in Guatemala, 60,000 dead in Nicaragua. As President Reagan had said, the U.S. border was out of control—but the Brownsville refugee crisis was a problem of Reagan's own making.[4]

On July 7, 1987, as the Contra war against Nicaragua collapsed in the wake of the Iran-Contra scandal, Attorney General Edwin Meese ordered the Immigration and Naturalization Service to stop deporting Nicaraguans and to grant all Nicaraguan political asylum applicants permits to work in the United States.[5] Not surprisingly, Nicaraguan immigration mushroomed. By September 1988, for the first time, more undocumented

Nicaraguans than Salvadorans were arrested in South Texas.[6] This posed a political problem for Ronald Reagan and George Bush.

The 1988 presidential election was five weeks away. The Iran-Contra hearings had been a major embarrassment for the Reagan administration, and key players in the scandal were awaiting trial. Lieutenant Colonel Oliver North's defense for his role in the arms deals was that the Democratic Congress had "turned its back" on the Contras. After the Contras were routed, thousands of them began entering the United States near Brownsville. Because of Meese's order, Nicaraguans arrested in Brownsville were allowed to apply for political asylum, given work permits, and set free: Most went to Miami. Salvadorans and Guatemalans, however, continued to be arrested, given an Order to Show Cause why they should not be deported, and told to stay in South Texas.[7]

To defend Salvadorans and Guatemalans, whose countries were still engulfed in civil wars, refugee defense groups were preparing a class action lawsuit charging the U.S. Department of Justice with discriminatory enforcement of law.[8] In an election year, Reagan's Justice Department had three choices: It could go to court, probably lose, and let a federal judge determine U.S. refugee policy. The federal judge who would hear the case in Brownsville was Filemon Vela. Vela had presided over trials in which juries convicted sanctuary workers Stacey Merkt and Jack Elder, who, because of their religious beliefs, had sheltered Salvadoran refugees at Casa Romero. Merkt served time in prison while she was pregnant; Elder was sentenced to prison but had his sentence reduced to community service and time in a halfway house. A U.S. attorney would have to persuade Judge Vela that friends of Nicaraguans could commit acts for which Merkt and Elder had been convicted and that Nicaraguans could have privileges in the United States that Salvadorans and Guatemalans were denied—the rights to work and travel.

The second option was just as unpleasant: Meese could deny Nicaraguans the right to work and confine them in South Texas with the Salvadorans and Guatemalans—the Reagan administration could "turn its back" on the Contras. That would be difficult with Oliver North's trial approaching, George Bush running for president, the Sandinistas still in control of Nicaragua, and the Reagan-Bush administration's defense for the Iran-Contra arms sales that the deals were necessary because the Democratic Congress had abandoned the Contras.

The only other possibility was to give Salvadorans and Guatemalans the right to submit an application for political asylum in South Texas and to work and travel in the United States. In September 1988, Reagan and Meese opened the gates: They gave Salvadorans and Guatemalans the same rights as Nicaraguans. The policy lasted until George Bush was elected. Less than one month later—on December 5, 1988—INS Deputy Commissioner James Buck rescinded Meese's 1987 order. He ordered the INS to stop granting work permits to political asylum applicants, to confine them to the INS district where they sought asylum, to speed up asylum decisions, and to lock up everyone whose claim was denied.[9]

The Justice Department began planning the biggest detention project since it had imprisoned Japanese Americans during World War II. The official capacity of Port Isabel immigration prison was expanded from 425 to 10,000.[10] Enormous revival-style tents were erected in the prison. The INS sent more than 500 officers to South Texas and made plans to interview 400 asylum applicants a day and decide 95 percent of the cases "within three hours of the completion of the interview."[11]

Class action lawsuits delayed but could not stop the detention policy, which began February 21, 1989. That day, 633 Central Americans waited in line to apply for political asylum at the Port Isabel prison. Virtually all of them were denied asylum, arrested, and incarcerated. Two days later, only ten people showed up at the prison to ask for asylum.[12] The INS said the tide of immigration had been "turned around." *New York Times* correspondent Larry Rohter reported that Central Americans were "abandoning shelters or detention centers in Brownsville or Bayview" and "swimming (south) across the Rio Grande from Texas" because of the new INS policy.[13] The national media left Brownsville. The INS had won.

It was a great story, but it wasn't true. Border Patrol arrests in the McAllen Sector rose from 6,474 in February 1989 to 10,838 in March. Arrests of "other than Mexicans"—who are overwhelmingly Central Americans in South Texas—rose from 2,351 in February to 3,786 in March.[14] And the only "refugee shelter" in Bayview was the Port Isabel immigration prison, which refugees cannot "abandon" without a pair of wire cutters and a head start. Rohter—whose story set the line that the national media followed—had been in Brownsville for less than half a day when he wrote his story. If he saw anyone "swimming south across the Rio Grande," it was probably Mexican domestic workers or shoppers who had spotted a Border Patrol van approaching. You can see them any day from the Gateway Bridge. Tourists and visiting journalists get excited about it, but it's just another day in Brownsville.

The South Texas detention project had two real effects: It swept the refugees from the streets, which made the national and international media lose interest, and it intensified abuses of law inside Port Isabel prison and in South Texas immigration courts. The South Texas detention project was the culmination of the Reagan and Bush administrations' refugee policies. In December 1991, a federal judge found that those policies so grossly abused the human and legal rights of refugees that they violated the Geneva Conventions. U.S. District Judge Robert Peckham ruled in *American Baptist Churches v. Thornburgh* that every Salvadoran and Guatemalan who had been denied political asylum in the 1980s had been tried unfairly. The U.S. Justice Department signed a consent decree admitting it.[15] Yet what had happened in the Port Isabel prison was no different from what went on in any other immigration prison on the southern border of the United States.

The Hot Gulag

The Immigration and Naturalization Service calls its prisons "service and processing centers"—an antiseptic name for an enormous prison system that systematically terrorized refugees and violated U.S. laws throughout the 1980s. From 1984 to 1987, I worked as a legal assistant in immigration prisons at Port Isabel and Laredo, Texas; at Oakdale, Louisiana; and at Florence, Arizona. I entered the prisons at El Paso and Houston with attorneys and interviewed refugees there; the INS refused to allow me entrance to the prison at El Centro, California.[16] My clients were Salvadorans and Guatemalans who had fled war to seek asylum in the United States. Inside these U.S. immigration prisons refugees were beaten and drugged by guards; refugee children were strip-searched and sexually propositioned by guards; refugees were put into solitary confinement for as long as seventy-seven days with no hearing and no explanation of the charges against them, or with no charges against them; refugees' mail was stolen and photocopied to be used as evidence against them; guards stole money orders, checks, and cash from refugees' mail; refugees' phone calls to their attorneys were tapped; they were denied access to lawyers; their court testimony was purposely mistranslated; they were deported illegally; they were tortured; they were force-fed drugs and injected with drugs; INS officials gave information from refugees' asylum applications to the Central Intelligence Agency and the Defense Intelligence Agency; and U.S. officials conspired with the Salvadoran military to deport refugees to their death.

These were not aberrations or abuses of the immigration system. This was how the system operated under the administrations of Ronald Reagan and George Bush. I saw it. I saw the bullet and bayonet wounds, and the bruises from guards' beatings. I saw children put into solitary confinement for standing too close to a bulletproof, wire-reinforced prison window. I saw teenage rape victims become hysterical after being repeatedly strip-searched. I saw clients who were disoriented and bruised from being beaten and drugged on an expanding metal bed in a solitary confinement cell. I saw clients ordered deported for "failing to appear" in court because prison guards would not take them from their cells to the courtroom inside the prison. I heard the testimony of Salvadoran clients with bullet wounds mistranslated so badly that simple statements of fact were turned on their heads, and I heard the judge cite the mistranslated statements as he ordered the refugees deported. I took testimony from refugees who had been beaten and robbed by prison guards and from witnesses to the robberies and beatings, and I presented the testimony and photographs of the wounds to the prison director—to no avail.

The worst abuses were inflicted in the prisons run by contractors: Laredo and Oakdale. The U.S. Justice Department began to privatize the immigration prison system at the same time the Reagan White House privatized the war against Nicaragua. The Laredo prison opened in March 1985 on a contract with the Corrections Corporation of America. It was the first U.S. immigration prison built to imprison infants and children—"with the cribs right in the cells," the INS district director said.[17] All prisoners, including babies, had their body cavities searched before and after each meeting with a legal representative. The only way to avoid being strip-searched was not to ask to see a lawyer.

One year after opening the prison at Laredo, the INS opened its prison at Oakdale on a contract with the U.S. Bureau of Prisons. Guards at Oakdale strip-searched, tapped phones, violated the mail, and tortured people. Cuban detainees burned the prison down in 1987. The next year Brownsville was awash with refugees, and the INS opened the tent city at Port Isabel.

From Fantasy Toward Chaos

The Reagan and Bush administrations' illegal and inhuman treatment of refugees stemmed from an ideology so at odds with reality that reality barely mattered in formulating policy decisions. As a result, many policies exacerbated the problems they were meant to solve. The South Texas detention project was the fifth stage of the U.S. refugee crisis that originated in the civil wars in Central America. The unfortunate U.S. foreign policy there—which propped up a succession of repressive governments through massive arms sales and foreign aid—became a domestic problem because Central America is close enough to the United States that hundreds of thousands of refugees could enter the country during Reagan's first term. The State Department estimated that 500,000 Salvadorans had entered the United States illegally by 1984—10 percent of El Salvador's population.[18] The refugee problem was compounded by immigration policies that were contradictory, that sometimes invited illegal immigration, and that often were simply illegal.

The first wave of Central American refugees began arriving in the late 1970s as political repression in El Salvador reached levels unapproached since the massacre of 1932, when 10,000 to 30,000 farmers, union members, and students were killed in a matter of weeks.[19] Then, in 1980, the Ninety-sixth Congress passed Public Law 96-210—the 1980 Refugee Act—

which gave political refugees putative legal rights in the United States. The 1980 Refugee Act changed U.S. law—but not policy—in a fundamental way. Under the Immigration and Nationality Act of 1952, people fleeing from communist nations could be granted political asylum in the United States. The 1980 Refugee Act intended to do away with the ideological distinction: People fleeing a repressive regime that was not communist became eligible for political asylum too. Anyone who had been persecuted in his or her homeland or who had "a well-founded fear of persecution on account of race, religion, nationality, membership in a particular social group, or political opinion" became eligible for political asylum in the United States.[20]

President Jimmy Carter signed the act on March 17, 1980. Ten months later, Ronald Reagan became president. He immediately increased military aid to El Salvador and fired Ambassador Robert White, who had been a strong proponent of human rights. Death squad killings increased, and so did immigration to the United States.

The crisis in U.S. immigration prisons began in 1981, when Attorney General William French Smith decreed that undocumented people who applied for political asylum under the 1980 Refugee Act should be detained until a decision was made in their case.[21] U.S. immigration prisons immediately filled beyond capacity—and refugees continued to come.

President Reagan had said he would "roll back communism," and he used El Salvador as a test case. As Marxists, the Salvadoran guerrillas were the United States' ideological enemies. Salvadorans who claimed persecution, therefore, must be communists themselves and were not to be admitted into the United States. The policy was stated publicly on several occasions. Maurice C. Inman Jr., general counsel for the INS in Washington, D.C., told the *Los Angeles Times* in June 1986: "All of those persons who have been detained will lose their asylum cases. All of them. Otherwise they would not be detained."[22] E. Michael Trominski, director of the INS office in Mexico City and later director of the INS Harlingen District, said bluntly, "We won't let FMLN types into the United States as refugees. ... They don't fit into the program."[23]

The policies described by Inman and Trominski were illegal, yet they remained in effect throughout Reagan's two terms. Administrative fiat overrode the law. The only chance an imprisoned refugee had in the United States was to get a lawyer. And the lawyer's only hope was delay. It was impossible for a Salvadoran in a U.S. immigration prison to win political asylum in the United States until the Iran-Contra scandal broke. It never happened.[24] All an immigration attorney could do was delay deportation or try to get clients out of jail. So the immigration prisons filled up with Salvadorans and Guatemalans who were willing to stay in jail in the United States—anything to avoid being deported. With no place to put newly arrested refugees, the Border Patrol and INS began systematically denying Salvadorans the right to legal counsel—by threats, lies, beatings, sexual abuse, drugs, and occasionally by torture—anything to get a refugee to sign INS form I-274, which waives the right to seek asylum and requests "voluntary repatriation" to Central America.[25]

U.S. Citizens Respond

With death squad murders in El Salvador averaging 500 a month,[26] with U.S. immigration prisons full and repression increasing along the U.S.-Mexican border, the United States entered the second stage of the refugee crisis. In the summer of 1982, U.S. citizens began organizing to protest Reagan's Central American and refugee policies. The resistance took two forms: legal pressure and civil disobedience.

In South Texas, immigration attorney Lisa Brodyaga witnessed the enormous abuses inflicted on refugees in the Port Isabel immigration prison and the refugees' need for legal help. In 1982 she organized a nonprofit law office, Proyecto Libertad (Project Liberty), the first law office in the United States dedicated to securing legal rights for imprisoned Central American refugees. Other lawyers and religious groups opened law offices to represent refugees imprisoned in Miami, Florida; El Centro, California; and Florence, Arizona. When the INS opened new prisons at Houston and Laredo, in Texas, and in Oakdale, Louisiana, prison projects sprang up to represent refugees there too.

When refugees gained access to legal representation, it increased pressure on the entire INS system: It takes longer to deport a person who is represented by counsel. Many clients of Proyecto Libertad stayed in Port Isabel prison for more than a year, fighting deportation. Unrepresented refugees could be deported in less than a month. With the prisons overflowing and no place to put new arrivals, the refugees who had lawyers not only used up bed space, they slowed up courtroom proceedings. Court dockets were overloaded, and it took the INS longer to call each Salvadoran's case.

With more pressure on the streets and in the prisons, the INS and Border Patrol increased the physical and legal abuse of refugees to try to keep them out of the U.S. legal system. As the abuses became flagrant, Brodyaga and others filed class action lawsuits against the INS, and federal judges ordered the INS to obey the law and its own policies and to stop the abuses. Two major lawsuits were filed against the INS in 1982: *Nuñez v. Boldin,* based on abuses of Salvadorans in Port Isabel prison, and *Orantes-Hernandez v. Smith,* based on abuses in the prison at El Centro, California.

Nuñez v. Boldin, a class action lawsuit, was filed against Harlingen INS District Director Hal Boldin. The named plaintiffs were four Salvadorans and a Guatemalan who were detained at the Port Isabel detention center. In that case, the INS conceded it had prohibited detained refugees access to legal material and to pencils and paper; had seized legal documents and personal papers from refugees and had read them; did not always notify refugees' attorneys when their clients had court hearings at the prison; did not inform Salvadorans or Guatemalans of their right to remain silent or to seek political asylum until after an INS officer had interrogated the refugee and asked him to waive his right to asylum; did not make INS forms available in Spanish, except for the form to request repatriation to Central America; and restricted attorneys' and paralegals' access to clients.

U.S. District Judge Filemon B. Vela issued restraining orders against the INS on December 4, 1981, and January 5, 1982. Vela ordered the INS to stop those coercive practices, to grant Salvadorans and Guatemalans access to legal material, to inform them of their right to request political asylum, and to give legal workers, including paralegals, access to detained refugees.

The *Nuñez v. Boldin* injunction granted those rights only to Salvadorans and Guatemalans detained in the jurisdiction of the U.S. Court of Appeals for the Fifth Circuit, which includes South Texas. Three months later, U.S. District Judge David Kenyon, in the Ninth Circuit of Central California, granted a similar injunction in *Orantes-Hernandez v. Smith* to protect refugees detained at El Centro immigration prison. Testimony in the Orantes case showed that immigration officials in El Centro INS District had arrested a Salvadoran woman who had seen her daughter raped by Salvadoran soldiers after they forced her to watch them execute her husband. To prevent her from applying for asylum, U.S. immigration agents forced Valium down her throat, then guided her hand to force her signature on form I-274, waiving her right to seek asylum. Judge Kenyon told the INS attorney, "You don't treat people like that. I wouldn't do that to the worst criminal who came into this courtroom."[27] He ordered the INS to send agents to El Salvador to bring the woman back to testify in his court, and he put her under a protective order to keep the INS away from her.

The INS and Border Patrol systematically violated the terms of *Orantes-Hernandez* and *Nuñez v. Boldin* throughout the decade, but refugees' increased access to legal counsel did slow the deportation mill. The legal pressure eventually won refugees some legal rights, but the legal struggle was all but invisible to the public, proceeding as it did in remote prisons. The most visible sign of citizens' opposition to the Reagan administration's Central American policies was the civil disobedience organized by church and peace activists that came to be known as the Sanctuary Movement.

On March 23, 1982, Reverend John Fife, minister of Southside Presbyterian Church in Tucson, sent a letter to the INS and to U.S. Attorney General William French Smith stating that he and his congregation would violate the law the next day by granting a Central American refugee sanctuary in Southside Presbyterian Church. Within three years, more than 200 churches joined the Sanctuary Movement. They told the U.S. government, and any newspaper reporters who cared to listen, that, as Fife wrote, "We believe our government is in violation of the 1980 Refugee Act and international law by continuing to arrest, detain, and forcibly return refugees to the terror, persecution, and murder in El Salvador and Guatemala."[28] Each time a sanctuary worker was arrested and prosecuted, more churches joined the movement.

Domestic Consequences of the Contra War

The third stage of the refugee crisis began when the CIA and the National Security Council intensified the Contra war against Nicaragua while Reagan's Justice Department began enticing Nicaraguans to come to the United States by offering them work permits and protection from deportation. These parallel policies of warfare and economic pressure against Nicaragua and the offer of safety and jobs in the United States were a powerful enticement for Nicaraguans to come here by any means possible—once across the Rio Grande, Nicaraguans were home free.

On May 1, 1985, President Reagan ordered the total economic embargo of Nicaragua. In August, Reagan approved secret arms sales to Iran in exchange for U.S. hostages held in Lebanon. Profits from the secret arms sales were used to arm the Contras, in defiance of a congressional ban on military aid. While warfare and economic pressure encouraged Nicaraguans to flee their country, lenient INS policies toward Nicaraguans encouraged them to come to the United States.

In April 1986, INS Miami District Director Perry Rivkind announced he would no longer deport Nicaraguans from Miami.[29] Until the Contra war heated up, the embargo began, and Rivkind started his own version of the Sanctuary Movement, Nicaraguans were a negligible element of the U.S. immigration problem. The INS did not even keep track of how many undocumented Nicaraguans the Border Patrol arrested until 1987; Nicaraguans were lumped together with other OTMs—Other Than Mexican—in INS statistics. Most of the population pressure in the immigration prisons came from Guatemalans and Salvadorans. Arrests of undocumented Salvadorans rose from 8,968 in INS fiscal year 1978 (October 1, 1977, to September 30, 1978) to 16,688 in fiscal year 1983 and 18,936 in fiscal year 1984.[30] INS and Border Patrol officials estimate they apprehend from one-tenth to one-third of the people who enter the country illegally.[31] The total capacity of the five immigration prisons on the southern U.S. border in 1984 was 1,774.[32] Even if the prisons had been empty, every five weeks the Border Patrol arrested enough Salvadorans to fill them beyond capacity. And now Nicaraguans were coming.

The increased immigration pressure caused the INS to open new prisons at Houston and Laredo. Like the Contra war, these prisons were run by private contractors, in this case the Corrections Corporation of America. The INS also reopened an old federal prison at Florence, Arizona, that had been used to incarcerate Japanese Americans during World War II. These three prisons gave the INS 700 more beds for detainees. But the Border Patrol was arresting more than 360 Salvadorans a week. Newly arrested Salvadorans alone would fill the three prisons beyond capacity in a fortnight. So the INS made plans to open the biggest U.S. immigration prison in history, a $27 million, thousand-bed facility in Oakdale, Louisiana. Oakdale prison would have an emergency capacity of 6,000, its own airstrip for deportations, six full-time immigration judges, and twelve INS trial attorneys. And in the swamps of southwest Louisiana, there were no immigration attorneys.[33]

The effect of the embargo and of Rivkind's special dispensations to Nicaraguans in Miami became apparent almost immediately at Casa Oscar Romero, the sanctuary run by the Catholic Diocese of Brownsville in San Benito, sixteen miles from the Mexican border. In the summer of 1984, Casa Romero housed about twenty Central Americans a night, mostly Salvadorans and Guatemalans. By December, the average nightly occupancy had doubled to forty. In April 1985, sixty to seventy people slept at Casa Romero each night. President Reagan announced the economic embargo of Nicaragua on May 1. By August, 100 people were sleeping at Casa Romero every night. Nightly occupancy rose to 300 in December, and by the summer of 1986, 600 people were sleeping at Casa Romero, most of them Nicaraguans.[34] The city of San Benito asked the diocese to close the shelter, and Brownsville's Bishop John Joseph Fitzpatrick, the house sponsor, agreed to move the sanctuary to a bigger compound just outside the Brownsville city limits.

Throughout this period, the INS was trying to discourage undocumented immigration through a blanket policy of denying asylum to Salvadorans and Guatemalans. Proyecto Libertad represented more than 6,000 asylum applicants from 1982 to 1986 without winning a single case. But when thousands of Nicaraguans began applying for asylum along with the Salvadorans, Reagan's refugee policies came crashing down. To deny asylum to Nicaraguans would be a political statement that the Sandinistas were not repressive. Yet to grant asylum to Nicaraguans whose stories of persecution were mild compared to Salvadorans' would invite more class action lawsuits that could open the door to Salvadorans.

The administration's immigration policy crashed at the same time its foreign policy did, on October 5, 1986. At about noon on that day, nineteen-year-old José Fernando Canales, a member of a Sandinista army patrol lost in the jungle of southern Nicaragua, shot down a C-123 cargo plane on a resupply mission to the Contras. The plane's sole survivor, Eugene Hasenfus, parachuted to safety and was captured.[35] President Reagan, CIA Director William Casey, and Deputy Assistant Secretary of State for Inter-American Affairs Elliott Abrams spent a combative month denying U.S. involvement with Hasenfus. Then, on November 3, a left-wing magazine in Beirut, *Al-Shiraa,* published the first report of the United States' secret arms deals with Iran. The next day, during the midterm elections, the Democratic Party regained control of the U.S. Senate, and Reagan lost control of Congress. Three weeks later, on November 25, Attorney General Meese announced that Lieutenant Colonel Oliver North had diverted millions of dollars of profits from the arms sales to Iran to resupply the Contras.

The Iran-Contra scandal undermined the Contra war and eventually brought it to an end. As the Contras disbanded, thousands headed for the United States. The closest point of entry by land was Brownsville, Texas. The arrival of the Contras marked the fourth stage of the refugee crisis, which progressed rapidly to chaos. Ironically, the illegality of Reagan's refugee policies became obvious, even to citizens who didn't care about refugees at all, only when Reagan at last made a halfhearted attempt to mend some injustices.

Chaos in South Texas

With the Contra war in shambles and the Sandinistas still in power, Reagan and Meese opened the doors to Nicaraguans. Meese's protective order for Nicaraguans was issued the day Oliver North began his public testimony to Congress. The rate of approval of Nicaraguan asylum applications rose from 27 percent in fiscal year 1986 to 84 percent in fiscal year 1987. The approval rate for Salvadorans and Guatemalans continued to hover between 1 percent and 3 percent, as it had throughout the 1980s.[36] Nicaraguans were granted other benefits as well. The INS processed Nicaraguan applications more quickly than those of Salvadorans and set up a special asylum review unit in the State Department so that even if a Nicaraguan were denied asylum, he or she would not be deported.[37] Meese's July 7, 1987, memo ordered the INS to grant all Nicaraguan asylum applicants work permits and permission to travel in the United States—rights that were summarily denied to Salvadorans and Guatemalans. To refugee defense workers, this was an invitation to a class action lawsuit. But primarily it was an open invitation for Nicaraguans to move to the United States.

By the autumn of 1988, South Texas was in chaos. More than 2,000 Central Americans were crossing the river every week. Nicaraguans got on buses to Miami while Salvadorans and Guatemalans squatted in fields and in abandoned buildings in Brownsville. Conjunctivitis and respiratory diseases spread among the dwellers of the fields. South Texas's overburdened public health clinics could barely keep up with the needs of U.S. citizens, let alone the problems of thousands of refugees. The Nicaraguan community in Miami grew to more than 100,000. Legal Nicaraguans clamored for public assistance for the new arrivals, and their ideological soul mates, the politically powerful Cuban Americans, added their voices to the outcry.

On January 17, 1989, as thousands of Nicaraguans were arriving in the city, a Miami policeman shot to death a black motorcyclist, and riots erupted in which two people died. Although the Nicaraguans were not receiving public assistance, many in the black community did not believe it. Some accused the U.S. government of helping foreigners but shooting its own citizens.[38] The Nicaraguans became another contentious issue in racially torn Miami. The riots caused cancellation of an NBA playoff game between the Phoenix Suns and the Miami Heat.

Refugees had made the sports pages—the situation in Brownsville became a national issue.

A Decade of Abuse

The South Texas detention project cleared the streets, but the ultimate cost to the Reagan and Bush administrations was that ten years of refugee policies were declared illegal. The December 1990 decision in *American Baptist Churches v. Richard Thornburgh* overturned more than 100,000 cases— more judicial decisions than any other case in U.S. history. U.S. District Court Judge Robert Peckham found that every Salvadoran and Guatemalan who had been denied political asylum in the United States in the 1980s had been tried illegally. He ordered the Justice Department to give a new trial to every such Salvadoran or Guatemalan who was still in the United States, if the refugee asked for it within one year. New procedures were established for political asylum applicants. The U.S. government was ordered to consider human rights reports from nongovernmental sources, such as Amnesty International, in determining native country conditions of asylum applicants. The INS was ordered to release Salvadorans and Guatemalans from the immigration prisons. The settlement agreement in the *American Baptist Churches v. Richard Thornburgh* case stipulated that

under the new asylum regulations as well as the old: foreign policy and border enforcement considerations are not relevant to the determination of whether an applicant for asylum has a well-founded fear of persecution; the fact that an individual is from a country whose government the United States supports or with which it has favorable relations is not relevant to the determination of whether an applicant for asylum has a well-founded fear of persecution; [and] whether or not the United States Government agrees with the political or ideological beliefs of the individual is not relevant to the determination of whether an applicant for asylum has a well-founded fear of persecution.[39]

The government was ordered to pay $200,000 to a special fund to be used to educate refugees and refugee rights groups about the provisions of the new asylum procedures. The fund was to be administered by the refugees' attorneys. And refugee rights groups—the very people the Justice Department had been prosecuting, burglarizing, and intimidating since 1980—were to help train INS officers in the new asylum procedures.[40]

For many people, the *American Baptist Churches* decision came too late. The 30,000 Salvadorans who had been deported were still deported. More than 100 Salvadoran deportees were known to be dead.[41] Salvadorans and Guatemalans who were still in the United States could get a new trial—but in the same system where they had been stripped, robbed, beaten, and humiliated and only if they voluntarily appeared at an immigration office and asked to go through the process again. Nicaraguans on the street who had been denied asylum were safe because the INS still refused to deport them. Other Nicaraguans were denied asylum and being held in U.S. immigration prisons throughout the appeals process, but even if they lost every appeal, they still would not be deported.

The Human Cost

This book describes conditions in U.S. immigration prisons at Port Isabel and Laredo, Texas; at Florence, Arizona; and at Oakdale, Louisiana, in the 1980s; it also describes what happened when the U.S. Justice Department deliberately caused the system to break down during the 1988 presidential campaign, bringing chaos to the streets of South Texas.

Some people who defended refugees in the 1980s believe the prisons were used not only to detain refugees but to keep them from informing the U.S. public about the reality of life in Central America. I doubt that Reagan's policymakers thought that deeply. To them, refugees were a good political issue, but as individual human beings, they simply didn't matter.

The history of this systematic abuse of refugees has never entered the public consciousness of the United States. Yet in their willful disregard of law and in their indulgence in rhetoric unsupported by fact, the policymakers of the Reagan decade laid the groundwork for another decade of U.S. anger toward and fear of immigrants.

Notes

1. Victor Clark Alfaro, telephone interviews with author, March–April 1989.
2. "The surge of Central American asylum claims in South Texas shows no signs of abating ... Asylum claims in Harlingen, Texas have risen from 400 per month in spring of 1988 to over 400 a day since January 15." U.S. Immigration and Naturalization Service, *Enhancement Plan for the Southern Border,* February 16, 1989, p. 1.

3. The only reliable history of Constanzo's drug ring is Edward Humes, *Buried Secrets* (New York: Dutton, 1991).

4. President Reagan first said the U.S. border was out of control in a press conference on June 14, 1984. In response to a question about the Simpson-Mazzoli immigration bill, then before the House, Reagan said, "The simple truth is that we've lost control of our own borders, and no nation can do that and survive."

5. Associated Press dispatch of July 8, "Immigration Rules Are Eased for Nicaraguan Exiles in U.S.," *New York Times,* July 9, 1987.

6. All INS statistics come from the INS statistics office in Washington, D.C., and from the Border Patrol intelligence office in McAllen Sector headquarters, McAllen, Texas.

7. Issuance of the Order to Show Cause is the first step in the deportation process. This Border Patrol document states the name and nationality of the arrestee, the date and place he or she entered the United States without authorization, and demands that the recipient show cause why he or she should not be deported.

8. Stipulated Settlement Agreement, *American Baptist Churches, et al. v. Richard L. Thornburgh, Gene McNary, and James A. Baker III,* Civil Case no. C-85-3255 PFP, U.S. District Court, Northern District of California. The case, which was filed in San Francisco in 1985, successfully charged the U.S. Department of Justice with discriminatory enforcement of law based upon political asylum applicants' country of origin. South Texas attorneys' class action lawsuits filed during the Bayview detention project were essentially holding actions designed to limit legal abuses at the Bayview prison. Abuses documented in these lawsuits buttressed the plaintiffs' cases in the *American Baptist Churches* case and in *Orantes-Hernandez v. Thornburgh.*

9. U.S. Immigration and Naturalization Service, *Nicaraguan Asylum/Harlingen Situation,* Office of the Deputy Commissioner, December 5, 1988, 3–4.

10. INS Commissioner Gene McNary traveled to Bayview, Texas, on February 7, 1990, to announce the new detention policy. Rebecca Thatcher, "INS Cracks Down, Bayview Center Capacity Raised to 10,000," *Brownsville Herald,* February 8, 1990.

11. *Enhancement Plan for the Southern Border,* 14.

12. The author was a reporter for the *Brownsville Herald* throughout the INS detention project. Statistics of arrests and political asylum applications came from INS public affairs spokeswoman Virginia Kice, and from Border Patrol headquarters in McAllen, Texas.

13. "Latin Refugees Fleeing Texas for Mexican Haven," *New York Times,* March 5, 1989.

14. The Border Patrol intelligence office in McAllen provided the author daily arrest statistics during this period.

15. *American Baptist Churches, et al. v. Richard L. Thornburgh, Gene McNary, and James Baker III,* Civil Case no. C-85-3255 PFP, U.S. District Court, Northern District of California. Stipulated Settlement Agreement, December 14, 1990. Thornburgh was U.S. attorney general at the time, McNary was INS commissioner, Baker was secretary of state.

16. The INS prohibited the author from entering El Centro prison on June 13, 1984.

17. INS San Antonio District Director Ricardo Casillas, telephone interview with author, April 30, 1985. The INS does not detain juveniles in its six major prisons along the southern border: El Centro, California; Florence, Arizona; El Paso, Los Fresnos, and Houston, Texas; and Krome Avenue, Miami, Florida.

18. General Accounting Office, *Central American Refugees: Regional Conditions and Prospects and Potential Impact on the United States,* Publication NSIAD-84-106, July 20, 1984, 3.

19. Thomas Anderson, *Matanza* (New York: Curbstone Press, 1992). The massacre is related from the peasants' viewpoint in Roque Dalton's *Miguel Marmol* (New York: Curbstone Press, 1987).

20. Public Law 96-212, 96th Cong., 2d sess. It was passed March 17, 1980, as Senate Bill 643.

21. "Administration Presses Policy of Incarcerating Illegal Aliens," *Congressional Quarterly,* February 16, 1985, p. 325. The *Congressional Quarterly* states that the "aggressive policy of detaining illegal aliens" began in July 1981 yet also cites "a policy directive issued April 16, 1982, cit[ing] a provision of immigration law stating that except in very specific cases, aliens 'who may not appear to the examining officer at the port of arrival to be clearly and beyond a doubt entitled to land shall be detained for further inquiry. ...'"

In response to requests from the author, INS officials in Washington stated that there was no memo of April 16, 1982, or any written directive from the U.S. attorney general ordering that asylum applicants be detained. However, in other cases, INS officials told the author that INS documents did not exist—sometimes, in the case of statistics, when the author was holding the disputed documents in his hand. In another case, the INS February 16, 1989, *Enhancement Plan for the Southern Border* refers to the "INS Enforcement Enhancement Plan for the Southern Border of the United States, February 1984," yet INS officials told the author the 1984 plan does not exist.

Interviews with more than a dozen immigration attorneys along the U.S.-Mexican border indicate that the detention policy began in 1981. The Reagan administration's defense of its policy, as stated in the April 16, 1982, memorandum cited in *Congressional Quarterly,* was based on specious reasoning, as it clearly referred to aliens who had not yet entered the country and could be excluded, rather than to asylum seekers who entered without passing through a "port of arrival." For the legal distinction between the deportation process and the exclusion process, see "Florence Prison."

22. Inman was quoted in "To This Illegal Alien It's a New Kind of 'Freedom Fight,'" *Los Angeles Times,* June 26, 1986.

23. Trominski is quoted in Bill Frelick's "Running the Gauntlet: The Central American Journey Through Mexico," U.S. Committee for Refugees, Washington, D.C., January 1991, 5. The FMLN—the Farabundo Martí Front for National Liberation—was the coalition of guerrilla opposition groups in El Salvador. It is now a legal political party.

24. Spokesmen for the Department of Justice and State Department could not cite any case of a Salvadoran winning political asylum while in detention before 1987. INS spokesman Duke Austin said he was prohibited from discussing specific cases. The author interviewed the primary refugee defense attorneys in San Fran-

cisco, Los Angeles, Phoenix, Tucson, El Paso, Laredo, Brownsville, Harlingen, Dallas, Houston, Oakdale, Miami, Chicago, New York, and Washington, D.C., from 1984 through 1991. These attorneys, who represented more than 10,000 Salvadoran and Guatemalan asylum applicants, could not cite a single case of a Salvadoran or Guatemalan winning political asylum while detained in a U.S. immigration prison until the Iran-Contra scandal discredited the Reagan administration's Central American policies.

25. Virtually all these INS abuses, including the murder of Salvadoran deportees, were reported less than two months after President Reagan took office. John Crewdson, "U.S. Returns Illegal Immigrants Who Are Fleeing Salvador War," *New York Times,* March 2, 1981.

26. Americas Watch Committee and the American Civil Liberties Union, *Report on Human Rights in El Salvador,* January 20, 1983, 16. The report presents monthly violence statistics as reported by *Tutela Legal* and *Socorro Jurídico,* legal and human rights offices associated with the Roman Catholic Archdiocese of San Salvador and the Human Rights Commission. Because of these groups' strict reporting requirements—signed statements by an eyewitness or family member—violence statistics were widely assumed to be underreported.

27. "Was Doped, Forced to Sign Papers, Refugee Says (-) Testifies in Salvadorans' Suit Against INS," *Los Angeles Times,* February 5, 1986.

28. The Reverend John Fife, letter to U.S. Attorney General William French Smith, March 23, 1982.

29. "Key Federal Aide Refuses to Deport Any Nicaraguans (-) Cites Sandinista Cruelty (-) Official in Florida Acts as U.S. Drafts Plan on Refugees of Communist Countries," *New York Times,* April 17, 1986.

30. Immigration and Naturalization Service Office of Statistics, Washington, D.C.

31. The author interviewed Border Patrol officers and supervisors in all nine sectors along the U.S.-Mexican border from 1984 to 1989. John Crewdson reported, "Border Patrol Agents estimate that for every illegal alien they catch, from two to five others evade detection, which would put the number of new [Salvadoran] arrivals at 25,000 to 60,000 a year." *New York Times,* March 2, 1981.

32. INS Commissioner Alan Nelson, letter to Sharon House, Congressional Research Service, Education and Public Welfare Division, Library of Congress, June 26, 1984.

33. *Congressional Quarterly* (February 16, 1985): 326–327. As Oakdale prison was being built, the Louisiana Bar Association asked 650 attorneys within a 10,000-square-mile radius of the prison site whether they would provide free legal services for refuge seekers detained at the prison. Three lawyers said they might be able to take a few cases.

34. Author's personal observations and interviews with Jack Elder, director of Casa Romero, in 1984, and Reverend Jonathan T. Jones, paralegal coordinator for Proyecto Libertad.

35. Roy Gutman, *Banana Diplomacy: The Making of American Policy in Nicaragua, 1981–1987* (New York: Simon & Schuster, 1988), 337–338; and contemporary news reports.

36. The author compiled yearly reports of asylum adjudications issued by the U.S. Department of Justice.

37. U.S. Attorney General Edwin Meese created the Nicaraguan Asylum Review Unit on July 2, 1987, to prevent Nicaraguans from being deported. All asylum applications from Nicaraguans whose claims were denied were sent to the office, which could overturn the denial and grant asylum, or in an absolutely meritless case simply hold the application indefinitely, enabling the applicant to stay in the United States. Nicaraguans are the only nationality for which there exists such an office.

38. *New York Times,* January 18 and 19, 1989.

39. Stipulated Settlement Agreement, *American Baptist Churches,* 2.

40. The history of the Justice Department's threats, intimidation, and burglary of the offices of the Central American support movement is told in Ross Gelbspan's *Break-ins, Death Threats and the FBI: The Covert War Against the Central America Movement* (Boston: South End Press, 1991).

41. For the murders of Salvadoran deportees, see "Murder by Remote Control."

Murder by Remote Control

I haven't seen my wife and family since they took me from them and cut my throat.

—Refugee from Aguilares

◇◇◇
⧂⧂
⧂⧂
⧂⧂
⧂⧂
⧂⧂
◇◇◇ Tʜᴇ Rᴇᴀɢᴀɴ ᴀᴅᴍɪɴɪsᴛʀᴀᴛɪᴏɴ's Central American policies were at heart fantasies based on perceptions so far removed from reality that when facts showed the policies were self-defeating and contradictory, that they were murderous and did not accomplish what they claimed to, then the facts—not the policies—were brushed aside. This was possible because no one—not Reagan, nor the U.S. Congress, nor the average U.S. citizen— actually knew or cared much about El Salvador. And with good reason: "The United States really has no vital interest in the country," former U.S. Ambassador Ignacio Lozano told Congress in 1977.[1]

El Salvador has no oil, no strategic minerals, no transoceanic canal; it produces nothing the United States cannot get easily elsewhere. Its main exports are human labor, coffee, and sugar. Yet throughout his two terms as president, Ronald Reagan made support of the corrupt, murderous Salvadoran military a central part of his foreign policy.[2] Because to most U.S. citizens El Salvador meant nothing, Reagan was able to give El Salvador an assigned meaning—to make it a symbol. Reagan changed the terms of the Salvadoran conflict to bring them into line with a worldview that simply did not exist in Salvadoran reality; in doing so, he did not elevate the Salvadoran people's suffering, he debased it: He made the suffering meaningless.[3]

Early in his first term, Reagan declared that El Salvador was a "textbook case" of U.S. ability to withstand "Soviet aggression."[4] By making this small, remote country a symbol of a clash between two great powers, Reagan in a sense made El Salvador disappear. Because El Salvador suddenly stood for so much—Reagan's ability to stand up to the Soviet Union—the real problems of El Salvador no longer mattered in Washington. The issues invoked were so enormous that reality receded and shrank. Thus it became impossible for Reagan to address or even identify the real problems in El Salvador.

The Reagan administration studied El Salvador by looking elsewhere: at Cuba, Nicaragua, and the Soviet Union. Yet El Salvador had had one of the hemisphere's longest-running insurgencies and one of its most repressive governments long before the 1979 Sandinista revolution, even before Castro's revolution in 1959. The players had changed, but the Salvadoran system remained essentially the same as it was in 1932, when the army and

National Guard killed 10,000 to 30,000 people in a ten-day massacre known as *la matanza*. The *matanza* virtually exterminated Indian language and culture in El Salvador and remains the greatest massacre ever perpetrated in the hemisphere.[5]

Then, as now, El Salvador's main problems were overpopulation, poverty, illness and malnutrition, illiteracy, and corrupt, repressive government. Obviously, the problems are related. El Salvador is the second poorest country in the Americas; per capita income was $680 a year—$13 a week—in 1982. It is the smallest country on the American mainland—8,236 square miles, the same size as Massachusetts—yet it is the most densely populated, with about 600 people per square mile. Illiteracy is about 50 percent. One in five children in the countryside dies before age five; most children are malnourished.[6] El Salvador suffers from land hunger, physical hunger, and a history of repression that has kept two-thirds of the country's wealth in the hands of 1 percent of the population.[7]

Even if one accepts at face value Reagan's justification of his Central American policy—that the United States had to keep El Salvador from falling to leftist guerrillas, as had Nicaragua—the fact remains that the United States did virtually nothing in the 1980s and has done virtually nothing since then to help El Salvador solve its problems of hunger, poverty, illness, and illiteracy. What the United States did do was to send El Salvador guns.

From 1950 to 1979, U.S. military aid to El Salvador averaged $545,000 a year. Reagan spent that much on armaments and military support *every day* for eight years.[8] Only after Reagan left office and the Cold War had collapsed along with the Soviet Union could U.S. policymakers admit, as the RAND Corporation noted in a 1991 report prepared for the Pentagon, that:

> Those involved in the American effort appreciated from the start that Salvadoran society was truly one of the sickest in Latin America and that the rebels had ample cause to lead a revolution. ... that between 1965 and 1977 the United States had trained the majority of the Salvadoran officer corps and that it was precisely these officers who carried out the worst bloodletting in Central American history ... that all the individuals interviewed for this report who have served there in the past two years believe that the Salvadoran military does not wish to win the war because in so doing it would lose the American aid that has enriched it for the past decade. ... It is precisely this new generation of officers that has been most intoxicated by the extreme right's vision; thus it is the one that most resents American influence over the conduct of the Salvadoran civil war and that favors the most ruthless crushing of dissent. ... As one former high-ranking State Department official declared in frustration, the Salvadoran armed forces have "always found it a lot easier to kill labor leaders than guerrillas."[9]

From Fantasy to Experiment

In the aftermath of the Iran-Contra hearings, it was easy to become lost in the rush to apportion guilt, in the maze of retroactive findings, in the varying interpretations of congressional intent and executive privilege. The perfervid defense offered for the Reagan administration's support of the Central American wars obscured the simple truth that the entire policy was an ideological charade in Nicaragua, in El Salvador, and in Washington. In Nicaragua, the charade was that the Contras were not led by brutal, corrupt officers from Somoza's National Guard.[10] In El Salvador, the fantasy was that the ultraright-wing ARENA party was a moderate, democratic movement with no ties to military-based death squads.[11]

Citing these unfortunate misrepresentations, President Reagan announced that popular uprisings in El Salvador and Nicaragua threatened U.S. security and were part of a worldwide communist aggression aimed ultimately at the United States.[12] He invested the enormous power of his administration's propaganda apparatus in trying to prove that the poor people of Central America were a tool of the Soviet Union, and therefore a threat to the United States. The Pentagon, chary of entering the conflicts the White House strategists were brewing, made Central America an experiment.

"American strategists have described the civil war in El Salvador as the 'ideal testing ground' for implementing low-intensity conflict doctrine," the RAND Corporation noted in 1991.[13] Four lieutenant colonels in the U.S. Army wrote much the same thing in a 1988 report, *American Military Policy in Small Wars: The Case of El Salvador:*

> For the United States, on the other hand, El Salvador represents an experiment, an attempt to reverse the record of American failure in waging small wars, an effort to defeat an insurgency by providing training and material support without committing American troops to combat. ... we view El Salvador as providing fertile ground—until now largely uncultivated—for teaching Americans how to fight small wars.[14]

When the Cold War ended after the collapse of the Soviet Union in 1991, the Pentagon declassified documents that show Washington was aware of the continuing massacres in El Salvador throughout the 1980s yet continued arming the government to prolong the ideological charade. In a 1981 report on El Salvador by General Fred Woerner that was declassified in 1993, Woerner wrote, "The Armed Forces, as an institution, has demonstrated a remarkable capacity for tolerating unprofessional and improper conduct," and is "reluctant to admonish its own for errors of professional judgment, acts of violence and impropriety."[15] Yet Woerner suggested spending $6 billion to fight the Salvadoran civil war—a suggestion with which the White House concurred.

Colonel John Waghelstein submitted a similar report to the Pentagon on January 1, 1985, based on his "experience as commander of the US Military Group, El Salvador during the period of March 1982 through June 1983."[16] Waghelstein professed no illusions that the United States was defending democracy in El Salvador. He wrote, "Mutual interest in maintaining the status quo united the military and the oligarchy and together they created a police state."[17] He was just as blunt about government involvement in death squads, which he traced back to 1972, when "the ruling elite launched, with the support of the military, a counterterror campaign using death squads."[18]

U.S. diplomatic cables prove the White House and State Department knew by 1980 that El Salvador was controlled by ultraright military officers and death squads. But just as disturbing as the contents of the cables is the degree to which the State Department censored its own political reporting once Reagan took office, suppressing facts or forcing them into alignment with the administration's Potemkin village version of Central America.[19]

When Reagan took office on January 20, 1981, the most troublesome problem in El Salvador from a U.S. public relations standpoint was not the continuing massacre of the Salvadoran people but the lack of progress in solving the murders of six U.S. citizens there: the four religious workers who were raped and murdered on December 2, 1980, and U.S. land reform advisers Michael Hammer and Mark Pearlman, who were shot to death on January 4, 1981, in the coffee shop of the San Salvador Sheraton.[20] On Reagan's inauguration day, Ambassador Robert White wrote to the Secretary of State, "All the evidence we have, and it has been reported fully, is that the Salvadoran government has made no serious effort to investigate the killings of the murdered American churchwomen."[21] Ten years later, the RAND Corporation pointed out that "those who conceived of the crime and the two officers who concealed it went unpunished, as did Colonel Carlos Eugenio Vides Casanova, then head of the National Guard and later the minister of defense, who undoubtedly was aware of and acquiesced in the cover up."[22]

Ambassador White's reporting from El Salvador was brutally frank:

[CENSORED] at dinner of Dec. 30 (1980) ... the worrisome new development, in his view, is the growing arrogance of the ultraright ... promising purges in the State Department, an end to any human rights considerations in U.S. policy and no further support for social reforms in Central America, raise the specter of a return to power of the Miami millionaires. "These people are scum," he said in English. "For decades they have bribed politicians and military officers to block any change that could threaten their interests. Now they are financing death squads and bribing the security forces to sow terror in the countryside. They are behind the [CENSORED]."[23]

It's evident why White was one of the first diplomats fired by the Reagan administration.[24] The "growing arrogance of the ultraright ... promising purges in the State Department" clearly refers to the U.S. ultraright. Salvadorans could not purge the State Department, nor put "an end to any human rights considerations in U.S. policy."

Cables from White in December 1980 describe institutionalized torture:

> [CENSORED] this morning recounted details of large-scale commission of atrocities allegedly under way at El Zapote barracks next to the Casa Presidencial in El Salvador. His information comes from someone confined there for 36 hours and released yesterday. Torture, beating and gang rape are taking place at this army installation. ...[25]

After extensive deletions, which do not obliterate all the details of torture by electroshock, White's cable continues:

> Before his release, however, he had already been taken to a hidden prison at El Churro, a resort area some 14 miles from San Salvador. There in underground cells many prisoners are being held in terrible conditions. [CENSORED] most are dying from the results of torture and beatings. [CENSORED] The young man said some of the prisoners probably were common criminals or subversives but that most were picked up randomly because they were of an age and class the military suspects.[26]

Suppression of reality in diplomatic cables could not be done overnight. In Reagan's first term, reality continued to intrude in reports from the U.S. embassy in San Salvador, but by 1985 the political reporting had been muzzled, even in classified cables from the embassy to the Secretary of State.

White was sacked almost as soon as Reagan took office. He was replaced briefly by Frederic Chapin, then by Deane R. Hinton, who served as ambassador from June 1981 to August 1983. In a September 1981 cable to the Secretary of State, Hinton described José Napoleon Duarte, the Reagan administration's designate as the man who would democratize El Salvador: "He has deftly and at length handled a wide variety of U.S. inquisitions rareipping [sic] into serious gaffs wtih [sic] an international press seeking to exploit [CENSORED]. *His tendency on occasions to present the truth is a potential problem.*"[27]

Hinton's cable sums up the problem Reagan had created for himself in El Salvador: He had given El Salvador a much greater political and symbolic importance for his administration than the country occupied in geopolitical reality. Precisely because it was a symbol, it was a country Reagan could not afford to "lose." When the Salvadoran army committed the greatest massacre of the war, at Mozote and nearby villages in December 1981, diplomatic cables confirmed it. The State Department denied it. Reality was reported, then suppressed, in 1981. But by Reagan's second term, State Department officials perverted political reporting from El Salvador even in their internal cables: Reality no longer existed.

The Mozote Massacre

From December 8 to 16, 1981, the U.S.-trained Atlacatl Battalion, led by Lieutenant Colonel Domingo Monterrosa, killed at least 794 people in the towns of Mozote, La Joya, Cerro Pando, Ranchería, Los Toriles, and Jocote Amarillo, in northern Morazan Province. Most of the victims were children, women, and old men. Most were killed from December 11 to 14 in and around Mozote.[28]

Only three U.S. citizens visited the scene in the weeks after the massacre: Raymond Bonner of the *New York Times,* Alma Guillermoprieto of the *Washington Post,* and a photographer who accompanied them. Bonner's and Guillermoprieto's reports were published on January 27, 1982. Bonner wrote, "The carnage was everywhere. I saw skulls, rib cages, femurs, tibias protruding from the rubble of cracked roofing tiles. ... Fourteen bodies lay in a heap at the edge of a cornfield, under the swooping green leaves of banana trees."[29] Bonner was shown a handwritten list of 733 victims; more were found later. Of 482 victims in Mozote, 280 were children younger than fourteen. Children and babies had been thrown into the air and caught on the points of bayonets.[30]

News of the massacre at Mozote reached Washington even before Bonner's and Guillermoprieto's reports were published. On December 30, 1981, Senators Thomas Eagleton, Mark Hatfield, and Lowell Weicker wrote to Secretary of State Alexander Haig, asking for information about the massacres. The senators wrote that they had seen

> convincing documentation of killings, at least one of which could be classified as a massacre, committed by Salvadoran and Honduran troops against innocent refugees attempting to flee violence in El Salvador. ... mass killings, drownings and disappearances on a horrifying scale have occurred on the border. In several instances, these atrocities were clearly the result of joint operations between Salvadoran and Honduran troops.[31]

The White House and the U.S. embassy in San Salvador denied the massacre had taken place and continued to deny it through 1992, when forensic scientists began unearthing mass graves of women and children in Mozote.[32] Yet State Department cables confirmed the massacre shortly after the three senators wrote to Haig. In response to the senators' inquiry, John Negroponte, U.S. Ambassador to Honduras, wrote to Haig on February 17, 1982:

During February 4 visit to Salvadoran refugee camp at Colomoncagua, Poloff [U.S. embassy political officer] and visiting House Foreign Affairs Committee Staffer Tom Smeeton interviewed several newly arrived Salvadoran families from Morazan Department. Latter reported a military sweep in Morazan December 7 to 17 which they claim resulted in large numbers of civilian casualties and physical destruction, leading to their exodus. Names of village cited coincide with *New York Times* article of January 20, same subject.

Comment: Most significant element in refugees' reports was their decision to flee at this time when in the past they had remained during sweeps. This lends credibility to reportedly greater magnitude and intensity of the GOES [government of El Salvador] military operations in northern Morazan. —Negroponte.[33]

Negroponte was no liberal. He was ambassador to Honduras from November 1981 until May 1985 and helped oversee the buildup of the U.S.-backed Contra army. Yet even this type of neutral political reporting disappeared from U.S. embassies in Central America by Reagan's second term.

Refugees from Mozote and other massacres sought shelter in refugee camps run by the Catholic Church in San Salvador. A contemptuous cable from the U.S. embassy to the secretary of state on April 7, 1985, describes the "church-run displaced person camps which frequently house family members of guerrilla combatants. There, residents are trundled out to visiting delegations to deliver well-rehearsed testimonials of alleged government atrocities that occurred years ago."[34]

An embassy cable of October 31, 1985, estimates there were 3,275 refugees living in four church-run camps in San Salvador. The average length of stay in a refugee camp was estimated as one to three years. The embassy officer described these places of human suffering as devices of guerrilla propaganda:

Note: San Roque [refugee camp] has been a regular stop for visiting human rights groups and non-official Codels [congressional delegations] with residents tearily presenting well-rehearsed briefings on the ills of the government and abuses committed by the Salvadoran Armed Forces (ESAF). The sight of 675 *deplazados* [sic: *desplazados*—displaced people] living inside a church, without adequate sanitation facilities, and without a yard for the children, rarely fails to have the desired effect.[35]

Ambassador Pickering described another Catholic refugee camp, San José de la Montaña, as a "Rest and Recreation camp for guerrillas."[36] Thus, suffering was reported as subversion, and war orphans were considered instruments of propaganda for guerrillas and congressional liberals.

That the United States' Central American policy was hijacked by the ultraright is confirmed by no less a light than Lieutenant Colonel Oliver North. In his book *Under Fire,* North wrote that congressional staffers called him "soft on communism" in 1983 because he acknowledged that death squads existed under the direction of Roberto D'Aubuisson.

> I made several trips to El Salvador, and in the summer of 1983 I wrote a paper about the death squads. From talking with our ambassador, our military liaison personnel, and with CIA people who knew the area, it was clear there were numerous allegations that the murders were connected to a leader of the right-wing Republican National Alliance Party, also known as ARENA. Back in Washington, I met with those who were lobbying the Congress on behalf of El Salvador. "Stay away from this guy and his cronies," I'd tell them. "Don't try to whitewash the problem. The death squads are real, and they must be stopped. Yes, we have to support the fight against Communism, but our ultimate goal isn't just to prevent Central America from going Communist—it's to help these countries become real democracies."
>
> I made the same point in briefings to congressmen and senators, and to their staffs. Most of them were open to the evidence, although two or three congressional staffers advised their principals that I was soft on Communism. I've been called a lot of things, but that was a first.[37]

The Disinformation Campaign

So sharply drawn were the ideological lines that U.S. Justice Department officials were willing to conspire to murder a Salvadoran deportee to make an ideological point. Ana Estela Guevara Flores was arrested by the Border Patrol with twelve other Salvadorans on June 24, 1981, in Cotulla, Texas, midway between Laredo and San Antonio. The Border Patrol singled her out and notified the FBI "because a leftist-appearing letter was found hidden in her underwear."[38] FBI agent Sal Escobedo interrogated Guevara on June 25.[39] The FBI asked the Border Patrol to keep Guevara in jail "until Agent Escobedo completes his interview of this subject."[40]

The FBI then sent a cable to CIA Deputy Chief of Station Fred Bruger in San Salvador to ask whether Guevara was a known "subversive." The U.S. legal attaché in Panama replied in a July 1 cable:

> On the evening of June 30, 1981, Fred Bruger, deputy chief of station, PARS, U.S. Embassy, San Salvador, El Salvador, advised that El Salvadoran authorities determined that subject is not a known guerrilla/subversive. ... Authorities do not believe subject is identical to Norma Guevara, for whom they have arrest warrants. They stated, however, that it is against the laws of El Salvador to possess subversive literature and she could be detained in El Salvador for possession of same. ...

El Salvadoran authorities requested that copies of all documents found in subject's possession be forwarded to them for analysis. In addition, if subject is deported back to El Salvador, they would desire to be notified of the date and flight number. It should be noted that the El Salvadoran airline, TACA, has the only direct flights from Houston to El Salvador, and perhaps copies of documents found on subject could be furnished the captain of TACA for passage to El Salvador National Guard, to the attention of Col. Eugenio Vides Casanova, director general. Bureau is requested to furnish above to Dallas, San Antonio and San Juan by teletype.[41]

The "subversive documents" confiscated from Ana Guevara were a cassette tape recording of a sermon by the late Salvadoran Archbishop Oscar Arnulfo Romero, who was murdered on March 24, 1980, while saying Mass at a cancer clinic; a cassette tape of Christian music; and books about the role of women in the church.[42]

Colonel, now General, Vides Casanova assumed command of the Salvadoran National Guard in 1979. Death squad killings reached a peak of more than 800 a month for more than a year while he directed the National Guard. Vides Casanova participated in the cover-up of the Salvadoran military's involvement in the rape and murder of four U.S. church workers in December 1980 and in the murders of two U.S. land reform advisers and the director of the office of Salvadoran land reform in January 1981. His cousin, Colonel Oscar Edgardo Casanova, was in charge of the military zone from which the four churchwomen were abducted, and gave the order to kill them.[43] The military zone the Casanovas commanded included the only road from the international airport. Many Salvadoran deportees disappeared on that road in the 1980s, then turned up dead, tortured, and decapitated.[44]

The attaché's cable shows that the FBI knew by July 1 that Ana Guevara was not "Commander Norma." Yet six days later, Julian de la Rosa, FBI agent in charge of the San Antonio office, publicly accused Guevara of being Commander Norma, a communist terrorist. De la Rosa told the Associated Press on July 7 that FBI agents had been sent to the Nueces County Jail in Corpus Christi to investigate Ana Estela Guevara Flores, who had been arrested with documents that showed she might be a communist terrorist. A Border Patrol agent told the AP that Ana Guevara had been sent to the United States to kill Salvadorans.

A 32-year-old woman who is thought to be a former Communist party leader who fled from El Salvador was in the Nueces County Jail today. Ana Guevarra [sic] Flores ... is thought to be "Commander Norma Guevarra [sic]," a member of ... a Communist Party front organization in El Salvador.

The woman was being investigated because she allegedly belonged to a terrorist group trying to topple the government of El Salvador, according to an FBI agent who asked not to be identified.[45]

The AP quoted a Border Patrol agent who said Guevara had come to "do a number" on Salvadorans in the United States. The article quoted a "Washington source ... an acknowledged expert on Central American guerilla activity," who said "Ms. Guevarra [sic] was known as 'Commander Norma Guevara.'" She supposedly had sent an "anti-government communique" to El Salvador from Cuba. FBI agent de la Rosa "declined to comment on what documents had been taken from Ms. Guevarra."[46]

The CIA cable from Panama proves that the FBI knew by July 1 that Ana Guevara was not "Commander Norma," a "communist terrorist." Yet six days later, agents of the FBI and the Border Patrol told the Associated Press a story they knew was false, that they knew would be reprinted in hundreds or thousands of newspapers around the world, and that they had reason to believe could have caused an innocent young woman to be deported, tortured, and killed. The only possible reason for the FBI to release this false information was to stir up fear and hatred of Salvadorans in the United States.

On July 10, the Associated Press released another story repeating the charge that Guevara was a communist terrorist, this time with a picture of her in a jail cell.[47] By that day the INS already had denied her request for political asylum and ordered her deported. With astonishing rapidity, the State Department's Bureau of Human Rights and Humanitarian Affairs—headed by Elliott Abrams—had provided a written opinion that Guevara would not be in danger in El Salvador, despite the fact that the FBI and Border Patrol had publicly accused her of being a communist terrorist and conspiratorial assassin and had broadcast the accusation to the world via the Associated Press, along with her picture, and that the CIA had asked the FBI to tell the Salvadoran National Guard the date and number of the poor woman's deportation flight.

Murder by Remote Control

Ana Guevara was not an exceptional case. The only unusual thing was that a U.S. immigration attorney—Lisa Brodyaga—was able to force the Justice Department to produce the memos from the Border Patrol, INS, FBI, and CIA, and thereby protect Guevara from deportation.

While Brodyaga forced Guevara's case through the courts, the INS continued to deport Salvadorans to their deaths. José Humberto Santacruz Elias, twenty-two, was deported on January 15, 1981, and disappeared upon arrival in El Salvador.[48] Santana Chirino Amaya, twenty-four, was ordered deported on June 10, 1981, and was found in late August, headless after being tortured, with the body of his fourteen-year-old cousin, in Amalupapa, San Vicente Province.[49] José Enriquez Orellano, nineteen, was shot three times in the chest and decapitated in November 1983, two weeks after he had been deported from South Texas.[50] Octavio Osegueda was shot to death in San Salvador on July 13, 1983—one day after he was deported from the United States. His brother Juan Antonio was killed with him.[51]

By the end of Reagan's first term, more than 100 Salvadoran deportees had been murdered after they were deported. When provided with proof of the continuing murders, the Reagan administration did not change its policy; it simply denied the proof existed.

On June 20, 1984, attorneys for the American Civil Liberties Union (ACLU) Political Asylum Project gave the U.S. House Subcommittee on Rules a list of 112 Salvadoran deportees believed to have suffered human rights abuses after they were deported. A copy of the list was given to Elliott Abrams, director of the State Department's Bureau of Human Rights and Humanitarian Affairs. The victims' last names were deleted from the record of the subcommittee hearings, but Abrams and the members of the subcommittee were given the 112 deportees' full names.[52]

The State Department looked into the matter. On July 6, 1984, Gloria Escalon, political desk officer at the U.S. embassy in San Salvador, wrote to two Salvadoran human rights organizations affiliated with the Catholic Archdiocese of San Salvador, *Socorro Jurídico* and *Tutela Legal,* to request information about 26 deportees chosen from the ACLU's list. Escalon's letter listed the twenty-six deportees by their full names.[53]

Socorro Jurídico and *Tutela Legal* replied in letters of July 13 and July 25 that their offices were not accustomed to provide that sort of information and lacked the staff and equipment to conduct a thorough search of their records. Still, they confirmed eight of the twenty-six cases and provided the U.S. embassy with eyewitness testimonies to them.[54]

The U.S. embassy was given sworn testimony to the following cases: A sixteen-year-old deportee was abducted by members of the U.S.-trained Atlacatl Battalion, who also abducted his mother and five younger brothers and sisters, who ranged in age from eighteen months to thirteen years. They were abducted at two in the afternoon in the presence of numerous eyewitnesses. The family never reappeared.[55] (A U.S. reporter later found the sole surviving family member, the deportee's father, in a church-run refugee camp in San Salvador. The man was too psychologically traumatized to talk.)

Four deportees were captured in daylight by heavily armed civilians while nearby security forces ignored the abductions. One was abducted by soldiers while bathing in a river. Two were taken from their homes in the city at night—one by heavily armed civilians armed with G-3 rifles, standard government issue in El Salvador.[56] Because of El Salvador's state-of-siege laws, there was at that time a strict nighttime curfew. Armed bands operating at night in the cities were commonly assumed to be associated with government forces.

This information was given to Elliott Abrams, as was an April 1984 document, "Salvadorans in the United States," by the ACLU National Immigration and Alien Rights Project. This 124-page document described the torture, death, and decapitation of five deportees and included Salvadoran newspaper accounts of their deaths, photos, descriptions of the torture, and letters from family members.[57] The report contained the sworn statement of José Rosales, a twenty-seven-year-old Salvadoran army sergeant who deserted in 1980 and came to the United States to seek asylum, "because I did not agree with the current government policies of kidnapping, torture and murder of innocent civilians under the guise of fighting subversion."[58]

Rosales described tortures and executions he witnessed as a member of the army and in support of actions of the National Guard:

> I have strong reasons to believe that the dangers faced by all young male civilians in El Salvador are greatly enhanced for those who are returned to El Salvador after being deported from other countries. I am aware of this increased danger because I was stationed at the San Salvador airport in the latter part of 1979. I recall one particular incident in November 1979, when an airplane arrived carrying, among others, nine Salvadorans being deported from Mexico. The nine deportees were detained at the airport, "investigated," that is, tortured and killed. Pictures of their bodies appeared in the newspaper. During my duties at the San Salvador airport I learned from conversations with superior officers that young men who are returned to El Salvador deported from other countries must be presumed to have left the country in order to avoid military service. This is considered a form of subversion or communism, because of the assumption that a young man who resists entering the army must be in opposition to the government.[59]

Rosales's nine-page deposition concludes:

> I am also familiar with the operation of the so-called death squads. Early in 1980, I volunteered to join what is referred to in El Salvador as a death squad. However, in my experience the death squad has no independent existence outside of the Salvadoran military and security forces. It is simply a form of duty which the military personnel are ordered to carry out while not in uniform. Within the military, these operations are not referred to as "death squads," but simply as "missions." ... I myself volunteered for one such mission in March of 1980. I then received verbal orders from a National Guardsman to take part in an operation involving a thirty-seven-year-old man in a suburb of San Salvador. An army colonel coordinated the operation. The man was captured and tortured for two hours, but gave no information. He said he knew he would be killed anyway, so there was no reason to talk. This was true, since the leaders of the mission planned to kill him, whether or not he gave any information. I did not participate in the torture, but I witnessed it. A nail was driven up one

of his nostrils. All the fingers on one hand were broken and a hypodermic needle was jammed into his wrist. After the soldiers were finished torturing him they shot him and stole his watch. Many soldiers volunteer for this duty to rob their victims. ... In El Salvador, a suspected subversive who is captured by the military, as a deportee, would be lucky if he were only shot. The unlucky ones are subjected to brutal torture before their execution.[60]

Despite this wealth of documentation, and the repeated pleas of Salvadoran Archbishop Arturo Rivera y Damas and Auxiliary Bishop Gregorio Chavez denouncing the continuing murders of deportees, Elliott Abrams told the *Washington Post* in March 1985, "If those people who go back [to El Salvador] are killed, as the activists maintain, we'd simply change our policy. But that is not true ... it isn't happening."[61]

Duke Austin, the chief INS spokesman in Washington, repeatedly told me from 1985 until 1991, "There is not a single case where there's proof of a Salvadoran being killed after deportation."[62] Yet the State Department and INS not only knew it was happening, they rigged it so it would continue to happen. An internal INS memorandum written in 1982 at the request of INS Commissioner Alan Nelson describes how the INS and the State Department systematically denied Salvadorans political asylum in order to deport them.

The ninety-three-page memorandum, "Asylum Adjudications: An Evolving Concept and Responsibility for the Immigration and Naturalization Service," was based on interviews and site visits with commissioned officer staff, INS regional commissioners, supervisory personnel, district directors, and immigration judges. It shows how the INS methodically violated the law by denying asylum to people of particular nationalities while granting it to others for ideological reasons.[63]

Different criteria sometimes may be applied to different nationalities. ... In some cases, different levels of proof are required of different asylum applicants. In other words, certain nationalities appear to benefit from presumptive status while others do not.

For example, for an El Salvadoran asylum applicant to receive a favorable asylum advisory opinion, he or she must have a "classic textbook case." On the other hand, BHRHA [Abrams's Bureau of Human Rights and Humanitarian Affairs] sometimes recommends favorable action where the applicant cannot meet the individual well-founded fear of persecution test.[64]

The memo describes an incident in which "seven Polish crewmen jumped ship and applied for asylum in Alaska."

Even before seeing the asylum applications, a State Department official said, "We're going to approve them." All the applications, in the view of INS senior officials, were extremely weak. In one instance, the crewman said the reason he feared returning to Poland was that he had once attended a Solidarity rally (he was one of more than 100,000 participants at the rally). The crewman had never been a member of Solidarity, never participated in any political activity, etc. His claim was approved within forty-eight hours.[65]

The Polish sailors were granted asylum, even though their cases were weak, because they fled from a communist country. Salvadorans were denied asylum no matter how badly they had been persecuted because they fled from a U.S. ally. The INS memo spells this out:

> No opinion is ever issued unless the (State Department) political desk agrees. ... One district office ... gives a receipt to the applicant filing the petition, holds no interview (an interview is required by law); forwards the application to State; and records State's decision as the INS decision.[66]

The high-ranking INS employee who wrote the memo at Commissioner Nelson's request delivered it to him in December 1982, then resigned.

Catch-22

The State Department had hijacked the asylum process and the Justice Department consented to ignore federal law for ideological reasons. The abuses were systematic. As one step of the political asylum process, the immigration judge sends the applicant's I-589—the application for political asylum—and any documents submitted with it to the State Department. The State Department then issues an "advisory opinion" letter, suggesting whether asylum should be granted. For Salvadorans, this was a form letter stating that the State Department did not believe the applicant would be persecuted in El Salvador. The form letter generally did not refer to any details of the Salvadorans' cases. Though immigration judges are not bound to follow the State Department's opinion, they did so nearly 100 percent of the time until the Iran-Contra scandal discredited the Reagan administration's Central American policies. In interviews across the country with attorneys who had represented more than 10,000 Salvadoran and Guatemalan asylum applicants from 1981 to 1986, I found one case in which an immigration judge overturned the State Department's opinion letter.[67]

In 1986, the State Department squared the circle and made it formally impossible for a member of the Salvadoran political opposition to win political asylum. In its advisory opinion letter, the State Department wrote that even if the judge found an applicant had reason to fear persecution by the government because he belonged to an organization of the political opposition, the judge should bear in mind that the FMLN is a "Marxist-

Leninist guerrilla organization ... attempting the violent overthrow of the legitimate, democratically elected government of El Salvador," and that if applicants belonged to any group associated with the FMLN, they could be "exclude(d) from admission to the United States ... even if they meet the well-founded fear criteria."[68]

So there was no way out. To win political asylum, a Salvadoran must fear persecution from the government; but any Salvadoran who feared persecution from the government was a guerrilla and could be excluded. Salvadorans didn't have a chance.

With no hope of justice in the immigration courts, a Salvadoran's only chance for asylum in the United States was to appeal to federal courts. Though the abuses Salvadorans suffered in the immigration system were mild compared to the tortures of El Salvador, it was the continued systematic abuses in U.S. immigration courts and prisons that forced federal judges to declare the entire system fraudulent and overturn more than 100,000 asylum decisions in December 1990.[69] To document those abuses, U.S. attorneys and prison workers had to force our way into the immigration system. We had to sue the U.S. government to get into prison.

Notes

1. Lozano is quoted in Raymond Bonner's *Weakness and Deceit: U.S. Policy and El Salvador* (New York: Times Books, 1984), 234.

2. Corruption in the Salvadoran military is detailed in Benjamin Schwartz, *American Counterinsurgency Doctrine and El Salvador,* the RAND Corporation, Santa Monica, California, 1991, prepared for the undersecretary of defense for policy. Schwartz concluded the Salvadoran military had little interest in winning the war, as this would cut off the U.S. aid that enriched it. "Every year, 20,000 pay slots for soldiers are divided among the Salvadoran Army's regional commanders. Since the Salvadoran armed forces have no central roster and hence no way to detect fraud, most commanders fill a portion of these slots with nonexistent soldiers, collecting the 'ghost soldier' salaries themselves. Brigades generally have at least one 50-man 'ghost' company that brings the brigade commander $60,000 annually" (19). Salvadoran conscripts are forced to contribute to a military social security fund, but "the benefits of the fund are not available to conscripts. ... The only members of the armed forces eligible to receive these benefits are officers and a very small number of re-enlistees" (20). The army also enriches itself through death squads, which steal the belongings of their victims, and one or more kidnapping rings. The kidnapping rings strained relations between the military and the Salvadoran oligarchy it serves (20, 28–31).

3. The extent to which Salvadoran reality was reported through a distorting U.S. lens was evident in a November 16, 1984, press conference on Maryland Avenue in Washington, D.C. Four representatives of the FMLN spoke: Guillermo Ungo, Salvador Samayoa, Hector Oqueli, and Oscar Acevedo. Reporters asked for a comment on Reagan administration statements that U.S. military aid was hurting the guerrillas, offering as proof the fact there had been no "fall offensive" that year.

Samayoa replied: "The autumn offensive is an invention of Ronald Reagan, in the first place, because we have no autumn in El Salvador." El Salvador has two seasons, wet and dry.

4. "U.S. Says Salvador Is 'Textbook Case' of Communist Plot (-) Embassies Get Memorandum (-) State Dept. Accuses Soviet Bloc of Indirect Armed Aggression in Supplying the Rebels," *New York Times,* February 20, 1981. The State Department memo concludes: "The political direction, organization and arming of the Salvadoran insurgency is coordinated and heavily influenced by Cuba—with active support of the Soviet Union, East Germany, Vietnam and other Communist states. ... In short, over the past year, the insurgency in El Salvador has been progressively transformed into a textbook case of armed aggression by Communist powers through Cuba." "Text of State Department Report on Communist Support of Salvadoran Rebels," *New York Times,* February 24, 1981. The Reagan administration used the arguments of this memorandum throughout the decade to justify its military attacks on Nicaragua and military support for El Salvador.

5. Thomas Anderson, *Matanza* (New York: Curbstone Press, 1992); Roque Dalton, *Miguel Marmol* (New York: Curbstone Press, 1987).

6. Walter LaFeber, *Inevitable Revolutions: The United States in Central America* (New York: W. W. Norton, 1983), 10.

7. William Durham's *Scarcity and Survival in Central America: Ecological Origins of the Soccer War* (Palo Alto, Calif.: Stanford University Press, 1979) is an excellent study of the relationship of land tenure to social structures in Central America.

8. U.S. military expenditures for the Military Assistance Program and Foreign Military Sales program are from U.S. government sources, cited in Michael McClintock, *The American Connection,* vol. 1 of *State Terror and Popular Resistance in El Salvador* (Avon, England: Zed Books, 1985), 326–328. This is the best one-volume history of U.S. military policy in El Salvador. Volume 2 deals with Guatemala.

9. Schwartz, *American Counterinsurgency Doctrine and El Salvador,* 8, 35, 21, 38, 25.

10. The best history of the Contras is Sam Dillon's *Comandos: The CIA and Nicaragua's Contra Rebels* (New York: Henry Holt, 1991). See, too, Christopher Dickey's *With the Contras* (New York: Simon & Schuster, 1985).

11. ARENA, the Republican National Alliance, founded by death squad leader Roberto D'Aubuisson, grew out of ORDEN, the Democratic Nationalist Organization, founded by D'Aubuisson's mentor, Colonel Alberto "Chele" Medrano. Both groups were organized as a network of anti-union, anti-Catholic paramilitary informers and assassins with compartmentalized secret cells under the direction of Salvadoran military officers. See McClintock, *The American Connection,* chapter 13.

12. In responding to a question about El Salvador in a news conference on March 6, 1981, President Reagan said: "What we're doing in going to the aid of a government that asked that aid of a neighboring country—and a friendly country in our hemisphere—is try to halt the infiltration into the Americas, by terrorists and by outside interference, and those who aren't just aiming at El Salvador but, I think, are aiming at the whole of Central and possibly later South America and, I'm sure, eventually North America. But this is what we're doing: is trying to stop this destabilizing force of terrorism and guerrilla warfare and revolution from being exported

in here, backed by the Soviet Union and Cuba and those others that we've named." "Transcript of the President's News Conference," *New York Times,* March 7, 1981.

13. Schwartz, *American Counterinsurgency Doctrine,* v, quoting unspecified "American strategists."

14. Lieutenant Colonels A. J. Bacevich, James D. Hallums, Richard H. White, and Thomas F. Young, *American Military Policy in Small Wars: The Case of El Salvador* (Washington, D.C.: Pergamon-Brassey's International Defense Publishers, Institute for Foreign Policy Analysis, Inc., 1988), 2.

15. General Fred F. Woerner was principal author of a 210-page report written for the Pentagon in 1981. Selections from the heavily censored "Woerner Report," obtained through a Freedom of Information Act request, were reported in a January 14, 1993, Associated Press dispatch from Washington.

16. Colonel John D. Waghelstein, *El Salvador: Observations and Experiences in Counterinsurgency,* U.S. Army War College, Carlisle, Pa., January 1, 1985, ix.

17. Ibid., 5.

18. Ibid., 7.

19. The State Department released more than 2,000 pages of cables and correspondence in 1992 in response to the author's Freedom of Information Act requests. These documents shall henceforth be referred to as FOIA, which will appear with the State Department's microfiche file number.

20. Ita Ford, Maura Clarke, Dorothy Kazel, and Jean Donovan were raped and murdered on the road from the international airport to San Salvador. Hammer and Pearlman, of the American Institute for Free Labor Development (AIFLD), were shot to death with Rodolfo Viera, head of the Salvadoran Institute for Agrarian Transformation (ISTA). The murders were ordered by high-ranking Salvadoran army intelligence officers. Schwartz and the RAND Corporation named the officers in *American Counterinsurgency Doctrine,* 27, 33.

21. White to U.S. Secretary of State, January 20, 1981, FOIA #8701016.

22. Schwartz, *American Counterinsurgency Doctrine,* 27.

23. White to U.S. Secretary of State, January 20, 1981, FOIA #8701016.

24. Ambassador Robert White was fired February 1, 1981, ten days after President Reagan took office. "Haig Said to Remove Ambassador to Salvador in Signal of New Policy," *New York Times,* February 2, 1981. The *Times* reported, "Secretary of State Alexander M. Haig Jr. has relieved Robert E. White of his duties as United States Ambassador to El Salvador as a sign of a new policy in Central America, according to State Department sources. Mr. White, a career Foreign Service officer, has been strongly criticized by many Republican conservatives. He was called here for consultations last week by Mr. Haig and informed that the Reagan administration would soon appoint a new Ambassador to El Salvador to signal the new United States policy, the sources said. ... Mr. Haig has ordered an interdepartmental review of United States policy toward El Salvador, which is now under way, but the decision to remove Mr. White was reportedly made before the completion of the review. ... United States support for land redistribution, and Mr. White's demand that there be a serious investigation into the killing last December of three American Roman Catholic nuns and a lay missionary, angered right-wing Salvadorans, who can get a hearing from Republican conservatives, such as Senator Jesse Helms,

chairman of the Senate Foreign Relations Subcommittee on Latin America, and Michael Deaver, a White House aide to President Reagan."

25. White to U.S. Secretary of State, January 20, 1981, FOIA #8701016.

26. Ibid. U.S. immigration attorneys tried and failed for a decade to persuade immigration judges that young male Salvadoran civilians of draft age constituted a social class likely to be singled out for persecution. White's informant and hundreds of Salvadorans interviewed by the author said the Salvadoran military considered young men out of uniform draft dodgers and guerrilla sympathizers. Immigration judges never conceded this.

27. Hinton to U.S. Secretary of State, September 1981, FOIA #8402021. Emphasis added.

28. The Mozote massacres are reported in detail in Mark Danner, "The Truth of El Mozote," *New Yorker,* December 6, 1993. Americas Watch summarized the pathetic U.S. response in "The Massacre at El Mozote: The Need to Remember," vol. IV, no. 2 (Washington, D.C.), March 4, 1992. The massacres were reported in numerous reports of Americas Watch and Amnesty International in the 1980s, and in Bonner, *Weakness and Deceit,* 112–113, 337–343.

29. Bonner, *Weakness and Deceit,* 113.

30. Raymond Bonner, "Massacre of Hundreds Is Reported in El Salvador," *New York Times,* January 27, 1982; and *Weakness and Deceit,* 338.

31. Senators Eagleton, Hatfield, and Weicker to U.S. Secretary of State Alexander Haig, December 30, 1981, FOIA #8701333.

32. Americas Watch, "The Massacre at El Mozote"; Mike Hoyt, "The Massacre at Mozote," *Columbia Journalism Review* (January/February 1993): 31–35; Danner, "The Truth of El Mozote."

33. Negroponte to U.S. Secretary of State, February 17, 1982, FOIA #8701333.

34. U.S. Embassy, San Salvador, to U.S. Secretary of State, April 7, 1985, FOIA #8701333.

35. U.S. Embassy, San Salvador, to U.S. Secretary of State, October 31, 1985, FOIA #8701526.

36. Pickering to U.S. Secretary of State, January 25, 1985, FOIA #8701379.

37. Oliver North with William Novak, *Under Fire* (New York: HarperCollins, 1991), 224–225.

38. Memo of July 13, 1981, by Border Patrol intelligence agent James W. Knight to Chief Patrol Agent, Laredo, Texas. Photocopy of two-page document in author's possession.

39. Border Patrol agent William B. Worley, Cotulla, Texas, to Chief Patrol Agent, Laredo, dated June 26, 1891 [sic]: "At approximately 1400, June 25, 1981, Agent Sal Escobedo, of the San Antonio Office of the FBI, interviewed the subject at the Frio County Jail and advised this agent that he wished to continue the interview of the subject and requested that she not be returned to El Salvador as scheduled on June 26, 1981." Photocopy of document in author's possession.

40. Ibid.

41. Teletype communication from "Legal Attaché Panama (199-NEW) to Director Immediate 158-01 ... (and) to Supervisor Carter Cornick, FBIHQ, July 1, 1981." Classified as secret, declassified September 27, 1983. Photocopy of document in author's possession.

42. Ana Guevara's "subversive documents" were described by an attorney familiar with the case.

43. Schwartz, *American Counterinsurgency Doctrine,* 33.

44. American Civil Liberties Union, "Salvadorans in the United States: The Case for Extended Voluntary Departure" (ACLU National Immigration and Alien Rights Project, Report no. 1, Washington, D.C., April 1984). The continuing murder of deportees was reported by the author in "U.S. Should Grant Asylum to Salvadorans," *Baltimore Sun,* March 1, 1985; and in "Memos Prove Aliens Die After Deportation," *National Catholic Reporter,* June 7, 1985.

45. Associated Press dispatch of July 7, 1981, reported in the *Brownsville Herald,* July 8, 1981.

46. Ibid.

47. Associated Press dispatch of July 10, 1981, reported in the *Brownsville Herald,* July 11, 1981.

48. ACLU, "Salvadorans in the United States," appendix III, containing open letter from Santacruz's grandmother, published in December 9, 1981, issue of *El Diario de Hoy,* daily newspaper in San Salvador.

49. ACLU, "Salvadorans in the United States," appendix III, with copy of U.S. INS deportation order of June 10, 1981, and death announcements in September 1, 1981, issues of *El Diario de Hoy* and *La Prensa Gráfica,* both daily newspapers in San Salvador.

50. ACLU, "Salvadorans in the United States," appendix III, with the *Brownsville Herald* news report of July 15, 1983, quoting letter of Enriquez's brother to Brownsville immigration attorney Linda Yañez.

51. "Salvadorans in the United States," appendix III, containing November 10, 1983, report of *El Diario de Hoy* announcing Osegueda's murder on July 13 of that year.

52. The author was not permitted to photocopy these documents but was allowed to make handwritten copies, which are in his possession.

53. Gloria Chacon, letter to *Socorro Jurídico,* July 6, 1984, written on U.S. embassy letterhead. Photocopy of document in author's possession.

54. Ernesto Chacon, coordinator of *Socorro Jurídico,* letter to Gloria Escalon, U.S. embassy political section, July 13, 1984. Maria Julia Hernandez, director of *Tutela Legal,* letter to Gloria Escalon, July 25, 1984. *Socorro Jurídico* and *Tutela Legal* report only those human rights abuses reported to them in sworn statements by eyewitnesses or family members of the victims. Photocopies of documents in author's possession.

55. *Socorro Jurídico* report of April 6, 1983.

56. *Tutela Legal* letter to U.S. embassy, July 25, 1984.

57. ACLU, "Salvadorans in the United States."

58. Affidavit of José Rosales, signed and sworn September 16, 1981. "Salvadorans in the United States," ACLU, appendix III, 2.

59. Ibid., 6.

60. Ibid., 8–9.

61. Abrams was quoted in the *Washington Post* on March 25, 1985.

62. The author spoke frequently with Austin from 1985 to 1991 as a freelance reporter, then as a reporter for and city editor of the *Brownsville Herald.*

63. INS, "Asylum Adjudications: An Evolving Concept and Responsibility for the Immigration and Naturalization Service" (unsigned INS report, Washington, D.C., June and December 1982).

64. Ibid., 59.

65. Ibid.

66. Ibid., 59, 37. Words in parentheses in original.

67. Author's interviews with attorneys in San Francisco, Los Angeles, Tucson, Phoenix, El Paso, Brownsville, Harlingen, Houston, Dallas, Chicago, New York City, Long Island, and Washington, D.C., 1984–1986. The one instance in which a judge overturned the State Department letter was the case of a Guatemalan who had been abducted and tortured by the army. In the following weeks he was followed on the street, shot at, threatened, and finally left Guatemala. The State Department wrote he did not have a well-founded fear of persecution.

68. Edward H. Wilkinson, director, Office of Asylum Affairs in the State Department's Bureau of Human Rights and Humanitarian Affairs, advisory opinion letter to Sharon Craven, clerk in the Executive Office of Immigration Review, Oakdale, Louisiana, July 29, 1986. Photocopy of document in author's possession.

69. *American Baptist Churches v. Richard Thornburgh, Gene McNary, and James Baker III,* Stipulated Settlement Agreement, United States District Court, Northern District of California, December 14, 1990.

THE CORRALÓN

It's a banality of evil, like Hannah Arendt wrote about. They're not evil people. They're just working. Like Adolf Eichmann said, "I never killed a Jew personally, with my own hands."

—Attorney Sam Williamson

THE BIGGEST IMMIGRATION PRISON in the United States sits at the end of Farm to Market Road 510 twenty-six miles east of Harlingen, Texas, and twenty-five miles northeast of Brownsville, next to a bird sanctuary and alligator breeding ground on the Gulf of Mexico. The prisoners wear fluorescent orange jumpsuits. The government calls it the Port Isabel Service and Processing Center. Newspapers call it the Bayview detention center or Los Fresnos immigration prison. The prisoners call it the *corralón*—the big corral. The *corralón* does not appear on any road map: The closest towns are the poor fishing villages of Los Fresnos and Port Isabel, and Bayview, an unincorporated village of mansions and citrus groves.

The *corralón* was opened as an immigration prison in 1977, with an official capacity of 236. Its capacity grew to 450 by 1984, though the prison held from 600 to 700 people at a time throughout the 1980s. During the winter of 1988–1989, after tents were erected inside its gates, the prison capacity was listed as 10,000.[1]

The remote 347-acre site was a U.S. Navy air station until it was turned over to the INS in 1961 to be used as a Border Patrol academy and training center. In those days, the U.S. Public Safety Program also used it as a training ground for foreign police officers and intelligence officials. Salvadoran military and police officers attended the courses with other Latin American officers. Among the subjects the Public Safety Program offered its Latin American students at Los Fresnos was a course in "bomb handling."[2] After four weeks' instruction at the International Police Academy in Washington, D.C., the officers were assigned four weeks of "practical exercises," blowing up things in Texas. Though the "Technical Investigations Course" at Los Fresnos ostensibly taught Latin American military and police officers how to prevent terrorist bombings, no instruction was given in dismantling bombs; however, courses were offered in bomb manufacture, including "booby traps" and "incendiaries." A course outline of skills taught at Los Fresnos includes "Terrorist Devices: Fabrication and Functioning of Devices, Improvised Triggering Devices," and lectures and demonstrations on "Assassination Weapons: A discussion of various weapons which may be used by the assassin."[3]

One graduate of the International Police Academy program was Lieutenant Roberto D'Aubuisson, the reputed godfather of the Salvadoran death squads. D'Aubuisson attended the program in 1970 after being booted out of El Salvador for his close association with Colonel José Alberto "Chele" Medrano, whom the government suspected of plotting a coup. Medrano was the founder of the right-wing paramilitary group ORDEN. When his protégé D'Aubuisson returned to El Salvador after finishing the courses in the United States, he was promoted to major and assigned to the National Guard as an intelligence officer. From that post, and then as deputy director of the National Security Agency, ANSESAL, D'Aubuisson is believed to have reorganized ORDEN as the death squads.[4] The Public Safety Program and the U.S. Agency for International Development (AID) also worked in El Salvador then, training the National Police, Treasury Police, and other security forces in "Special Investigations." Many of their victims and family members of victims were imprisoned ten years later near the graduate assassins' old classrooms at Los Fresnos.

The Public Safety Program's bomb and terrorism course became public knowledge in September 1973, when Senator James Abourezk forced the U.S. AID to release information about the program. The U.S. AID and Public Safety Program phased out its work in El Salvador in late 1974.[5] In 1977, the Justice Department opened a new Border Patrol academy in Glynco, Georgia, and in April of that year the site near Los Fresnos became a full-time immigration detention center.

In late 1981, as the prison filled beyond capacity with refugees from the Central American wars, immigration attorney Lisa Brodyaga founded the law office Proyecto Libertad to defend refugees imprisoned at the *corralón*. The FBI began investigating Brodyaga and her law office in 1982.[6]

The FBI Investigation of Proyecto Libertad

I went to work in the *corralón* in September 1984 as a paralegal for Proyecto Libertad. It was a terrible job, under terrible conditions. We were in prison, constantly watched by guards. The caseload was enormous, and unless the client had relatives in the United States, we were his or her only hope. Because of the pressure and isolation, we tended to become friends with our clients, many of whom had been raped or tortured. And we had to make them talk about it while they were in prison. The only hope we could offer was to try to raise the money to pay their bond, and we couldn't promise to find bond money for everyone.

Paralegals were the only link between the prisoners and the attorneys, who did not have time to do intake interviews and who generally met their clients just in time to prepare for the political asylum hearing. Proyecto attorneys had fifteen to twenty hearings a day in courtrooms at the *corralón* and in Harlingen in 1984 and accepted about seventy-five new cases each month. The law office had 3,000 open cases and a perfect score of no asylum victories in 1,000 trials.[7] The paralegals kept a list of potential clients who called from the *corralón*—the list was usually a few dozen names long.

I lived above the Proyecto office in the attic of an enormous unfinished firetrap at 301 East Madison Street in Harlingen. The office was furnished with rickety card tables and chairs, two ratty couches, a few banged-up file cabinets, and box after cardboard box crammed full of manila folders—the active files. There was one photocopy machine and half a dozen telephones. Wooden studs without walls lined the narrow staircase that led to the lawyers' unfinished offices on the second floor, where manila folders lay strewn about the floors, piled in boxes, and spilling off chairs. The office furnishings suited our pay scale of $75 a week—about a dollar an hour. There was no air-conditioning in the prison or in the office where we worked fourteen-hour days in the humid 100-degree heat of South Texas. Lisa Brodyaga did not demand those hours—we were all volunteers.

At 6 A.M. every morning in the autumn of 1984, the phone rang in the office of Proyecto Libertad. I would answer it and hear a click, then the caller would hang up. I assumed it was an FBI phone tap, or the FBI simply letting us know it could tap us if it wanted. The FBI file on Proyecto Libertad shows the bureau was investigating the office then, photographing visitors, clients, and office workers; investigating volunteers and financial donors; and trying to find out what books Lisa Brodyaga read.[8] The FBI even investigated a newspaper reporter who wrote an article that quoted Brodyaga speaking at a university-sponsored public forum on Central America.[9]

Documents from the FBI investigation, coordinated from the bureau's San Antonio office, are titled "El Salvador—Terrorism." The investigation began in 1982 and continued at least until September 1985—the date of the last file the bureau released from its 362-page investigation of Proyecto Libertad. The bureau released only 128 pages and blacked out more than half the text in them. A May 10, 1985, cable to FBI headquarters in Washington states, "No information has been received by the San Antonio office to indicate that captioned organization is directly connected with any terrorist organization. Furthermore, there are no specific or articulable facts to indicate Proyecto Libertad [CENSORED] or in any activity in support thereof."[10]

The FBI investigation of constitutionally protected activity violated a 1981 consent decree in which the FBI agreed to cease illegal spying upon activities protected by the First Amendment.[11] The FBI intrusion upon civil liberties was widespread. An INS officer at the Bayview prison provided the

FBI with information from political asylum applications Brodyaga filed for Salvadoran clients, though the INS has always claimed that political asylum applications are confidential.[12] The FBI reported information about Brodyaga to the Internal Revenue Service.[13] The bureau compiled photographs of Proyecto office workers—all of which were deleted from the FBI files that the bureau released under the Freedom of Information Act.[14] The FBI investigated the political views of Scott Lind, a reporter for the *McAllen Monitor,* after he wrote an article about a Pan-American University public forum on U.S. Central America policy at which Brodyaga spoke.[15] The bureau broadened its terrorism investigation to include the Texas Farm Workers Union (TFWU), after a TFWU organizer spoke at the university forum.[16] And the FBI investigated financial contributors to Proyecto Libertad, a nonprofit corporation, including "an unidentified 'young millionaire' from Austin, Texas, who [CENSORED] described as a 'liberal.'"[17]

One FBI informant told the bureau that Lisa Brodyaga "is a [sic] avid reader" and that the informant "will discretely [sic] try to obtain any information [CENSORED] is willing to provide about [CENSORED] and her activities."[18] The bureau also collected license plate numbers of Proyecto office workers and visitors,[19] and refused the author's request to declassify them. The FBI claimed it would compromise national security to tell me my own license plate number.[20]

The expurgated Proyecto file, released in 1992 in response to a Freedom of Information Act request, shows the Justice Department had decided by 1983 that all Salvadorans would be denied asylum and deported. An FBI agent in San Antonio wrote on September 30, 1983, that Brodyaga represented Salvadoran asylum applicants "knowing full well that these aliens will ultimately be deported to El Salvador, thus keeping the USINS camp busy and keeping the United States/Central American policy controversy alive in the Rio Grande Valley, Texas."[21]

These government documents and others show that Proyecto Libertad had no chance to win asylum for Salvadoran clients. Our only victories were bonding people out before they had to go to trial in the prison so that they might get a more fair trial in a northern district, and documenting the abuses in the prisons and in prison courts to use in federal appeals and class action lawsuits. While Proyecto workers defended victims of rape and torture from the governments of the United States and El Salvador, we were the ones suspected of being terrorists.

The Corralón

The Reverend Jonathan Torvik Jones, a Lutheran minister, was my fellow paralegal at Proyecto. Five days a week, we split up the new client list with the other paralegals, if there were any, then drove the twenty-six miles to the *corralón*, past San Benito through flat river bottomland, past white wooden houses on stilts overlooking fields where undocumented Mexicans and Central Americans picked tomatoes and strawberries, bending over the black earth in humid air that reeked of pesticides. For the last quarter-hour, we drove through miles of flat green nothing. Turtles crawled across the road in the morning, turtle shells lay smashed on the road in the evening; scissortails and hawks flew overhead while a few spindly-legged white cranes stalked over the wet ground past Brahma bulls munching grasses with long-billed cattle egrets on their back feeding on the insects that fed on the cattle.

The *corralón* is at the east end of a narrow 600-meter driveway lined by decapitated palm trees killed in the 1983 freeze. To the right is a little village of trailer homes and prefabs, built for INS officers who want to live in government housing. Beyond the checkpoint that is like a freeway toll-booth, the long driveway winds toward the prison, which sits behind chain-link fence topped with television cameras and concertina wire. To the southeast, ahead and to the right, are the women's dorms, separated from the men's section by more fences. Behind the parking lot, dead ahead, are two sliding chain-link fences, also topped with razor wire. Deportees line up inside the gates to be marched onto the bus that will take them to the Houston airport. Beyond the double gates is the prison's dusty dirt yard, with a few volleyball nets and a makeshift soccer field. Prison director Cecilio Ruiz convinced the INS to build a couple of open-air shelters for protection from the sun in the late 1980s, but the shelters were not there in 1984. Beyond the dusty yard are the men's dorms. To the right of the parking lot are trailers that house INS offices, and immigration courts during the winter of 1988–1989. To the left, far off to the north, are brick buildings that housed the prison's administrative offices. During the refugee crisis of 1988–1989, the INS chartered Boeing 747s and deported Central Americans from a county airstrip just beyond the fence north of the administration buildings. Immediately to the left of the parking lot is the only way into the prison—up the sidewalk to a metal door with a window of reinforced glass. Access is controlled by an officer in the control room, who sits behind another fortified window.

Behind the tiny foyer, the control room is equipped with microphones, telephones, radios, and three banks of six-inch TV screens along two walls. The TV screens show the prison perimeter, the dorms, the yard, the kitchen and cafeteria. To the left, a narrow hall branches left again to the prison offices and immigration courts. At the mouth of the hall, to the right, is a waiting room with a few picnic-style tables. Access to it is regulated from the control room. Behind the waiting room is an even narrower hall, one person wide, with four private rooms off it to the left. Each room is about six by eight feet in area, with a tiny table and two chairs. That's where we interviewed clients. The back wall of each interview room had a window through which prison officers could look, though they seldom bothered. In a separate building south of the parking lot was the smaller women's section, with just two interview cubicles directly under the eye of the guard in the entrance hall.

Systematic Abuse

In the three months I worked in the *corralón* I saw prison guards, immigration judges, and court workers break so many laws that recording these abuses became as big a project as the bare-bones legal work and refugee interviews I continued to do. Among the most egregious abuses to which the INS subjected refugees were beatings, sexual assault, theft of mail, theft of property, theft of bond money, denial of access to counsel, theft of legal documents, willful mistranslation of court testimony, woefully inadequate medical care, and unconstitutional interference with the right to counsel.[22]

Prison guards demanded that detainees tell them what their lawyers had said, and INS guards misinformed refugees about U.S. immigration law to dissuade them from seeking asylum. Except for the thefts, sexual assaults, and drug dealing, most of this was done openly. On occasion, the prison guard who led a refugee away from me after an intake interview would return to the cubicle and recite what I had told the refugee and what the refugee had told me. Prisons are about power, and in this demoralizing setting, petty harassment was one of the perks.

Because of the *Nuñez v. Boldin* and *Orantes-Hernandez v. Meese* (formerly *Orantes-Hernandez v. Smith*) federal court orders, the INS had to inform Salvadorans of their right to seek political asylum, but it would be more accurate to say that the INS misinformed Salvadorans about their right to seek asylum. Virtually every man processed through Los Fresnos immigration prison was told that if he applied for political asylum, he would have to stay in jail for a year or more. Most were told that if they applied for asylum, they could never return to their homeland again. This happened to more than 90 percent of the 300 people I interviewed inside the *corralón*. Many said that a prison guard had "explained the law" to him the night he entered the prison, after he took a shower and was deloused. As the refugees stood naked with chemicals on their genitals, prison guards misinformed them about U.S. law to discourage them from seeking political asylum. Other guards repeated the misinformation later, in the dorms. Prison guards did not misinform the women prisoners as often as they misinformed the men.

Prison officials then subjected them to an unending string of harassment and petty humiliations. Guards, for example, kept the toilet paper. "Each barrack has a toilet, yes, but you're not allowed in the barracks during the day," a college-educated Colombian told me. "During the day, there's one toilet for five hundred people. And toilet paper? They don't put it in the toilets; they don't give it to you. They give it to the guard, and you have to ask the guard for it. He'll give you one piece."[23]

A guard named Vasquez liked to torment prisoners by ruining their meals. South Texas temperatures hit the nineties and hundreds from April through October, with humidity almost as high as the mercury. Lunch at the *corralón* tended to be beans, bread, and Kool-Aid. "If you ask Vasquez for a second cup of Kool-Aid, he pours it over your beans," two Salvadorans told me. "How can you eat that?"[24]

Guards left the lights on all night in the dorms and rousted prisoners from bed at midnight and in the early morning to be searched. Guards charged prisoners ten cents on the dollar to give change for the cigarette and pop machines and overcharged for postage stamps. More enterprising guards sold drugs to detainees—$3 a joint. A few guards sold cocaine.[25]

Petty graft and abuse cannot be prevented by a court order, nor did it do as much damage as did the judges' and guards' calculated violations of immigration law. The *Nuñez v. Boldin* and *Orantes-Hernandez* orders directed the INS to provide Salvadoran detainees access to legal counsel. The INS responded by giving detainees a list of legal organizations—none of which did political asylum work. Despite years of requests, the INS refused to put Proyecto Libertad on the list given to refugees, though it was the only office in South Texas that did pro bono refugee work. The INS list included Texas Rural Legal Aid, which is prohibited by law from doing legal work for undocumented immigrants; the Texas Bar Association; and other referral agencies that do not offer direct services to refugees. And even the most far-reaching court orders, such as *Nuñez v. Boldin* and *Orantes-Hernandez,* did not affect the way Salvadorans were treated by immigration judges.

So if a refugee got Proyecto's phone number from another detainee and decided to stand up to the guards and take a chance on spending a year in jail, and if we called him to an interview before the INS called him to a deportation hearing, and if the prison guards actually called the man to the interview, and if he believed me and not the prison guards and was so terrified of being deported that he preferred to stay in jail, then we could help him apply for political asylum.

The average immigration prisoner was moved in and out of an immigration prison in thirteen days in 1984.[26] The only way out was to pay the bond—usually $3,000 at the *corralón*—or be deported. That gave refugees thirteen days to find an attorney, get called to an interview, and convince a Proyecto Libertad paralegal to accept the case. It gave us thirteen days to interview the people who had called first, to work our way down to the new arrivals, to decide whether to accept the case, to file a G-28 form to notify the INS that the prisoner had an attorney who had to be notified before each hearing, to inform the prisoner of his rights, to appear with him at an initial hearing, and to start the interviews to prepare government form I-589—the application for political asylum. More refugees arrived almost every day.

A few refugees had family members or friends who agreed to pay their bonds. Most didn't. In that case, depending on his or her degree of desperation and the danger he or she would face at home, we might try to help him or her pay the bond. The most desperate cases were union workers, victims of rape or torture, army deserters, community organizers, students, and people from villages that had been obliterated by bombing or army sweeps. Finding bond money was up to each paralegal or lawyer. I promised to try to raise $2,000 for the first prisoner I met when I went to work for Proyecto. I had no idea how I would do it.

Life in the Corralón

Carlos was a skinny Guatemalan with a blood bruise on his eyeball where a prison guard had punched him. Carlos spoke English with a peculiar accent, more German than Spanish. I saw him at least once a week for six weeks as he became more desperate each day—losing weight, forgetting to shave, clutching his Bible, a cornered look in his eye. Carlos was a born-again Christian who had been beaten "too many times" in Guatemala. He came into the tiny interview room dressed in an orange jumpsuit. He said in English:

> You see my eye? A guard slapped me in the face, here. There was a guy calling me and I asked the guard, "Sir? Can I go? Someone is calling me," and he said, "Shut up." I didn't understand this, and said, "What is this, 'Shut up?'" and he slapped me here, in the eye. Then they put me in solitary for five days. There's supposed to be a limit of seventy-two hours. I was in there for five days.[27]

INS regulations limit solitary confinement to three days. It was typical that Carlos was put into solitary after being beaten. That made it harder for him to register a complaint and harder for an attorney to find him, if he had an attorney. It served as "evidence" that he was "guilty" of something, and if there were bruises, they would fade by the time he was released. After a severe beating, the INS often transferred the victim to a county jail until the bruises went away.[28] I asked Carlos why he had been put into solitary confinement.

"They wrote a paper and it said that I was having abuse, that I was abusing a guard. And that's not right. I was only asking to talk to a guy. The paper said seventy-two hours. I was there for five days. The room was about as big as this. Every morning when I was sleeping, they'd throw water on me through the window. Every morning. And then they'd laugh at me. That's not right."

"Why are the guards picking on you?"

"The guards don't like me because I speak English."

"What's wrong with that?"

"I don't know. They speak half and half, half English and half Spanish in every sentence, but they tell me not to speak English.[29] I say, 'What is wrong in here? Can't I speak English?' but they don't want me to speak English. Maybe I'm not supposed to speak English because they think I'm an alien."

Already Carlos's desperation took physical form in the constant, slow rocking of his body, the hunted look in his eyes. I asked him to tell me about the prison.

"I was having a hard time here, because I had no shoes. When I came here, I put all my things together to take a shower, and when I came out there were no shoes. It was like three weeks I had no shoes. At noon time they call the people to stand in line and count you before you eat, and the stones were real hot. I had to try to find some shadow to stand in. Then a guy from Guatemala told me, 'I got an extra pair of shoes I'll give you if I get out.' And now he got deported, I guess. He give me the shoes and they're all dirty, like he'd been working with cattle. So I wash them up and they're drying now. Another guy from Guatemala gave me these sandals, 'cause he saw my suffering.

"There's some other guys from Guatemala. We get together and read the Scriptures, and that's the only pleasure I have. I don't smoke. I don't drink. I'm a Christian. I preach the Word in here. I have a Bible here. It's beautiful, with a concordance and all. Beautiful. I got one in English and one in Spanish. But the guards always be picking on me, always, especially if I'm laughing or smiling. Maybe they think I'm laughing at them, I don't know. I'm not. I respect myself. I respect everybody."

"Did they hit you besides the time they hit your eye?"

"No, they just push me from behind, from the back. They're always pushing. They always get into how your mother is, everybody's mother. That's hard. There's a lot of people who get this kind of treatment, but they are afraid. They are afraid of the solitary room, they are afraid to be deported, they are afraid to go to the county jail."

"Why do they send you to the county jail?"

"I don't know. They told me that I had one more week before they sent me to the county jail. I was in the county jail in Laredo for three weeks before they brought me here. In Laredo there was one American in there that I think was out of his mind. He was laughing, like he was out of his mind. Jimmy ———. I remember that guy.

"Over here, whatever you say, whatever you touch, whatever you do, everybody knows it."

"Why don't you want to go back to Guatemala?"

"I was having such a hard time with the Guatemalan government. Every place you go, all the time, there's the army, the police, all the time with guns, asking for papers, asking for money. The police. The army. It was bad. Always stopping me, always asking me, beating me up."

"Why did they beat you up?"

"They wanted to know the truth, and that's the only way they know how to find the truth, is to beat you up. Because I don't talk like a Guatemalan anymore. Or they saw me talking with some Americans. I know a lot of things. I know a lot of people there. But I don't want to go there and get killed.

"Last time I went to Guatemala the cops got me right in the airport. Boy, they didn't waste any time. Straight off the plane they took me right over to jail. Two weeks. Boy, that was terrible. I wasn't having much papers when I got there, but they knew who I was."

Carlos had been deported from the United States, arrested at the Guatemala City airport, and imprisoned and beaten for two weeks.

"[After two weeks] They threw me out. Then they started stopping me wherever I'm going: Guatemala City, in the whole country. They was checking all the people around, everywhere. This was because of the elections. If you didn't have the papers to vote in the elections, they take you to jail. I was beaten up too many times. I don't deserve it. They told me after they beat me that if I don't get me out of the country they will disappear me. Man, I don't need that. I need to survive. I need to be in peace."

I told Carlos I would do whatever I could to get him out of prison. Since there was nothing else I could do but get a lawyer to file a G-28, I shook his hand and escorted him to the door of the tiny interview room, which means· I stood up and turned around. Carlos was not used to prison. He never did get used to prison.

Six weeks later, a religious organization paid Carlos's bond and helped him get political asylum in Canada. He came to see me at Proyecto the day before the church group took him north. He hugged me and promised to write from Canada. He did send a postcard, thanking me and praising the Lord. It was my first victory.

Yet Carlos didn't have much of a case for political asylum. He certainly would have been denied asylum in the United States. After all, he had been deported before and had lived. He had come back after being deported, for which he could have been charged with criminal reentry. Though our attorney would have argued that that shows how afraid he was to stay in Guatemala, the INS attorney and the judge would take it as evidence that Carlos was in no danger in Guatemala.

The average Proyecto client had a much sadder story than Carlos, but Carlos had three advantages: He was educated and articulate in two languages, he was religious, and he was not political. Because he was educated and spoke English, he was able to get a religious worker interested in his case. Being a born-again evangelical Christian didn't hurt. And though political asylum, by definition, is for victims of political repression, neither the U.S. government nor most religious groups looked kindly upon people who had been involved with the guerrillas. Most churches preferred victims to people who fought back.[30]

After Carlos left, I sat in the little room until a guard brought me Adrian, the smiling refugee. Adrian was five feet two inches tall and weighed about 110 pounds. Every time I saw him he made me laugh, though he was in prison and I wasn't. While he was in the *corralón,* Adrian taught an illiterate Salvadoran army deserter who had been tortured how to read and write. He helped another Salvadoran, who did not trust lawyers, to fill out an application for political asylum.

Adrian got out of prison because a U.S. citizen, a stranger who had hired him to do yard work for a few weeks, had learned a little bit about Adrian's life and was so appalled to learn the INS wanted to deport Adrian to El Salvador that he called me to ask how to pay Adrian's $2,000 bond "and whatever else it takes to get him out of there."[31]

For refugees who managed to bond out of immigration prison, this was not unusual, though sometimes refugees were bonded out by unscrupulous employers who used the debt to impose virtual slavery upon them. In one case in South Texas, a U.S. businessman bonded out a Salvadoran and employed him in debt servitude. When the man's pregnant wife arrived, the businessman promptly drove her to the airport and deported her himself—and added the cost of the plane ticket to her husband's indenture. The man had been tortured in El Salvador; the Salvadoran government had murdered members of his wife's family. This de facto deportation by a private citizen heaped untold misery on the poor Salvadoran, who continued to work for the businessman because he felt that working off the cost of his bond—and his wife's plane ticket south—was a debt of honor.[32]

Adrian was not so unlucky. The man who paid his bond wanted nothing in return. He could afford the $2,000 it cost to get Adrian out of prison, so he spent it. Adrian understood that Proyecto Libertad's purpose was to help refugees, and he encouraged the prisoners with the saddest stories to call us. If they didn't know how to use a telephone, Adrian called for them. The day I met him, I asked Adrian to describe a typical day in the *corralón.*

They get us up at five in the morning. There's about one hundred in our barracks. It's a mess when we have to leave; there's great disorder because everyone wants to get out. There are guards with radios up above saying when we leave, what's happening. We get about fifteen minutes to wash up.[33]

After we eat, we go back to the beds to be counted. A guard goes by and counts us. If he loses count, he has to go back and count us again. [Adrian laughed.] We say inside that he can't count. After we're counted, we can go to the phone to make phone calls. Most of us get together and talk about what we've suffered in the war in El Salvador.

Fights are very frequent. Someone will get offended by someone from another country, and they'll fight. Or someone will steal something from someone else—soap, a cookie, and then they'll fight. Then there's a few guards who like to insult and beat the refugees.

Being locked up like this affects the minds of some, who are not accustomed to it. There are many who don't have contacts with anyone; they have lost their whole family in El Salvador. Some of them start to behave like children. They stand in a corner talking to themselves as though there were someone else there, or they laugh or cry for no reason. Or they sit alone, playing with a comb and tissue paper. I want to get out of here as fast as I can. I don't want this to affect my mind.

I got out of El Salvador just in time. A week later the army came and took three of my friends. We were just like brothers. After a few weeks in the army one of them got a family visit. Listen, before they let him see his mother, the officers called him and said, "Look, you're going to get a visit. We're going to be watching you. If your mamá comes out of the visit with a sad face, it's going to be too bad for you. You just watch what you say."

Look, all he wanted to say was, "Mamá, get me out of here." He'd been beaten, see, like the others. But he had to say, "Mamá, everything's fine. They treat me well here," so that she wouldn't be crying when she came out. But he told her how it was, and they both wanted to cry, but she managed to be smiling when she came out. She smiled, you see, because she had to.[34]

Adrian made it safely to Washington, D.C., the best place for a Salvadoran refugee to live in the 1980s. I saw him there four months later. He lived in a two-bedroom apartment with at least ten other refugees, including two brothers, one who came to the United States legally with his wife and two children, and one who made it without being caught. Cousins, in-laws, and people from their neighborhood slept on the floor. Adrian was washing dishes to pay off his $2,000 debt.

No Help for Campesinos

Because of the long waits to which prison guards subjected refugees and prison workers, Carlos and Adrian were the only people I interviewed on my first morning in the *corralón*. They were lucky. Someone took an interest in them, so they got out of jail. Most refugees were not so lucky. *Campesinos* especially—the small farmers who arrived here with nothing:

poor, illiterate, inarticulate—often were unable to arouse enough interest from a legal worker that the worker would run up a phone bill trying to badger someone into paying the bond.

Reynaldo was a typical *campesino*, one of hundreds I interviewed in the prisons. He was about forty years old and looked about sixty. Reynaldo was a humble man. He had no schooling. He didn't know how old he was, or his birth date. Like most *campesinos,* he had never heard of political asylum, and when he learned what it was he said he didn't want it. He just wanted "a permit to stay here for a little while, if that would be possible?"[35]

"I live in ———, department of Usulutan. I'm a small farmer [*campesino*]."

"Have you had any problems?"

"No, it's calm enough there. I haven't had any problems, because I'm a *campesino*. At times they steal my animals, my cows, my oxen. I don't have any little animals now. I don't mix with things. If one of 'the boys' asks me for five, I'll give it to him.[36] If a soldier asks me for something, I'll give it to him. Maybe they ask me for my shirt, or my shoes. So I give it to them. I don't have any problems. I'm a *campesino*.

"Look, it's like being between two thorns, on either side. I stay away from both of them. I don't understand politics. Because I'm a *campesino*. I have no problems."

"You have no problems? There is no war in Usulutan?" [Usulutan was guerrilla territory.]

"Where I live, in my pueblo, no. Two kilometers away, there are bombardments, attacks, firefights. But where I live, everything is calm. Everyone lives in the town, now. You don't go inland, because 'the boys' are there, and the army—the Ramon Belloso Battalion.[37] The army is all around a big coffee estate there, guarding it. All around it.

"If you go on the roads, the army stops you and asks you for papers. You know, 'Hands up! Against the wall!' Like that. And they search you all over and if they find nothing then they let you go. There's no problem, if you're a *campesino*. It's not like being a teacher."

"What happens to the teachers?"

"I don't know."

"Tell me some more about Usulutan."

"Oh, it's very beautiful. There's mountains and forests. It's a beautiful country, El Salvador."

"What do you think of President Duarte?"

"Well, in some ways good, in some ways bad. Look, there are people in El Salvador with great amounts of land, thousands of *manzanas* [hectares].[38] If you live on the borders of their estate, and you have just a few *manzanas,* then they make you work on the big estate. And if you don't, they take your land away from you.

"I had an aunt who broke both her hands. And because she has no sons, there was no one to work the land for her. So they took it from her, because she couldn't work it, you see, because her hands were broken, and she has no sons."

"Who has the land now?"

"Señor Chacon. He has a lot of land around there. But I had no problems. I have the good luck that none of my relatives are in the guerrilla, nor the army. So when the army comes to investigate me and ask questions and search my papers, I have no problems. And when the guerrilla come to investigate me, I have no problems. Because I'm not with one nor the other. So I sleep tranquilly. I'm a *campesino*."

Reynaldo wanted nothing to do with political asylum. Prison guards had told him that if he applied for political asylum, his government would find out, would consider him a traitor, and would never let him go home again. He was deported to El Salvador.

The Court System

Many of the crimes prison guards committed were crimes of opportunity: theft of refugees' personal belongings, theft of bond money, physical and sexual assault. But the dissemination of false information to intimidate and discourage refugees from seeking political asylum was systematic. It happened to virtually every male prisoner I interviewed in the *corralón*. Though it violated U.S. law, interfered with the right to counsel, and violated the *Nuñez-Boldin* injunction, the abuse would be nearly impossible to prove in court, and even if we could prove it, a judge would be likely to dismiss it—perhaps the guard didn't understand the law. A greater abuse than all the beatings, thefts, robberies, and sexual assaults committed by Border Patrol personnel and INS prison guards was the lockstep behavior of immigration judges, who systematically violated federal law to deport refugees—many of them to their deaths.

Prison trials operated in a realm beyond logic—pure ideology and whim become judicial decree. The first prison hearings I ever witnessed, in El Paso prison, set the tone for the rest. El Paso prison was built to hold 342 detainees; its capacity was expanded to 410 in 1985.[39] Like all the other border prisons, it was filled to capacity throughout the 1980s.[40] Any U.S. citizen has the legal right to enter an immigration prison to watch deportation hearings, but prison officials generally won't allow members of the general public to enter unless they are accompanied by a lawyer. I got into El Paso prison with a sympathetic attorney, who led me to Judge William Weinert's courtroom, then left to interview clients. I saw fifteen Salvadorans ordered deported in as many minutes, and nine more brought in. The attorney who helped me appeared for about three minutes and got a client a continuance. The rest of the time there were just the judge and I, the refugees in orange jumpsuits, and, for a while, a white lawyer in a very expensive suit.

Judge Weinert could certainly rap out a quick deportation order on his push-button tape recorder. He ordered the first fifteen men deported to El

Salvador, noting that they could appeal his decision to a higher court in Falls Church, Virginia.[41] One nervous young man asked to appeal. As the prisoners were being led out, Judge Weinert and the well-heeled lawyer, to my surprise, discussed whether the Reverend Jesse Jackson, who was then seeking the Democratic nomination for president, was a Marxist-Leninist. Nine more Salvadorans were brought in wearing orange jumpsuits. The lawyer got one of them a bond reduction. Weinert gave the rest of them four days to get a lawyer or face deportation. There was no refugee law project in El Paso. Refugees without money couldn't get a lawyer.

The third young Salvadoran man to go before the judge asked if he could have his bond reduced without a lawyer. "Why?" asked Judge Weinert. "Aren't you ready to face the deportation hearing? Aren't you ready to face the deportation hearing? Aren't you ready to face the deportation hearing?"[42] Weinert and the lawyer laughed as Weinert taunted the prisoner. I was astonished at the judge's contempt for the people he was judging. He and the lawyer told cruel jokes with their eyes while the desperate eyes of *campesinos* from El Salvador looked to me and to the lawyer for an answer. I didn't know the answer, and if the lawyer did, it would cost money. So the Salvadorans were deported.

Judge Robert Brown, of Houston, was just as contemptuous of the prisoners upon whom he sat in judgment. Brown went to Oakdale as a visiting judge in September 1986. There he presided over the asylum trial of a Salvadoran man who had scars of torture all over his back. Soldiers had cut him with razors and poured salt on the wounds. He had been one of twelve men in an opposition group in 1981, ten of whom had been killed by death squads, usually after prolonged torture. One had been granted political asylum in the United States. In Oakdale immigration court I presented Judge Brown with an English translation of Omar's five-page single-spaced statement. It described the tortures to which he had been subjected and the fate of his eleven companions. Brown took less than three seconds to flip through the sworn statement and toss it aside. He refused to read it and refused to let the man testify about being tortured because, he said, torture was "irrelevant" to the man's claim for political asylum.[43]

The cruelty and contempt with which judges treated Salvadorans were reflected in the decisions they rendered. A typical case was Angel, an educated twenty-three-year-old Salvadoran who did office work for Proyecto Libertad after he was released on bond from the *corralón*. His asylum trial took place in October 1984 inside Los Fresnos prison. Angel had worked on a cooperative cotton farm in El Salvador. Cooperative farms were a favorite target of death squads because the land for many of them had been taken from large landowners as part of the U.S.-backed land reform. Death squads had killed two of Angel's coworkers and then had killed his cousin, Rigoberto Funes, and threw his body into a canyon. Angel retrieved his cousin's body; his eyes had been gouged out. Soon after that, while Angel was standing in the back of a truck on his way to work, a death squad stopped the truck, singled out Angel, and shot him in the stomach. The driver took him to a hospital, where one of the nurses knew him. She immediately had him transferred to another clinic because death squads follow their victims to hospitals to finish them off. The death squad looked for Angel at the first hospital but could not find him. They went to his house and asked for him. Angel lived in hiding for five months, recuperating, then fled to the United States.

I worked with Angel for weeks and saw him suffering the effects of his wounds. Some days he could barely stand up due to the nerve damage in his back. His lawyer, Clare Cherkasky, talked the prison director into letting her take Angel to a private doctor in Harlingen. The doctor examined him and wrote a description of the gunshot wound and the extensive nerve damage it had caused. Clare submitted the doctor's report as evidence after Angel told his story and showed the bullet entrance and exit wounds to immigration judge Daniel Kahn inside Los Fresnos prison.

Angel never had a chance. As usual, the INS translator consistently mistranslated his testimony in a prejudicial manner to assist the judge in denying him asylum. In Angel's case, the INS translator mistranslated his testimony, "*No dispararon a todos, solamente a mi*" (They didn't shoot at everyone, only at me) as, "They shot at everyone but only hit me." She mistranslated "*Amenicé reuniones*" (I livened up meetings) as "I threatened meetings" and she repeatedly refused to translate the words "*escuadrón de muerte*"—death squad.[44]

Not once, in the dozens of asylum trials I attended, did I hear an INS translator correctly translate "*escuadrón de muerte*." In Angel's case, the translator simply left the words out or stopped and refused to go on when it was clear she had to finish a sentence with those words. She blushed as Clare finally shouted, "Death squad! Come on, death squad!"[45]

The mistranslations were critical in Angel's case. In denying him asylum, Judge Kahn wrote, "I find no convincing evidence that the person or persons [who shot him] ... were specifically aiming at the respondent." This was contradicted by Angel's testimony, which had been mistranslated by the INS translator.[46]

Mistranslations in asylum trials were common, egregious, and consistently damaging to refugees' cases; they seemed intentional and systematic. Translators mistranslated judges' and attorneys' questions, mistranslated the refugees' responses, failed to translate refugees' statements, and inserted statements into the record that the refugees did not make. Most immigration judges do not speak Spanish.

The INS has no standards whatsoever for translators, who are employees of the same system that pays the prosecutors and the judges.[47]

The asylum trial of a Salvadoran named Ricardo inside Oakdale immigration prison was typical. Ricardo represented himself at the hearing. He called me afterward, terrified, because the judge had called him a "terrorist" and ordered him deported. I listened to the tape recording of Ricardo's trial before immigration judge Johnny Duck. The translator, Maria Reyes, mistranslated Ricardo's very first statement and continued to mistranslate his statements throughout the trial, seriously damaging his claim to asylum.

Reyes translated Ricardo's statement, *"las autoridades, ya que han matado a mis familiares,"* (now that the authorities have killed my relatives) as "[the authorities] have already killed some families." Ricardo asked if he could present evidence that his brother had been kidnapped and murdered, and Reyes told the judge that Ricardo wanted time to get information about his brother. Ricardo said his brother had been kidnapped by armed men dressed as civilians, which Reyes translated as, "We know they were people that had arms, but I don't know. I really couldn't tell." The INS attorney asked Ricardo if his children had been threatened in El Salvador, and he responded, *"No sé"* (I don't know). Reyes translated this as, "No. I don't know." Ricardo said he had gotten eleven traffic tickets while living in Los Angeles, and Reyes said he had got eleven tickets for drunk driving. The INS attorney asked Ricardo in English if he belonged to an armed group that advocated the violent overthrow of the Salvadoran government, and Reyes asked in Spanish if it was true that his group was against the government. Ricardo answered, "Yes."[48]

Judge Duck denied Ricardo asylum and ordered him excluded from the United States because "by his own admission" he had tried to overthrow the Salvadoran government by violence.[49] Ricardo had said only that he had once hidden some pamphlets that denounced the government. The translator had put words into his mouth.

It might be comforting to think that these were the worst asylum trials I ever witnessed, and that abuses in other trials were not so egregious. That is not the case. Zero grants of asylum out of 7,000 applications is fairly solid statistical proof.[50] Angel's and Ricardo's trials were commonplace. The murder and disappearance of relatives was a usual claim for a Salvadoran; the U.S. government's lack of any evidence that the claim was untrue was usual; the mistranslations that were so bad as to seem deliberate were usual; the denial of asylum from a judge who did not speak Spanish was usual. Ricardo and Angel got a better chance at asylum than most because most Salvadorans who were deported from the United States in the 1980s never got to speak with an attorney. The only unusual detail in the two cases is that Angel had a letter from a U.S. doctor describing his bullet wounds, but even that didn't convince the judge that Angel had suffered persecution in El Salvador.

Law as a Subset of Ideology

High-ranking officials in the Justice Department acknowledged the administration's asylum policies were illegal—and vowed that the policies would continue. While the INS was under federal court orders to inform Salvadorans of their right to seek asylum and provide them access to legal services, the general counsel for the INS in Washington, D.C., Maurice C. Inman, told the *Los Angeles Times,* "All of those persons who have been detained will lose their asylum cases. All of them."[51]

Inman's statement was not rhetorical excess, or an unfortunate slip-up: It was a definition of the way the Justice Department ran the immigration prisons under the Reagan administration. It was a totalitarian system in which judicial decisions were made in Washington and imposed throughout the country. Joseph Stalin called it "democratic centralism." Americans call it kangaroo courts.

Refugees were in prison because they came to the United States without a visa. Legally, and in reality, that has nothing to do with the strength of their cases for political asylum. Inman said that though the refugees were arrested for a minor infraction—failure to have a visa—that would be used to deny them a fair hearing on a far more important issue—whether their lives were in danger in their homeland.

The INS never executed Central American refugees directly, but a litany of abuses of law and human decency similar to what Aleksandr Solzhenitsyn reported about the gulag were repeated in U.S. immigration prisons throughout the years of the Reagan administration. These included:[52]

> Beating and torture of prisoners
> Denial of sleep and food
> Failure to explain charges until after interrogation
> Invasion and search of homes without warrant
> Handing down of indefinite sentences
> Strip searches during interrogations
> Sentences predetermined, with a blank space left to insert the "guilty" person's name
> Violation of the mail
> Banning of books
> Imputation of crime because prisoners refuse to answer questions[53]
> Reading of private correspondence to seek information about potential charges, to be determined only after the correspondence has been read
> Extreme secrecy in court proceedings, including *running*, rather than walking, prisoners to court to keep them away from lawyers and the media[54]

Refusal to provide transcripts of court proceedings
Judging prisoners by class not by case
Slandering of private defense lawyers by government employees
Forbidding hunger strikes[55]
Forbidding outsiders from bringing food to prisoners
Prohibiting prisoners from viewing sunlight or talking
Holding prisoners in solitary confinement longer than the maximum
    period prescribed by law
Confining civil prisoners with the insane
Leaving on electric lights twenty-four hours a day
Prohibiting children from wearing shoes
Theft of prisoners' belongings by jailers
Prohibiting prisoners from sleeping or from warming themselves with
    blankets during the day
Detaining felons and violent criminals together with political prisoners
Denial by prison officials of knowledge of prisoners detained
Inadequate medical care
Recruiting and placing spies and stool pigeons inside the prisons
Manipulation of the press
Transfer of prisoners to remote locations with no notice to prisoners,
    their attorneys, or families
Arrest and imprisonment of family members before the prisoner's guilt
    has been proved and before formal presentation of charges
Threats to transfer a prisoner to a worse prison
Lying to and misinforming prisoners about matters of law to intimi-
    date, threaten, confuse, deny rights, and force confession

These abuses were carried out within an administrative court system that
operated on the assumption of guilty until proven innocent and one in
which the prosecutor, judge, and court translator were all working for the
same employer.

And if we didn't get the forms completed in time—the I-589, the G-
325 form containing biographical information, the fingerprints, the personal narrative, the documentation in support of the claim to political
asylum—the case was over: Welcome to Ilopango Airport. An excellent
metaphor for the system came to the Reverend Jonathan T. Jones in a
dream. After five years working for Proyecto Libertad and a season with
the Non-Governmental Human Rights Commission in El Salvador,
Jonathan was troubled with "weeks of violent nightmares. I remember in
one I'd been shot in the leg, and I dragged myself from room to room in
the office, bleeding everywhere, trying to get someone to look at my leg,
and nobody paid any attention to me." Jonathan laughed. "Just another
day at Proyecto."

Stealing from the Helpless

Our workday began with the 6 A.M. phone call and ended between 9 P.M. and midnight, when the INS released the people who had paid their bonds. Refugees who could pay the full amount of their bonds were given a date-stamped INS form and released after they reported an address where they could be notified of their next hearing. If the refugee attended all hearings and won the case or left the country within the time set by a judge, the bond money was returned with about 3 percent interest. But most refugees couldn't afford the $2,000 or $3,000 bond, so they used a bond company—in 1984 it was usually National Bail Bonds, which had an office right across the street from Proyecto. A bond company charged a percentage of the bond—from 10 to 75 percent, depending on the company's need for cash and what the traffic would bear—and if the refugee had a U.S. address and could provide the address and signature of someone who would be responsible for the rest of the bond should the refugee miss a court hearing, the bond company could arrange the refugee's release.

If a refugee failed to appear at a court hearing, the INS declared the bond breached: Unless the bond company could locate and return the refugee to the INS, the bond company had to pay INS the remaining amount of the bond. Unscrupulous bondsmen bilked refugees by demanding a monthly fee. Some worked with a notary public or an attorney to milk refugees of their last dollar, then failed to notify them of a court hearing and sent the INS to their home or workplace to arrest and deport them. The bondsman kept the money.

Many bail bondsmen are licensed to carry concealed weapons; they can enter homes without a warrant and have virtually unlimited power to make an arrest. "It's the closest thing to legalized slavery there is," one bail bondsman told me.[56] He offered me the use of his yacht and all the prostitutes, drinks, and drugs I wanted if I would recommend him to immigration detainees. I declined.

Just as unscrupulous as the bail bondsmen were the crooked notaries public, many of whom were based in Houston. In Central America, a *notario público* can do practically everything a lawyer does in the United States except represent people in court. I met dozens of refugees who had paid hundreds or thousands of dollars to *notarios públicos* in Texas to help detained relatives or to be bonded out themselves, only to find weeks later that a notary public cannot do legal work in the United States. The victims are deported, so there's no plaintiff to file a complaint against the notary.

The notary scam is so common in Texas that the state legislature passed a law limiting notaries' rights to advertise in Spanish or do immigration work. One notary, Jorge Santos of Houston, is under court order to stop taking money for "purported services" to immigrants, to refrain from using the words *notario público* in advertisements, and to refrain from preparing legal documents or documents to release people on bond.[57] Santos repeatedly violated the court order and continued to charge undocumented Salvadorans thousands of dollars for his "purported services." I met Jorge Santos's victims in Laredo, Houston, and Brownsville.

"The problem is always the same," said Houston attorney Meg Burkhart. "He says he's a lawyer, takes their money, and does nothing."[58] Angel, the Proyecto worker who had been shot in the stomach, was a Jorge Santos victim. He paid Santos $1,125 to be released from the *corralón*. Santos failed to notify him of a hearing, then sent the INS to arrest him.[59] Angel was sent to the *corralón* again, this time with a bond of $10,000. He was considered a bad bail risk because he had "absconded" from the hearing Santos hadn't told him about.[60] It's in the notaries' interest that their clients be deported; that way, the notary keeps the bond money: If the refugee wins asylum or goes to Canada, the notary would have to return it.

Houston notary Jorge Morales ran a scam with a lawyer, James T. Garrett, whose law license was suspended in 1983.[61] Garrett sold blank G-28 forms to refugees for $150. He told them it was a permit that would keep them from being deported. The G-28 form, Notice of Entrance of Appearance as Attorney or Representative, is a free government form available at any INS office. Unless an attorney files the form with the INS, the form is worthless.

One man was shot to death in Houston in 1986 in the office of a company that specialized in stealing from refugees.[62]

Proyecto Libertad never had any trouble with National Bail Bonds. We were glad to have an office close by that helped refugees get out of jail. After leaving the *corralón,* refugees filled out paperwork at the bond company; let the bondsmen photocopy every personal document they had; provided the names, addresses, and phone numbers of every relative and friend they had in the United States; and then they walked across the street to talk to me. I helped them fill out more forms, gave them the name of a lawyer in the city where they were headed, warned them about notaries, helped them make travel arrangements, told them that if they missed a single court date they could be arrested and deported, then drove them to Casa Romero, six miles away. There they could sleep and wait for their relatives in the north to send them bus fare out of South Texas. At that point, the refugees were no longer "illegal aliens"; they were legally in the United States seeking refuge, waiting for an asylum trial.[63]

The happiest times at Proyecto were between nine and eleven at night, when refugees were bonded out of prison. Husbands and wives were reunited after months of separation; brothers and sisters, lovers, entire families would meet again in Proyecto's office. After I had told them their legal rights, I'd say in Spanish, "Congratulations. Welcome to freedom in the United States."

They weren't really free, of course. They were in the process of being deported. One night a Salvadoran *campesino* and his wife were released on bond after spending a month in the *corralón*. She arrived at the office a few minutes before he did, beautifully madeup in a lacy black dress, heavily perfumed. I had carried messages between them for weeks. She sat on Proyecto's threadbare couch and I welcomed José as he stepped through the door. I shook his hand and asked him how it felt to be free. He looked over my shoulder at Maria as he shook my hand. Then he looked me in the eyes and said, "I just called my family in El Salvador. They came to my house, looking for me. They took away my little brother."

Maria and José left the next morning. I don't know what happened to them.

The Survivor Syndrome

Once a refugee bonded out of prison, the safest thing to do was to get out of South Texas into a northern district where judges occasionally granted asylum. As the refugee crisis continued, the INS devised ways to keep refugees confined to South Texas. INS Harlingen District Director Omer Sewell invented the "travel bond" in early 1986, charging refugees $1,000 above the cost of their bond for the right to leave the Harlingen INS District.[64] It was the only district in the country with such a policy. Then in 1988 the INS tried to stop refugees from leaving South Texas altogether.[65] But refugees whose only friends or family lived in South Texas had to stay there and return to the *corralón* or Harlingen for their trial, where they would be denied asylum.

Refugees who had an early morning trial stayed overnight in the Proyecto house. They had lived freely for a while, trusted Proyecto, and were nervous about their trial, so they usually talked more easily than did refugees who were still in prison. Benito told me his story the night before his asylum trial:[66]

> "I was jailed in the *corralón* for six months. After two months I went to see the doctor. I couldn't urinate for some time, and then when I could, it was a strange color. It felt as though my penis was going to fall off. The doctor said that all I had to do was wash with soap. Well, they don't give you any soap in there anyway, except when you first get in. It got worse, and I asked to go back to the doctor, and he said to get me out of there. He said there was nothing wrong with me. Then one day I woke up and there was blood all over the front of my pants. I went to the doctor and he said, 'Get him out of here. There's nothing wrong with him.'"

"You're telling me you were bleeding from the penis and the doctor said there was nothing wrong with you?"

"It's true. He said that it was because I was abusing myself. 'Get him out of here,' he said, 'There's nothing wrong with him.' Man, I was the first one in there that day, and I was the first one sent back to the barracks. I was sick the whole final four months. It was from the foul food they give you, food that even a dog wouldn't eat.

"When I finally got out after six months, I went to stay with my sister in Corpus Christi. She took my clothes to the laundromat to wash them. I stayed home, eating and eating, after that six months' food. My sister saw the blood in my pants when she washed them and she came back and asked me if I'd had sexual relations there in the jail. 'No, man,' I told her, 'I've been sick with this for four months.'[67]

"She took me to the doctor and he told me I was sick from lack of vitamins and that I had inflammation and a blood clot that interfered with my urination. He gave me antibiotics and vitamins. He took X rays and gave me an injection in the penis. That was pretty bad, man. It made me cry. I don't know what he injected me with. He told me to rest and eat. Man, I didn't need anyone to tell me that when I got out of the *corralón*. I ate ten times a day after I got out of there. I was eating with two hands.

"Do you have a guitar? No? Ah, that's too bad. I like the guitar. I know a lot of songs, popular songs, revolutionary songs. [Benito sang]:

> *Que triste se oye la lluvia*
> *en techos de cartón.*
> *Que triste vive mi gente*
> *por causa de explotación.*
>
> *Usted no lo va a creer*
> *pero hay escuelas de perros*
> *y les dan educación*
> *para que no muerdan los diarios*
> *pero el patrón.*[68]

> [How sad to hear the rain
> on roofs of cardboard.
> How sadly my people live
> because of exploitation.
>
> You won't believe this
> but there are schools for dogs
> and they teach them
> to not bite the workers
> but the boss.]

"I remember in Salvador a member of ———— gave me the words to some revolutionary songs. She photocopied them and gave me twenty or thirty and at night I nailed them to the walls and posts on the corners through the whole town, except in front of the Guard and the police. Next morning, the whole town was on the corners, reading the words. It's the only way you can inform yourself in Salvador, because the newspapers don't print anything. Not the truth. They print that the Left killed such and such, and it's not the truth, it's the Right. I know. A cousin of mine was killed by the Right, and the newspapers said that it was the Left.

"See these scars? This on my hands is from a machine gun. Man, I got my hands out of the way just in time. These on my face and on my head are from the army's boots. This is from a .22 bullet, here, in my leg. On my back and my thigh, here? Army boots.

"I was recruited in 1982. I spent five days in the army. Man, they beat you if you're not in the army, and they beat you when you're in the army. I couldn't stand the thought of killing the people. That's why I left Salvador.

"I remember when I was fifteen, just a kid. I was walking by the City Hall and there were five soldiers there. One of them picked me up from behind and he threw me toward another. He kneed me in the stomach and threw me to another, and he kicked me in the face. Then I was on the ground and another kicked me in the stomach, and the other stomped on my back. They point a rifle at me and say, 'Now, beg our pardon.'

"Man, I was just a kid. I'd never begged for anything. And there I was on my knees, begging their pardon. I remember them. I know them. And if one day I go back to Salvador ...

"My parents turned their back on me when they found I sympathized with the guerrilla. They turned their back on me. Man, that's hard. My father wouldn't talk to me. My mother, she'd talk to me just a little. I remember those five soldiers beating me up. I can see them like they're here in front of me right now. And if one day I go back to Salvador ..."

"How did you get the .22 wound?"

"That's because I was playing soccer. Every Sunday, every eight days, we'd play soccer.[69] I don't know, maybe one of the guys I played with informed on me, on how I thought, on my sentiments. When I was walking home after playing soccer they shot me, here, and then they stole my shoes, my soccer shoes.

"What I want to know is, why did they let me live? The soldiers had to come a long way to ———, to my village, just to steal my shoes. What I wonder is, why they let me live.

"No, it's a sad thing to know that the rich are eating banquets while the poor make a meal from dirt. Yes, the poor people eat dirt. That's the way it is. I remember the funeral of Señor Romero. You know Señor Romero? Señor Romero was a man who loved the people, and the people loved Señor Romero. There was a mountain of people there at Señor Romero's funeral. And when the shooting started, when the bombs went off, there was nowhere to run. People ran to this corner and poom! They ran into the machine guns. They ran to that corner and poom! Machine guns. ... There was no place to run.

"I hid in the cathedral. I grabbed a column and then I lay down and I stayed there for hours, till it was over. And I cried. But not from sentiment; I cried to see so many innocent people killed. I cried to see the blood flow like you see water flow in a river.[70]

"I don't have a master's degree. I don't have a college degree, but you don't have to be too smart to know that it was D'Aubuisson who killed Señor Romero, who had him shot with a bullet in the heart. Everyone knows it. It was D'Aubuisson who ordered the massacre at Señor Romero's funeral. You don't have to be smart to know that. Your people don't know what is being done with the arms you send to Salvador. Your people are being fucked by the Salvadoran press, by D'Aubuisson, because the truth never comes out."

In a dozen details, Benito's life was typical of hundreds of Salvadorans I met in the prisons and on the streets. He had been beaten by soldiers for no reason except that he was a young man out of uniform; he had been forcibly recruited, beaten, and had deserted; he had been shot for no clear reason. For having survived, he felt vaguely guilty. For fear that his friends would inform on him, he did not discuss his feelings. He was rejected by his own family for criticizing the government, yet his only involvement with the guerrilla was posting political propaganda. He loved Monsignor Romero and had witnessed the massacre at his funeral; he hated Roberto D'Aubuisson with an impotent rage. He had been mistreated in the *corralón*, yet he still had faith—greater faith than I did—that U.S. citizens did not know what was happening in El Salvador, that we had been tricked by the Salvadoran government and the press, and that if we did realize what was happening, we could stop it.

The "survivor syndrome"—guilt at not having been killed—was common among survivors of the Nazi concentration camps. But the average Salvadoran refugee is less educated than the average death camp survivor, has less faith in doctors and psychiatry, and has little or no access to medical and psychological help. There is no way to calculate the long-term damage these untreated psychological traumas will inflict upon refugees and their new homeland, the United States, but I saw some of it: the screaming nightmares, the refugee children's preoccupation with violence and death, the self-destructive and suicidal behavior that emanated from an inarticulable hate they feared to express and ended up turning upon themselves.

Medical Neglect

Medical care in the *corralón* was execrable. Tubercular prisoners were locked in the same dorms with healthy ones. This was reported by several prisoners and confirmed by a nurse.[71] Tuberculosis was just one of Federico's problems. Unknown men had beaten him at his home in Guatemala, for unknown reasons. He fled to the United States and was arrested in

Laredo in April 1984 and sent to the *corralón*. He had been there for six months when I interviewed him.

> They set a hearing for me for May 24, and I told the judge that I didn't want to be deported, that I wanted to ask for political asylum in the United States. He told me that I had to get a lawyer, or I'd have to represent myself. The next hearing was June 27, but I was never called. I've been waiting here since then. Nothing has happened. I've been forgotten here. I've just been waiting.[72]

A nurse confirmed that Federico had tested positive for tuberculosis when he was processed into prison. He was given daily medication for tuberculosis, but the INS refused to take him to court, presumably to avoid exposure. This continued for six months until Federico despaired and accepted deportation to Guatemala. Federico had no idea why he had been beaten in Guatemala and no idea what was happening to him in Los Fresnos. All he learned from his 4,000-mile round-trip and six months in jail was that he had tuberculosis.

Dozens of Salvadoran prisoners who reported to sick call at Los Fresnos were berated and called "communists" by the prison doctor, Lorenzo Pelley. Pelley is a Cuban American who claimed to be a member of Brigade 256, which invaded Cuba at the Bay of Pigs in 1961. In the four immigration prisons where I worked, more prisoners complained to me about Dr. Pelley than about any other person. Salvadorans resented it when they went to him in pain and he called them communists and told them they should be back in El Salvador fighting the communists instead of helping them.[73] On the other hand, when Nicaraguans were sleeping in the streets of Brownsville in the winter of 1988–1989, Pelley accepted numerous calls in the middle of the night to take care of them. Even providing medical care for Central American refugees was dictated by ideology.

Contra Recruiting

Perhaps the most blatant violation of U.S. law in the *corralón* happened on the day the Justice Department allowed right-wing U.S. citizens into prison to recruit fighters for the Contras. Recruiting foreigners on U.S. soil to fight in a foreign war is illegal—a violation of the United States Neutrality Act.

A Contra recruiter, a retired U.S. Army general, and a right-wing citizen entered the *corralón* on December 17, 1985, to recruit for the Contras. Father Lenny DePasquale, who conducted religious services inside the prison, spoke with several detainees who were recruited by the Contras that day.[74] Two attorneys who worked at the *corralón* said Contra representatives visited the prison on December 17 and offered to pay the bonds of detained Nicaraguans if they would join the Contras. Lisa Brodyaga spoke with two detainees who had been recruited: "I talked to them after they were out [of detention], and they said they had turned it down."[75]

Attorney Thelma Garcia said Contra representatives had also interviewed one of her clients in the *corralón:* After he refused to join the Contras he was interrogated by the FBI. "The FBI spoke to him after the Contras spoke to him and he refused to join up," Garcia said. "They accused him of being a Sandinista."[76]

FBI Special Agent Juan Gonzales acknowledged he had interviewed a Nicaraguan named Javier Pichardo Cuadras inside the *corralón* on December 17.[77] That day, Contra spokesman Mario Calero, the brother of Contra leader Adolfo Calero, was in Los Fresnos on a speaking and fund-raising tour with retired U.S. Army General John Singlaub, head of the World Anti-Communist League and a leading fund-raiser for the Contras.[78] Gonzales said the interviews concerned national security issues he could not discuss. Julian De la Rosa, FBI special agent in charge of the Los Fresnos area, refused to comment on the interviews. "We have no prohibition upon interviewing inside INS detention centers," De la Rosa said.[79]

Pichardo told his attorney, Thelma Garcia, that he had been taken to a private interview room in the prison on December 17 and introduced to a man who identified himself as Mario Calero. He said Calero offered to pay his bond if he would join the Contras. When Pichardo declined the offer, he was introduced to four other Nicaraguans in the prison who had agreed to go. "I don't know whether they actually paid the bond [for the four] or whether they were released on their own recognizance, as the government has that authority," Garcia said.

Pichardo's bond was $4,000; he had been detained for seven months. After the Contras and the FBI interviewed him, Pichardo became nervous and refused to talk to the press. When his story was printed in the *Brownsville Herald,* Pichardo lost his job in the prison, which paid a dollar a day.[80]

In 1985 the Reagan administration formed the United Nicaraguan Opposition, or UNO, whose chief spokesman, Bosco Matamoros, told me in a telephone interview from Washington that he had no knowledge of the recruitment interviews. Then he denied they ever took place. "We do not recruit anyone in the United States," Matamoros said in a booming baritone, "nor do we recruit any place in the world. People join our organization and leave our organization of their own free will."[81]

This was nonsense, of course. The Contras forcibly recruited, raped, tortured, and killed peasants who refused to join them.[82] The UNO spokesman who screened my call to Matamoros had told me, "Yes, we do call to volunteer, but we have to be careful about that. ... We've had a lot of restrictions on humanitarian aid. For example, we can't buy them tickets to send them down there. These sorts of restrictions."[83]

When I told Matamoros that a man who identified himself as Mario Calero had recruited Nicaraguans inside Los Fresnos prison, Matamoros responded, "There are many people who call themselves Bosco Matamoros." Someone impersonating Mario Calero might have conducted the interviews, he said.

However, Steve Walker, a Los Fresnos resident sympathetic to the Contras, told me he met with Singlaub and Mario Calero on their tour of the lower Rio Grande Valley. Walker denied that they had recruited Nicaraguans inside the detention center.[84] But Thelma Garcia contradicted this: Walker "called me here at the house. He told me that the Contras were coming through, and because he knew I represented a lot of Nicaraguan clients, that they wanted to meet with them."

When confronted with that information, Walker acknowledged he had tried to get the names of Nicaraguans detained at Los Fresnos because "we [Walker, Singlaub, and Calero] talked about what a shame it was that nothing could be done" about detained Nicaraguans. Walker said they went to the prison, but "the INS wouldn't let us in."

But John Luvender, acting assistant director for detention and deportation in the Harlingen INS District who was then in charge of the *corralón,* said the INS had admitted private citizens, whose names he could not reveal, into the prison on December 16 and 17, the days the Contra recruiting took place.[85] He claimed Pichardo was confronted with his statement that the Contras had recruited him inside the prison, and he retracted it. Luvender confirmed Brodyaga's statement that all the Nicaraguans who had been interviewed had left the prison except Pichardo, who was unable to pay his bond.

"The ones that are out of the [lower Rio Grande] Valley are the ones who were recruited and bonded out," Garcia said. "The people who were picked out [for recruitment] were people who had no attorneys." Garcia said that after he was interviewed by the Contras and the FBI, Pichardo "became kind of paranoid, and he withdrew his claim to political asylum."

Snapshots of Prison

What I remember most about the prisons, besides the rage, isolation, and frustration, is a few heartbreaking vignettes—not because the incidents were unusual but because they represent so well the lives of thousands of immigration detainees. I was talking with a young Salvadoran *campesina* in the *corralón.* Her village had been bombed, her husband killed. She had left her babies with her mother and fled to another village, then to the United States to find work. In El Salvador, she couldn't earn enough money to buy her children milk. She hoped that by getting a job in the United States she could send her mother enough money to feed her children. The Border Patrol arrested her the day she entered the United States. She knew no one here; she had no one to pay her bond. If she applied for political asylum she would lose, we would appeal the case, she would lose that too, and she would be deported back to the war after spending six to twelve months in prison.

Teresa wore the regulation orange jumpsuit. We talked in a tiny booth next to and visible from the control room in the women's section. A guard watched us through the window. I told Teresa she could apply for asylum but that her only real hope was to find $2,000 to bond out. I didn't have the money and I couldn't promise her anything. I asked what she wanted to do.

She decided to apply for asylum. I said that we would represent her, though I knew she didn't have a chance of winning and that if I found $2,000 I'd use it to help someone whose life was even sadder than hers. I told Teresa I'd come back to see her from time to time to prepare her case and so that she'd have someone to talk to. Was there anything else she wanted?

"Well, yes," she said. "A cookie."

"A cookie?"

"Yes," she said. "I'd like a cookie."

Smuggling food to detainees was prohibited. It was possible in the men's section, where the interview rooms were closed on three sides, but it was impossible to smuggle food to women, where the guard in the control room could see everything. So I lied. I told Teresa I'd bring her a cookie.

One day I went shopping with a beautiful young Salvadoran *campesina*. She too had left her children in El Salvador with her mother. I had talked a sympathetic woman into paying Ana's bond by telling a bit of her life. A death squad had dismembered her brother and raped her. Ana was afraid to leave the law office, but she relaxed as we strolled the aisles of a grocery store among other people speaking Spanish. She seemed fine until I turned to see she was not with me anymore. She was standing in front of the dairy case, tears streaming down her face. I went to her and asked what was wrong.

"Sixty-nine cents for milk," she said, crying. "The sons of bitches." She looked at me, still crying. "My children will never drink real milk. You *gringos* can have everything, and we can't have anything."

Women in prison often were afraid to speak. Many insisted they had nothing to say or that they wanted to say nothing. The average Salvadoran man I met in immigration prisons had perhaps four years of schooling. The average Salvadoran woman had less than that. I was able to coax Patricia into talking to me inside the *corralón* because I genuinely wanted to understand the life of a Salvadoran woman. Throughout the interview Patricia dabbed a wadded-up tissue at her eyes and nose, twisting it in her hands. When I interrupted and asked a question, Patricia broke into tears and begged me to let her go away.

> "It's so hard being locked up. I left my two children in El Salvador with my grandmother because there was nothing I could do for them in El Salvador. I

came to the north hoping I could find work and help them. Then the first day I fell to the *migra* and I've been locked up here for five weeks.[86]

"You understand we are very poor in El Salvador. And the president of El Salvador and the guerrilla both get money from the United States, but the poor people get nothing."

"The guerrilla get money from the United States?"

"Well, yes."

"How do you know that?"

"Because in San Vicente, where I live, there's lots of guerrilla. The guerrilla are everywhere, in the mountains, and they come down from the mountains to buy food and they always pay for it with dollars."

Patricia's eyes widened. I was questioning her about the guerrilla. She had admitted she had information about the guerrilla. She burst into tears. Her hands and then her entire body trembled. I put down my pen and said, "Look, it's all right. I won't write anymore." Patricia asked me to let her go, and she left the room, crying.

That was the hardest thing about working in the prisons. It was not the issues—the U.S. government arming, training, and covering up for death squads; prison officials and immigration judges violating the law; the prison doctor taunting torture victims, calling them communists; my own government covering up and excusing Salvadoran army massacres—but that these people, our clients, were human beings. They were not policy issues. They were human beings who had suffered tremendously, left their homeland unwillingly, and once in the United States were subjected to more abuse, which was not only illegal, unconstitutional, and inhuman, it was unnecessary. And there was nothing we could do about it. We could only document that it was happening.

In the *corralón* I met a young Salvadoran girl who had come home from school to find her mother's body in the yard, beheaded, stripped naked, with her head stuck on a bayonet that had been thrust into her vagina. Soldiers stood around to see how her daughter would react. I met a teenage boy who had seen Salvadoran soldiers rape and behead his mother. I met girls who had picked up pieces of their brothers. These people had no chance to win political asylum while Ronald Reagan was president of the United States. The abuses that forced the Justice Department to slowly, incrementally, grudgingly grant Central American refugees a few legal rights were the comparatively milder abuses to which they were subjected in the United States.

Waiting for Godot

Aside from misinforming Salvadorans about U.S. law in order to coerce them into waiving their right to request asylum, the most common legal abuse in the prisons was another form of interference with the right to counsel. Prison guards simply refused to bring us clients, or waited an hour or more to call a client to a twenty-minute interview, then made us wait another hour before calling the next one. This denial of access to clients was systematic, but it depended to some extent upon the mood of the guard in the control room.

In early October, as a guard brought me a client, I commented that things had gone pretty smoothly the day before. The guard, a burly young man with a short, bristly mustache, retorted, "I got reprimanded for bringing you clients too quickly."[87]

Almost daily, clients called the office late in the afternoon to ask why we hadn't called them that day. We had. We'd call them again the next day, but a prison guard would say they "didn't respond." That was the daily routine.

Another way the INS deliberately obstructed our work was to make us wait so long to see a prisoner that moments after a guard finally brought us a client, he'd return to take him away for the afternoon count. Thus the INS could show they had provided us access to prisoners, though no legal work could be done. On September 24, 1984, a prison guard in the *corralón* demonstrated how this could be done.[88]

Prison officials violated the United States Constitution by demanding that prisoners tell them what legal advice their lawyers or paralegals had given them. This was confirmed by a curious exchange I had with the prison director, Cecilio Ruiz, on the afternoon of September 28. It was a Friday, and because the long waits had prevented me from working, I told a client I would return the next day to talk with him. Proyecto workers hardly ever went to the *corralón* on Saturdays. As I left the men's section of the prison, Ruiz caught up to me and said, "Be sure to sign in tomorrow when you come."[89]

It was a gratuitous remark. Paralegals and attorneys have to sign in to enter the prison, and the only person who knew I planned to go back to the prison on Saturday was a Salvadoran prisoner I had interviewed alone in a closed room.

Violation of the Mail

The long waits to see prisoners led me to discover mail fraud at the *corralón*. I was sitting in the little vestibule of the prison after lunch, waiting for a client, when a young man entered, uttered a few urgent words in Spanish to the officer in the control room, then paced up and down the tiny foyer until I asked him what the matter was.

"A friend mailed a check to me from Port Arthur, Texas." He put his fists on his hips and said angrily, "The check never got to me and the letter was never returned to him."[90]

He was Salvadoran. He had bonded out of the *corralón* and was waiting for his asylum trial. He showed me a photocopy of both sides of the canceled check, endorsed with his name. "I just got back from Port Arthur," he said. "My friend gave this copy to me." He paced up and down. I asked him how mail was delivered inside the *corralón*. "I never got anything, man," he said. "I never got a letter."

I began asking clients if they had problems with the mail. Within two weeks, prisoners and bonded-out prisoners reported more than $4,000 worth of checks, money orders, and cash stolen from the mail. Mail fraud is virtually impossible to stop in the *corralón*. Incoming phone calls are not permitted, so prisoners don't know if they have a letter coming unless they have made a collect call to a friend or relative who promises to send money. Once a prisoner bonds out, he or she usually goes far away from South Texas and can't afford to return when the theft is discovered.

In early October, a client who had bonded out was sitting in Proyecto's office, waiting for a plane to New York.

"Roberto, maybe you can give me some advice. When I was in the *corralón* my friends from New York sent me $2,000 in postal money orders—four separate money orders for $500. I never got any of them. My friends sent me photocopies of the receipts. They called to investigate what had happened. All the money orders had been cashed. They had been signed with my name. Don't they ask for any identification when they cash them?"[91]

"I think they do. But let me tell you, this seems common in the *corralón*."

"I know it is. I know a Nicaraguan who had a check sent to him for $2,000. It never got to him and it appeared, cashed. There's a Salvadoran, Juan José ———, who had money sent to him in a registered letter. Registered, you understand, with seals. And the letter never arrived and the money disappeared. There's another one, a Colombian. He had a letter sent to him also, registered, with his bond. It was mailed a month before he was deported. He was deported one afternoon, and that same evening they called him, 'Mauricio, there is a registered letter for you.' They held that letter until he was deported."

"How do you know it wasn't held up in the mail from Colombia?"

"It was mailed from Los Angeles."

"How do you know when it was mailed?"

"Because he'd told us a month before that he'd had his bond sent to him by registered mail from Los Angeles. News goes around in there. He waited for a month, and they waited to call him until they'd already deported him."

Prison officials told me that prisoners opened their own mail in the presence of guards, who checked the contents for contraband. But prisoners on cleaning detail saw guards opening prisoners' mail while alone in their office.[92] In July 1989, immigration officers at the *corralón* refused to accept cash bonds after a $2,000 cash bond disappeared at the camp. The policy was changed after lawyers complained that the INS has no right to refuse bond payments. A few INS officials were transferred from one office to another, but the money was never recovered.[93]

Drugs and Sexual Abuse

Proyecto Libertad did not have the time or resources to investigate mail theft. Nor could we do anything about the guards who sold drugs to detainees. The going rate was $3 a joint in 1984.[94] Guards doled out to prisoners small amounts of the money they had had with them when they were arrested, and prisoners who accepted work details inside the prison were paid $1 a day. Guards sold drugs until June 15, 1989, when agents from the Justice Department's Internal Affairs division arrested seven officials at the *corralón*. They were charged with selling marijuana and cocaine at the prison. An INS guard and five security guards hired by INS on a private contract pleaded guilty to drug charges. One INS guard, Israel Perez, was acquitted on a charge of selling half a gram of cocaine to an undercover informant at the prison. The informant, twenty-year-old Dino Blancas, who worked as a cook, testified in court that the *corralón* was "a cesspool of corruption, prostitution and drugs. You name it, they had it."[95]

The week before Blancas testified against Perez, INS detention officer George Perales, thirty-eight, pleaded guilty to violating the civil rights of two sixteen-year-old boys who had been detained at the *corralón* in 1988—in violation of INS regulations that prohibit detention of minors with adults. The boys' attorney said they had been sexually molested.[96]

Drug dealing at the *corralón* contributed to an accident that left a young Honduran man a paraplegic. Twenty-year-old Juan José Gonzalez Cantillano fell and broke his neck after smoking marijuana inside the prison on March 17, 1989. Gonzalez was taken to a Harlingen hospital, then deported on June 3 in a chartered air ambulance that cost INS $12,700. INS officials and the consul general of Honduras in San Antonio, Rosa Argentina Pinal, said Gonzalez told them he broke his neck after smoking pot at the camp. After he was deported, a newspaper in Tegucigalpa staged a ten-kilometer run to raise money to pay for his medical treatment in Honduras.[97]

A bizarre incident of corruption at the *corralón* was the case of a pretty seventeen-year-old Salvadoran woman whom INS officials had promised to release if she'd dance the lambada with them. Two prison guards reported this to INS Harlingen District Director E. Michael Trominski in September 1990. It was one in a series of sexual harassment complaints that four prison guards filed with the Equal Employment Opportunity Commission and the U.S. Inspector General. Three female guards complained that they had been fired after rejecting sexual advances from a superior officer.[98]

The seventeen-year-old Salvadoran woman was scheduled for an immigration hearing at the prison on May 22, 1990. The Reverend Anthony Hefner, a Baptist minister who worked as a security guard at the *corralón*, showed me a copy of the INS court docket for May 22, which contained the woman's name and her immigration file number. Hefner said a woman guard took the Salvadoran teenager to the INS processing office "four or five times that day, and the INS officers said she had to dance the lambada dance and they would let her go."[99]

The twenty-five-year-old female guard who escorted the Salvadoran girl to the INS office confirmed the incident, and said she too had reported it to Trominski. She had been ordered to escort the Salvadoran to the INS processing office "at least four or five times in one day. ... She was coming out sweating and I asked her why and she said she had been doing the lambada and that she was going to leave that day or the next night, and she did."[100]

The Salvadoran girl's case was "administratively closed" on May 31. "I don't see there's any indication an asylum application was filed in the case," said Jerry Hurwitz, spokesman for the Executive Office of Immigration Review, in Falls Church, Virginia.[101]

Aside from seeking political asylum, marrying a U.S. citizen, or receiving special parole from the U.S. attorney general or humanitarian parole from an INS district director, there is no way a recently arrived undocumented immigrant can pursue a claim to remain in the United States, unless the INS simply chooses not to prosecute.

Bob Wallis, acting deputy district director of Harlingen INS District, told me, "I have no idea why the case was closed."[102]

Harlingen INS District director E. Michael Trominski did not return my phone calls for more than a year.[103]

Beating and Robbery Condoned

I never heard of a woman being beaten at the *corralón*, though consensual sex with guards was not uncommon.[104] Guards beat male prisoners frequently, and the beatings sometimes were condoned by the prison administration. Two INS guards beat and kicked Victor Julio Espinoza Valencia, a Colombian, in a storage room at the *corralón* on October 7, 1984, and stole from him a ring and a silver cigarette lighter embossed with an eagle. The guards admonished him not to report the incident or he would not live to see Colombia again.[105]

The attack was witnessed by two prisoners on cleaning detail, a Chilean and a Salvadoran. The college-educated Chilean had been tortured after General Augusto Pinochet's 1973 coup. He called me to demand that I take his sworn statement, and he persuaded the Salvadoran that it was his duty to talk about it as well. I interviewed the Chilean, the Colombian, and the Salvadoran separately. The Reverend Jonathan T. Jones took photos of the Colombian's head and chest wounds. All three prisoners said that while the guards were beating the Colombian, one went to the door of the equipment room to look out and said, "Go ahead, there's no one coming," then the guards continued to beat him. Both witnesses described the theft of the lighter and the guards' threat to kill the Colombian if he reported the attack.

I took the men's sworn statements on October 9 and 10, translated them into English, and presented the statements with photographs of the head and chest wounds to the prison director, Cecilio Ruiz. Ruiz interviewed the three men separately, in Spanish, then complimented me on the accuracy of my translation and my ability to take an affidavit. Nevertheless, he would not punish the guards because Espinoza had "abused officials."[106]

The Banality of Evil

Assault, theft, robbery, sexual assault, mail theft, drug deals, denial of access to counsel, interference with right to counsel, inadequate medical care—all this goes on in many prisons. At the new prisons at Laredo and Oakdale I saw how guards reacted to being placed suddenly in a position of power. Some became violent and abusive and tested the limits of their new-found power. A few became sensitive to the problems of the people inside. One guard—Kirk Bullock at Oakdale—started reading about Central America. But prison guards are not to blame for the U.S. immigration system. The most abusive guards, as detainees pointed out, were ignorant. Immigration judges, however, were not. They knew what was happening in Central America. They heard stories of rape, torture, and murder nearly every day in court. They had access to reports from Amnesty International, Americas Watch, and the State Department that detailed the savagery committed by the Salvadoran army and security forces. They saw the torture victims in their courts, and they heard Salvadoran army deserters describe the tortures to which government opponents were subjected—and the judges deported them anyway.

More harm was done to more refugees in the United States by bureaucrats in judges' robes—immigration judges Michael Horn, Daniel Kahn, Robert Brown, William Nail, and others—than by all the petty muggers and sexual predators in Border Patrol and prison guard uniforms. Of all Salvadoran asylum applicants whose cases reached federal appeals courts in 1984 and 1985, more than 60 percent were reversed or remanded.[107] That simple fact speaks volumes about the quality of justice doled out by U.S. immigration judges. It shouldn't have been necessary for Lisa Brodyaga to appeal a case to the U.S. Court of Appeals for the Fifth Circuit to argue that rape by Salvadoran soldiers is a form of persecution—

but it *was* necessary. And the Fifth Circuit agreed with the INS—that just because soldiers raped a Salvadoran woman doesn't mean they persecuted her.[108]

Accessory to Murder

Refugees in border prisons didn't have a chance to win political asylum, no matter what had happened to them in El Salvador or Guatemala. Their only hope was to bond out. Proyecto Libertad was not the Sanctuary Movement: We didn't help refugees get around the legal system; we walked them through it. I wanted to change the system, to make it comply with its own laws and regulations. Each torture victim and each rape victim I talked to pleaded with me to change it now. At the very least, I wanted the facts of these people's lives and the treatment to which they were subjected in the United States to be public information.

I didn't want anyone in my own country to be able to say he or she didn't know what the United States was doing in Central America. So, late at night I sat in front of a fan in Harlingen writing articles about Los Fresnos immigration prison, and the next day I'd send them off to newspapers and magazines. Not a single story was printed. I'd call the editors a week later and none of them knew who I was. They'd never seen a story from Harlingen. "Where is Harlingen?" And if I did find an editor who was interested, he wouldn't accept my article because I was an advocate. It wasn't news; it was just my point of view.

One day in November I went to the Harlingen Public Library to do some research for Raul, the Chilean detainee who had been tortured during Pinochet's coup. The library's only book about Chile had been printed in 1957—sixteen years before Raul was tortured. I walked back to the office and gave two weeks' notice. I had interviewed more than 1,000 refugees. I knew what refugees' problems were. Now I was going to Washington to force someone to listen.

Maybe in Washington I would find the answer to a question that bothered all of us at Proyecto—paralegals, lawyers, and our clients. Prison guards told refugees that if they applied for political asylum, the Salvadoran government would find out and would consider them traitors. Was it true? Did the State Department, the INS, or the CIA regularly send information from Salvadorans' asylum applications to the Salvadoran military? We knew that in Ana Guevara's case the State Department had sent information from FBI interviews to the Salvadoran military. The INS planning document for the 1989 detention project at the *corralón* states: "The INS Intelligence Program will continue on-going liaison with other government agencies, particularly the CIA, DIA [Defense Intelligence Agency] and the Department of State. ... The information provided by these agencies will be analyzed in conjunction with statements provided by aliens during debriefings."[109]

The INS wrote that its February 16, 1989, "Enhancement Plan for the Southern Border" was "founded on the principles established in the INS Enforcement Enhancement Plan for the Southern Border of the United States, February 1984."[110] INS officials told me the 1984 plan does not exist—yet the 1989 South Texas detention project was based upon it. The 1989 "Enhancement Plan" states: "The Port Isabel Service Processing Center will be effectively utilized to augment the services and proceedings conducted at the containment area. At this facility all the mechanisms for conducting hearings, communicating with foreign governments, and arranging air transportation exist and are utilized on a daily basiş."[111]

INS Harlingen District Director Omer Sewell told me the information the INS gathered would "not necessarily" come from asylum interviews or trials, "although ... there would be nothing to prohibit the disclosure of information [to the CIA] if it is related to national security or something like that."[112]

The agency's internal documents show the INS did share information from political asylum applications with the FBI, the CIA, and foreign governments—the very authorities from whom refugees fear persecution. Attorneys' requests for confidentiality had no effect on the practice. In an August 1984 brief to the Board of Immigration Appeals, attorney Bill Van Wyke wrote that his Salvadoran client "has a basis for believing that the information he gives [in his asylum application] will reach Salvadoran officials ... from the United States government, by way of the Central Intelligence Agency and other intelligence bodies."[113]

> Salvadoran officials collect intelligence information on their own citizens on a broad range of bases, including mere suspicion of being disloyal to the government ... simply being a member of a particular organization (including various legal organizations), or merely possessing any sort of literature deemed unacceptable to the authorities. ... This centralized intelligence bank serves as the nerve center for the notorious "death squads," which include both paramilitary organizations and the institutionalized military bodies themselves. ... The CIA and other U.S. intelligence-gathering bodies share information about Salvadorans outside their country with the Salvadoran authorities. ... The information available in political asylum applications is exactly the sort of data the Salvadoran authorities gather about their citizens ... [and] no laws restrict the CIA's access to political asylum applications.[114]

Van Wyke pointed out that Lawrence Arthur, Elliott Abrams's predecessor as head of the State Department's Bureau of Human Rights and Humanitarian Affairs, had stated, "We may and sometimes do share information with others who are charged with official responsibility for taking action on asylum requests or with those who have a direct and official need to know about the matter."[115]

Van Wyke asked the INS and the State Department to guarantee that his client's testimony would be protected from intelligence-sharing. The Board of Immigration Appeals never ruled on the issue.[116]

This was a serious problem for prison workers. Our two most important jobs were to decide who qualified for legal assistance and who did not and to help clients complete form I-589, the request for political asylum, a four-page document of forty-four questions that requires the names and addresses of all the applicant's immediate relatives. The questions include:

> Have you or any member of your immediate family ever belonged to any organization in your home country? __Yes __No. (If yes, provide the following information relating to each organization: Name of organization, dates of membership or affiliation, what, if any, were your official duties or responsibilities, and are you still an active member. (If not, explain.)
> Have you taken any action that you believe will result in persecution in your home country?[117]

These are reasonable questions, provided that the applicant knows the answers will not be sent to the government from which he or she fled. But refugees had no such assurance.

A competent paralegal would take a personal narrative from the refugee describing the persecution he or she had suffered and why he or she was afraid to return to El Salvador. The narrative was appended to the I-589. We never gave up hope that one day we would find a client with a history. so terrifying, so convincing, that a judge would have to grant asylum. So we made the personal narratives as complete as possible.

INS trial attorneys and judges used the narratives to impugn refugees' testimony:

> You were tortured for three days but you don't know what day you were released? ... You were tortured by a lieutenant? But your application says it was a captain. ... Your interrogators spoke English? How do you know it was English if you don't speak English? ... You joined a political organization when you were 12 years old? But your application says you were in school. How can you go to school and be in a political organization at the same time?

One mistaken date and the judge declared the refugee "unreliable."[118]

By 1990, paralegals at Proyecto Libertad had stopped writing personal narratives. Aside from the judge using it to attack a nervous refugee in court, there was no guarantee that the information in the statement would not make its way, one way or another, to El Salvador. All the effort I put into preparing asylum applications for refugees in Los Fresnos and Laredo, in Florence, and in Oakdale might not have helped them at all. The INS, FBI, CIA, and State Department could have done to any of my clients what they did to Ana Guevara—take the statements I had so carefully elicited from them and send the information to the Salvadoran government, which could use it to find, follow, and kill the people who were deported. Despite the best of intentions, I might have been an accomplice to murder.

Notes

1. Information from an INS press packet prepared during the 1989 Los Fresnos detention project, and from Harlingen District Assistant Director for Detention and Deportation Cecilio Ruiz, the officer in charge of the prison.

2. Michael McClintock, *The American Connection: State Terror and Popular Resistance in El Salvador* (Avon, England: Zed Books, 1985), 215.

3. Ibid., 59–61. McClintock cites the U.S. Office of Public Safety, "Termination Phase-Out Study, Public Safety Project El Salvador" (May 1974). This report assessed the Public Safety Program's work in El Salvador, which was terminated in late 1974.

4. Ibid., 218–221.

5. Ibid., 59–61.

6. The FBI released a heavily expurgated file on its investigation of Proyecto Libertad in response to the author's Freedom of Information Act request. This shall henceforth be referred to as FBI/Proyecto and will include the date of the cited document.

7. Proyecto Libertad supervising attorney Patrick Hughes, interview with the author, July 9, 1984.

8. FBI/Proyecto, February 25, 1983. "On 2-22-85, [CENSORED] (Protect) USINS Detention Camp, Los Fresnos, Texas, advised he had been invited to have a social drink by a group of three individuals, which group included [CENSORED] and her secretary, [CENSORED] and a male friend of [CENSORED]. ... On 2-25-83, [CENSORED], supra, telephonically advised that [CENSORED] is a avid reader, especially of books on Communism. [CENSORED] refered [sic] to [CENSORED] as a Communist. [CENSORED] stated he will discretely [sic] try to obtain any information [CENSORED] is willing to provide about [CENSORED] and her activities."

9. FBI/Proyecto, August 17, 1983. "Scott Lind was a staff writer for the McAllen, Texas newspaper 'The Monitor.' All news articles by Lind regarding 'struggle' of local farmworkers and regarding 'struggle' of leftist guerrillas attempting to overthrow the current Government of El Salvador have been highly critical of U.S. aid to El Salvador." Document classified Secret, declassified November 29, 1989.

10. FBI/Proyecto, San Antonio office to director, May 10, 1985. Classified Secret, declassified October 18, 1989.

11. U.S. District Judge Ann Claire Williams ruled on October 2, 1991, that the FBI investigation of CISPES, the Committee in Solidarity with the People of El Salvador, violated terms of the 1981 consent decree the Justice Department

signed to resolve lawsuits brought against the FBI for illegal activities of the 1970s. An October 5, 1988, document from the FBI investigation of Proyecto Libertad refers to the Proyecto investigation as "CISPES 'spin-off' files." The FBI used similar techniques against both groups. In ruling on the CISPES lawsuit filed in Chicago, Judge Williams wrote, "The court notes that certain especially intrusive investigating techniques were needlessly used in Chicago, including infiltration, gathering of telephone toll records, gathering of bank checking account records, photographic surveillance of a private residence and labeling a Chicago CISPES leader as a 'terrorist.'" Williams reordered the FBI to follow the terms of the consent decree.

12. FBI/Proyecto, January 13, 1982. "On 1/12/83, [CENSORED] USINS Detention Camp, Bayview, Texas, provided photocopies of documents which Attorney Lisa S. Brodyaga from captioned organization submits in support of Political Asylum applications she submits on behalf of Salvadoran illegal aliens who are her clients." This document lists four college professors, three "graduate student(s) and journalist(s)," and a former U.S. ambassador to El Salvador whose statements Brodyaga submitted in support of Salvadorans' requests for political asylum. It summarizes material taken from a political asylum application Brodyaga submitted, which included "a Request of Guarantees of Confidentiality [for Brodyaga's client]." A February 23, 1983, cable includes a list of documents Brodyaga submitted with asylum applications. A November 16, 1982, cable states that the INS has records of all Salvadorans Brodyaga has helped, and that "addresses for those aliens can also be obtained at the USINS District Office."

13. FBI/Proyecto, January 20, 1983. This report was sent to another agency with the note: "This document ... is the property of the FBI and is loaned to your agency; it and its contents are not to be distributed outside your agency." The name of the agency is blacked out, but a paragraph has been censored on page 2 with a handwritten note alongside, "per IRS." The September 30, 1983, report on Proyecto Libertad also was loaned to another unidentified agency.

14. FBI/Proyecto, November 17, 1982. Includes "Item 1—Photo of [CENSORED]." FBI/Proyecto, February 24, 1984. Includes "Item 5—Photo of [CENSORED]."

15. FBI/Proyecto, August 17, 1983, and FBI/Proyecto, January 13, 1982. This report states, "It should be noted that captioned organization has made use of Scott Lind, reporter, for the McAllen newspaper, 'The Monitor,' who is sympathetic to the plight of Salvadoran illegal aliens." The next paragraph is blacked out entirely and marked "b7d"—to "protect the identity of a confidential source."

16. FBI/Proyecto, December 9, 1982, and January 20, 1983. The January 20 cable is a heavily censored ten-page document that includes information on an "early morning fire" that "destroyed the headquarters of USPER #5, Hidalgo, Texas." It states that UFW organizer Jesus Perez Moya and TFWU director Antonio Orendain "suspected arson." The next page begins, "USPER #8 stated that the fire had destroyed all of USPER #5's records." The rest of the page is blacked out. The document includes a list of identities of USPERs #1 though 10, except for the informant, USPER #6. USPER #5 is the Texas Farm Workers Union. Orendain and Moya are further investigated in cables of January 12, 13, and 20, 1984.

17. FBI/Proyecto, March 5, 1984. "On 3-6-84 [CENSORED] (protect by request) [CENSORED] USINS Detention Center, Bayview, Texas, advised he had learned from [CENSORED] paralegal at Proyecto Libertad (PL) that PL is 'going down the drain' due to lack of funds. [CENSORED] told [CENSORED] that some financial contributions continue to come in to PL from an unidentified 'young millionaire' from Austin, Texas, who [CENSORED] described as a 'liberal.' [CENSORED] stated he will try to determine the identity of the young millionaire and advise the writer."

18. FBI/Proyecto, February 25, 1983.

19. FBI/Proyecto, June 5, 1984, and November 29, 1984. The November 29 report states, "On 11-27-84, the following vehicles bearing the following license plates were observed at the parking lot area used by captioned organization: ..." Five license plate numbers are blacked out, listed by plate number, state, and owner.

20. The FBI refused the author's Freedom of Information Act request to declassify his own license plate number in a July 23, 1993, letter from Richard L. Huff, codirector, Office of Information and Privacy. U.S. Department of Justice, Appeal no. 92-0207.

21. FBI/Proyecto, September 30, 1983. The FBI, the INS, the Border Patrol, and the Executive Office of Immigration Review, to which appeals of political asylum denials are sent, are all branches of the Department of Justice.

22. All interviews and conversations recorded in this book were taken down in writing by the author as they occurred. Interviews conducted in Spanish were written in English as they occurred and translated back into Spanish for informants who wanted to hear them. The author's supervising attorneys at all locations were aware he was conducting interviews for a book about Central American refugees. Statements from refugees who agreed to be interviewed for this book were recorded in separate notebooks, after they were interviewed for the law office.

The author testified to the abuses he witnessed inside immigration prisons in a sworn deposition submitted as evidence in the *Orantes-Hernandez* case. "Deposition of Robert Kahn," July 24, 1985, Phoenix, Arizona.

23. Detainee interview with the author inside Port Isabel Service and Processing Center, September 1984; confirmed in separate interviews at Proyecto Libertad office, Harlingen, September 1984. The INS keeps logbooks containing the names of all detainees Proyecto Libertad paralegals interviewed and the dates we interviewed them. To protect the identities of informants, generally only the place, month, and year of such interviews will be cited here.

24. Two detainee interviews with the author inside Port Isabel Service and Processing Center, July 1984.

25. The August 31, 1989, edition of the *Brownsville Herald* described the arrests of seven prison guards, and the guilty pleas of five of them, who ran a marijuana and cocaine ring inside Los Fresnos prison.

26. INS Commissioner Alan Nelson, letter to Sharon House, Congressional Research Service, Education and Public Welfare Division, Library of Congress, June 26, 1984. The letter was written in response to congressional inquiries about immigration prisons.

27. Detainee interview with the author inside Port Isabel Service and Processing Center, September 1984.

28. As a paralegal, I had two clients who were transferred to distant prisons after being beaten by prison guards. Proyecto Libertad attorneys Lisa Brodyaga and Clare Cherkasky had many such clients.

29. Bilingualism in South Texas often is expressed in the lingua franca of the border, called "Tex Mex" or "Spanglish." Each sentence in a conversation may contain words in both languages. Newspaper columnists have written entire articles in the patois, under tongue-in-cheek headlines such as "Reclamamos our derecho to Spanglish."

30. The author sought bond money for refugees as part of his work for three years and dealt with many religious organizations to do so. Some were diplomatic, others blunt about the "sort of refugee" they were willing to help.

31. Unsolicited phone call to the author at Proyecto Libertad, Harlingen, Texas, September 1984.

32. Attorney Patrick Hughes, interview with the author, May 1985.

33. Interview inside Port Isabel Service and Processing Center, September 1984.

34. Deserters from the U.S.-funded Salvadoran Army Center for Military Training (CEMFA), in La Union Province, said torturing suspected dissidents and watching other recruits torture them were part of their basic training. Immigration judge Glenn MacPhaul granted asylum in July 1990 to a seventeen-year-old who deserted rather than participate in the torture sessions and mutilation of bodies he was forced to watch in basic training. See "Brownsville," and the author's reports: "17-year-old Salvadoran Says Army Teaches Torture," *Brownsville Herald*, July 3, 1990; and "Salvadoran Deserter Gains Asylum," *Brownsville Herald,* July 10, 1990.

35. Detainee interview with the author inside Port Isabel Service and Processing Center, October 1984.

36. "The boys"—*los muchachos*—is the popular name for the Salvadoran guerrilla.

37. The Ramon Belloso Battalion was a rapid-response search-and-destroy "killer battalion" outfitted and trained by the U.S. military at Fort Benning, Georgia. It was the second such killer battalion formed and trained by U.S. advisers. The first was the Atlacatl Battalion, which carried out the massacres at Mozote.

38. A *manzana* is 1 hectare, or 2.47 acres.

39. The June 26, 1984, letter from INS Commissioner Alan Nelson to Sharon House of the Congressional Research Service in the Library of Congress lists the capacity of El Paso immigration prison as 342. In an interview inside the prison on May 24, 1985, INS Assistant District Director for Detention and Deportation Daniel McDonald told the author the prison capacity was 410. McDonald had been head of El Paso immigration prison since 1979.

40. The June 26, 1984, letter states El Paso held 336 detainees on May 31, 1984. McDonald said the prison held 395 on May 24, 1985. He estimated that one-fourth of the detainees were Salvadoran. While the author interviewed McDonald in his prison office, McDonald arranged for another half dozen detainees to be transferred to El Paso from Los Fresnos.

41. The headquarters of the Board of Immigration Appeals, a branch of the Executive Office of Immigration Review, is in Falls Church, Virginia. Deportation hearings and political asylum trials are recorded on tape. The tape recordings serve as a record of the hearings, and are used if a refugee's lawyer requests a transcript for an appeal.

42. Court hearings witnessed by the author inside El Paso immigration prison, July 6, 1984.

43. Political asylum trial witnessed by author inside Oakdale immigration prison, Oakdale, Louisiana, September 1986. The date is withheld to protect the defendant.

44. Political asylum trial witnessed by author inside Port Isabel Service and Processing Center, October 1984. The date is withheld to protect the defendant.

45. Los Angeles refugee organization El Rescate sued the INS and the Executive Office of Immigration Review (EOIR) in 1988, challenging the competency and completeness of its translations. U.S. District Court Judge William Gray granted El Rescate's motion for summary judgment on December 14, 1989. The INS appealed to the U.S. Court of Appeals for the Ninth Circuit, which dismissed *El Rescate v. EOIR and INS* without prejudice. But as a result of the lawsuit and Gray's order, the INS began requiring its translators to give complete translations of testimony. The INS still has no competency standards for translators. In the asylum trial of a Salvadoran client of Proyecto Libertad attorney Clare Cherkasky, the INS interpreter translated *escuadrón de muerte* as "the death of the squadrons."

46. Decision rendered by immigration judge Daniel Kahn, Port Isabel Service and Processing Center, February 21, 1985.

47. The Department of Justice created the Executive Office of Immigration Review in 1983 in response to criticism from human rights advocates who pointed out that immigration judges work for the same agency as do INS deportation officers, prosecuting attorneys, and prison guards. The immigration courts and the Board of Immigration Appeals were placed under the EOIR, which, like the INS and the Border Patrol, is a branch of the Justice Department. On paper, the EOIR became a separate branch from the INS, though most immigration judges were drawn from the ranks of INS trial attorneys, and both branches answer to the U.S. attorney general. Creation of the EOIR did not change any immigration policies.

48. Official court recording of asylum trial inside Oakdale immigration prison, November 1986. The author listened to the audiotape inside the Oakdale prison.

49. Ibid.

50. Proyecto Libertad represented more than 7,600 political asylum applicants before winning its first case in 1987. The man granted asylum was no longer in detention. Proyecto Libertad office director Danny Katz, interview with the author, August 26, 1986.

51. "To This Illegal Alien It's a New Kind of 'Freedom Fight,'" *Los Angeles Times*, June 26, 1985.

52. The author witnessed all these INS abuses or took testimony about each one from more than one client or detainee. The Soviet prison system is described by Aleksandr Solzhenitsyn, *The Gulag Archipelago*, 3 vols. (New York: Harper & Row, 1973).

53. Four clients of Proyecto Libertad were held in Los Fresnos prison for six months, even though the INS produced no evidence against them. The men simply refused to answer questions, "so for six months the guys just sat in prison," attorney Jeff Larsen said. "That's what you get for claiming your Fifth Amendment rights in South Texas." Three clients of Lisa Brodyaga were interrogated for three days, during which time they were denied food and sleep. The INS filed criminal

charges against the men, though the agency had no evidence against them; they had simply refused to answer questions. Brodyaga filed a writ of habeas corpus in federal court, and the men were released. "They're bringing criminal charges for exercising their right to remain silent," Brodyaga said. "As a punishment for exercising a constitutional right, that's illegal. It's illegal to even put them in [deportation] proceedings, unless they have evidence to prove that they are here in violation of law." These and other cases were reported by the author in "The High Cost of Silence," *Texas Observer,* August 15, 1986.

54. Abuses of Haitians in the prison on Krome Avenue in Miami were documented in the federal lawsuits *Jean v. Nelson,* 472 US 846 (1985); 105 S.Ct. 2992, 86 L.Ed.2d 664, 1985; and *Haitian Refugee Center v. Meese,* 791 F2d 1489–99 (11th Cir 1986). After the 1981 Haitian boatlift, "Prison officials actually ran Haitians to and from court," to keep them away from the press and attorneys. "It was really something," said Niels Frenzen, attorney for the Haitian Refugee Center in Miami. Niels Frenzen, interview with the author, June 3, 1986.

55. El Paso immigration prison director Daniel McDonald provided the author a list of prison rules during a May 24, 1985, interview inside the prison. The ninth rule states, "Engaging in or encouraging a group demonstration (hunger strikes) is prohibited." The words "hunger strikes" are in parentheses in the original document.

56. Unsolicited phone call from New Orleans bail bondsman to author at the office of Oakdale Legal Assistance, Oakdale, Louisiana, July 10, 1986.

57. Final Judgment and Agreed Permanent Injunction, *State of Texas v. Jorge A. Santos Corporation, and Jorge A. Santos, individually.* Harris County District Court, Houston, Texas, July 26, 1984.

58. Immigration attorney Margaret Burkhart, telephone interview with the author, April 23, 1985. Burkhart is now an immigration judge in the Harlingen INS District.

59. Because of the uncertainties of life in exile, many refugees gave the INS the address of their notary or bond company because that address was likely to be more stable than their own.

60. Attorney Clare Cherkasky, interview with the author, April 23, 1985.

61. The author reported on these dishonest notaries and others in two July 18, 1985, news dispatches for Pacific News Service. The articles were reprinted as "Central American Refugees Claim INS Agents Mistreat Them, Deny Their Rights," and "Coyotes, Thieves, Notarios Prey on Illegal Aliens," *Los Angeles Daily Journal,* July 22, 1985.

62. Raul Hoyos was shot to death on February 12, 1987, in the notaries' office. The shooting was reported in the February 13, 1987, *Houston Post.* The State of Texas later fined the owners of the office for defrauding refugees and immigrants. Final Judgment and Agreed Permanent Injunction, *State of Texas v. Bruce A. Shirley, Lawrence N. Shea and Fernando Luna, Sr. d/b/a Oficina de Relaciones Latinas and Servicios para Inmigrantes and Servicios para Inmigrantes, Inc.,* Harris County District Court, January 28, 1988. See "Oakdale."

63. U.S. law makes provisions for asylum seekers to remain in the United States pending the outcome of their cases. Technically, a refugee is a person who has been granted refugee status outside the borders of the United States. One way to get this

status is to apply for asylum at a U.S. embassy. Asylees, however, apply for political asylum after they have entered the United States.

64. The precise date which INS Harlingen District Director Omer G. Sewell invented the "travel bond" is uncertain, because it was established by unpublished internal memo—like most INS policy changes along the border in the 1980s. Sewell refused a request for an interview with the author in 1991, after he had retired from the INS.

65. "Nicaraguan Asylum/Harlingen Situation," U.S. Immigration and Naturalization Service, Office of the Deputy Commissioner, December 5, 1988; and "Enhancement Plan for the Southern Border," U.S. INS, February 16, 1989. See "Brownsville."

66. Refugee interview with the author in the office of Proyecto Libertad, September 1984.

67. "No, man," is an all-purpose Salvadoran expression. *No, hombre,* pronounced *"nombre,"* can indicate disbelief, protest, real disagreement, or teasing disagreement. Because *nombre* (name) is the initial word of other stronger expressions, such as *Nombre de Dios* (name of God, or, in English, "Oh, my God") *"nombre"* is a flexible and popular expression.

68. "Techos de cartón" (Rooves of Cardboard), copyright by Alejandro Primavera, Sociedad de Autores y Compositores Venezolanos. The rendition of Primavera's song by the Venezuelan group Guanaguao was so popular among refugees that it was a virtual national anthem of Salvadorans in exile.

69. Salvadorans count a week from a particular day until that day repeats—Sunday through the following Sunday, for example, or eight days.

70. The assassination of Archbishop Oscar Arnulfo Romero on March 24, 1980, and the massacre at his funeral four days later were defining moments for a generation of Salvadorans who speak of where they were when they heard of Romero's assassination in the same way a generation of U.S. citizens remember where they were when they heard that President Kennedy had been killed.

71. Nurse at the Port Isabel Service and Processing Center, interview with the author, October 1, 1984.

72. Federico, interview with the author, inside Port Isabel Service and Processing Center, October 1984.

73. Detainee interviews with the author in Port Isabel Service and Processing Center and in office of Proyecto Libertad, September–November 1984.

74. Father Lenny DePasquale, telephone interview with the author, July 1986. "Contras Accused of Illegal Recruiting," *National Catholic Reporter,* August 1, 1986.

75. Attorney Lisa Brodyaga, telephone interview with the author, July 1986.

76. Attorney Thelma Garcia, telephone interview with the author, July 1986.

77. FBI Special Agent Juan Gonzales, telephone interview with the author, July 1986.

78. The Contra recruiting in the *corralón* was first reported by *Brownsville Herald* reporter Ed Asher.

79. FBI Special Agent Julian De la Rosa, telephone interview with the author, July 1986.

80. Thelma Garcia, interview with the author, July 1986.

81. Bosco Matamoros, telephone interview with the author, July 1986.

82. Sam Dillon, *Comandos: The CIA and Nicaragua's Contra Rebels* (New York: Henry Holt, 1991); Christopher Dickey, *With the Contras* (New York: Simon & Schuster, 1985).

83. UNO spokesman, telephone interview with the author, July 1986.

84. Steve Walker, telephone interview with the author, July 1986.

85. INS Harlingen District Acting Assistant Director for Detention and Deportation John Luvender, telephone interview with the author, July 1986.

86. *La migra* is the common Spanish name for the Border Patrol.

87. *Orantes-Hernandez v. Meese,* Deposition of Robert Kahn, 1985, Phoenix, Arizona, 59–64.

88. Most of the author's prison interviews were recorded in nine hard-bound 120-page notebooks, which shall be called Kahn notebooks. This excerpt is from vol. III, 96.

89. Kahn notebooks, vol. IV, 6.

90. Salvadoran asylum seeker, interview with the author at Los Fresnos immigration prison, September 24, 1984.

91. Refugee interview with the author in office of Proyecto Libertad, October 6, 1984.

92. Detainees on cleaning detail at Los Fresnos and Oakdale gave the author eyewitness reports of prison officials stealing mail at those prisons.

93. "Officials Investigate Disappearing Bond Money at INS Center," *Brownsville Herald,* July 4, 1989.

94. Guards at the immigration prison on Krome Avenue in Miami, Florida, charged detainees $5 a joint in 1986. Three detainees transferred from Krome to Oakdale prison; interviews with the author, June 1986.

95. Blancas testified in court on August 30, 1989. The court session was reported in the *Brownsville Herald,* August 31, 1989.

96. *Brownsville Herald,* August 31, 1989. Perales was sentenced to ten months in prison: *Brownsville Herald,* October 27, 1989.

97. "Injured Man Returned to Honduras," *Brownsville Herald,* June 12, 1989; "Injured Honduran Puffed Pot at Camp," *Brownsville Herald,* June 21, 1989. The cost of the chartered air ambulance was provided by Cecilio Ruiz, the INS officer in charge of Los Fresnos prison. Ruiz said the INS spent more than $133,000 on Gonzalez's medical bills. Serapio Umanzor, a reporter for *El Tiempo* newspaper in San Pedro Sula, Honduras, helped organize a footrace to raise money for Gonzalez's hospital expenses in Honduras. Serapio Umanzor, telephone interview with the author, June 21, 1989.

98. "INS Investigates Alleged Sexual Harassment," *Brownsville Herald,* September 27, 1990.

99. Reverend Anthony Hefner, interview with the author, September 25, 1990.

100. Telephone interview with female guard, September 26, 1990.

101. Jerry Hurwitz, telephone interview with the author, September 26, 1990.

102. Bob Wallis, telephone interview with the author, September 26, 1990.

103. The author called Trominski's office twice a day for a month seeking comment on this case and other irregularities at INS. Trominski did not accept phone calls or return them from 1990 until 1993, when the author stopped calling.

104. Detainees at the *corralón* and at Oakdale regularly reported consensual sex between women detainees and male prison guards.

105. Affidavit of Victor Julio Espinoza Valencia, signed and sworn inside Port Isabel Service and Processing Center, October 10, 1984; and affidavits of two witnesses, October 10, 1984. The author declines to identify the witnesses.

106. Cecilio Ruiz, interview with the author, October 11, 1984.

107. Carolyn Patty Blum, "Salvadoran Refugee Cases on Appeal: Somebody Up There Is Listening," *Immigration Newsletter,* 15 (March–April 1986). National Immigration Project of the National Lawyers Guild, Boston.

108. The U.S. Court of Appeals for the Fifth Circuit Court ruled in 1987 in *Campos-Guardado v. INS* that rape is not necessarily a form of persecution. Campos-Guardado's uncle, a trade union activist, was murdered by a death squad. The death squad then raped Campos-Guardado. The INS argued, and the Fifth Circuit agreed, that though rape is a form of persecution, Campos-Guardado was not necessarily raped because of her political opinion and therefore did not deserve political asylum.

109. "Enhancement Plan for the Southern Border," U.S. INS, February 16, 1989, 18.

110. Ibid., 8.

111. Ibid., 12–13.

112. INS Harlingen District Director Omer G. Sewell, telephone interview with the author, May 10, 1989, reported in "INS Document Reveals Intelligence-sharing with CIA," *Brownsville Herald,* May 11, 1989.

113. "In the Matter of José E., Respondent's Brief on Appeal," August 27, 1984, Washington, D.C. Van Wyke was appealing to the Board of Immigration Appeals in Falls Church, Virginia, an immigration judge's denial of political asylum to José E. Van Wyke then was an attorney for the Central American Refugee Center, CARECEN, in Washington. He is now an immigration judge in New York City.

114. Ibid., 2–4.

115. Ibid., 4.

116. Personal communication from William Van Wyke.

117. Request for Asylum in the United States, U.S. Immigration and Naturalization Service form I-589, questions 34 and 35.

118. Political asylum trials witnessed by the author in Los Fresnos immigration prison in 1984, and in Oakdale prison in 1986.

WASHINGTON, D.C.

He has to have proof it might happen again.

*—Lee Johnson, director of the State Depart-
ment's Office of Asylum Affairs, explaining
why a Salvadoran was denied asylum even
though the National Guard had cut his throat
and stabbed him twice under the heart.*

SALVADORANS FACED LESS INS PRESSURE in Washington, D.C., than anywhere else in the country. The employment situation was better, too: There are hundreds of hotels, restaurants, and office buildings that need janitors and dishwashers, and many people could afford maids. Salvadorans were safer in Washington because of easy access to lawyers, the presence of the media, and the absence of a large detention center where asylum trials could be conducted out of sight.

Most Washington-area refugees are from the eastern departments, or states, of La Union and San Miguel, areas of heavy warfare and frequent government bombing during the Salvadoran civil war. Entire towns had picked up and moved to Washington. "A famous case is the city of Intipucá, where practically the only people left are old people and women," a Salvadoran priest told me.[1] "Here in Washington there are about 5,000 Salvadorans from Intipucá. This is because of the massive repression there. There are two soccer clubs from Intipucá and one band from Intipucá here in Washington. Another case is a city near Intipucá called Chirilagua. There is a soccer club here from Chirilagua, too."

Another priest who worked in the Salvadoran community delighted in telling how a soccer game between refugees from two villages changed INS policy in Washington. Early in Reagan's first term, the INS raided a game between two Salvadoran soccer clubs playing on a field by the Potomac River. Nearly everyone on both teams was a Salvadoran refugee. Rather than face arrest and deportation to El Salvador, many jumped into the river to escape. Several nearly drowned. The INS raid was covered by local TV stations, which mentioned the Salvadorans' fear of deportation and the conditions they had fled in El Salvador. "Since then, the INS has been very well behaved in Washington," the priest said with a smile.[2]

I searched the files of the *Washington Post* for news of the soccer raid in vain. Perhaps the story is apocryphal. But Washington was the best place in the United States for a Salvadoran refugee to live. The INS accommodated defense attorneys there. Continuances of six months to prepare an asylum case were common, and the judge might grant a further continuance.[3] At Proyecto Libertad, we got two weeks. In Florence, Arizona, Judge William Nail gave Salvadorans three to seven days to seek asylum. During the South Texas detention project in 1989, the entire asylum process took three hours.

Though INS pressure was slack, Salvadorans lived a shadow life in Washington, paying taxes and Social Security though they were ineligible for benefits. Every situation cut two ways: If a Salvadoran applied for political asylum, he would probably be ordered deported. If her employer deducted taxes from her paycheck, she was not eligible for the benefits; if the employer did not, he might ask her to work for less than minimum wage. If a Salvadoran were robbed or if his employer refused to pay him, he was afraid to go to the police for fear they would ask for papers. If her children learned English they'd have an easier time of it in the United States, but they might forget they were Salvadoran. To be Salvadoran was to live with Uncle Sam's hands gently but firmly around your neck.[4]

After businessmen went home, Salvadorans cleaned their offices. After patrons ate in a restaurant, Salvadorans washed their dishes. When guests checked out of a hotel, a Salvadoran maid changed the sheets. But official Washington and the people from Maryland and Virginia who worked there did not interact with Salvadorans. They didn't see them and they didn't understand them. Of Washington's 3,880 police officers in 1984, forty-three were Hispanic and thirty-six spoke Spanish.[5] Because of the inertia of bureaucracy and the ghostlike existence of Salvadorans, the city did not react to their presence; it ignored them. This may have been a better reaction than the street sweeps in South Texas, but the long slow-burning fuse finally exploded in May 1991, when the Salvadoran community rioted for two days after a monolingual black police officer shot a Salvadoran.[6]

Already in 1984 tension was brewing among Washington's Latin American communities. What little outreach there was from city agencies was directed at Cuban American and Puerto Rican businessmen. Although Salvadorans outnumbered all other Latin Americans combined by the mid-1980s, they had no voice in community affairs. The Mayor's Committee on Latino Economic Development was dominated by Puerto Ricans and Cuban Americans, who were politically at odds with Salvadorans. The Puerto Ricans and Cubans had documents; Salvadorans did not. The mayor's committee and city government were more concerned with promoting business than with helping refugees.[7]

But there was less pressure on refugees in Washington than anywhere else in the country not just because of the relatively well-behaved INS there but because the Salvadoran community has a geographical center, the Adams Morgan neighborhood. Salvadoran organizations worked openly there. The Committee of Central American Refugees (CARE-CEN), the Central American Refugee Center (CRECEN), and Casa El Salvador posted flyers on telephone poles a few blocks from the White House announcing meetings, fund-raisers, concerts, films, and speeches.

Representatives of the FMLN spoke in public and walked home without incident. Aside from sanctuary work and campaigning against military aid, most political organizing was directed at trying to stop the Simpson-Mazzoli Bill, which would have made it illegal for undocumented people to work.[8]

Salvadorans had to learn English in order to do political work. That meant walking the streets, holding public meetings, risking arrest. Victor, a member of Casa El Salvador, worked out of a room in a church on V Street. "We are illegal here," he said. "We can't vote. We can't lobby Congress. Our only recourse is to go over the president's head, directly to the American people. Refugees come here and we have relations with people. We don't have relations with the government. Many North American people sympathize with the things for which our people are fighting. Of course we don't resent the people, but the government has made the situation difficult. It's a very complex situation."[9]

Salvadorans' only hope for asylum in the United States was to appeal to federal courts. The Simpson-Mazzoli Bill would have denied them even this by prohibiting political asylum applicants the right to appeal a denial of asylum. Yet so fantastic and deluded were the politics of immigration in 1984 that Representative Mazzoli's office insisted that was not the case. The bill did not deny refugees the right to appeal, a member of Mazzoli's staff told me. "It combines the appeal with the original application."

I asked for an explanation.

"It combines the two steps into one."

"You mean to tell me that it denies them asylum and then denies their appeal at the same time, and you say that preserves their right to appeal?"

"Right. It combines the two steps into one."[10]

"The aliens don't object to Simpson-Mazzoli," Mazzoli's spokeswoman assured me. The only people who disliked Simpson-Mazzoli, according to her, were "the lawyers, who don't like some of the provisions because it'll cut down on their litigation."

This absurdly implied that refugee defense lawyers did political asylum "litigation" for the money and that the more refugees they defended, the more money they made. That may be a fair statement about the average lawyer in Washington, D.C., but it has nothing to do with the lawyers who were actually doing political asylum work. Attorneys at Proyecto Libertad earned less than minimum wage for their eighty-hour weeks. Clare Cherkasky didn't make any more money "litigating" cases than she did hollering "Death squad!" at prison translators. Lisa Brodyaga didn't make any money writing appeals to the U.S. District Court of Appeals for the Fifth Circuit to try to save Ana Guevara's life. The paralegals I worked with made about a dollar an hour—$75 a week. Any refugee who could find a job made more money than the legal workers who were "litigating" cases in prison courtrooms.

The gulf between Salvadoran reality and Washington politics was absolute. The continuing stream of refugees had no influence on U.S. policy, and policymakers showed no understanding of the lives of El Salvador's poor majority and no inclination to try to understand them. The officials charged with implementing U.S. human rights policy dismissed reality with a facility that was beyond distressing—it was cartoonish. Lee Johnson, the director of the State Department's Office of Asylum Affairs in Elliott Abrams's Bureau of Human Rights and Humanitarian Affairs, told me, "There is no prejudice against Salvadorans. All we're looking for is a meritorious case."[11]

I told Johnson about Reynaldo, a Salvadoran whose throat had been cut by a member of the National Guard, who had then bayoneted him twice under the heart. I had seen the scars. How is it possible that this man was denied asylum? He not only had a "well-founded fear of persecution," he already *had* been persecuted. Johnson replied, "He has to have proof it might happen again."[12]

I described Reynaldo's case to Paula Kuzmich, assistant to Laura Jordan Dietrich, one of Elliott Abrams's chief deputies in the State Department's Bureau of Human Rights. Kuzmich said Reynaldo was lying, even though I had seen his scars. "I have a scar on my forehead, where I fell on my tricycle when I was three," Kuzmich said. "I can claim torture."[13]

The Theme of the Day

Just as political campaigns have been run on a "theme of the day" since Reagan's 1984 landslide, U.S. officials in charge of refugee policies had three themes from which they never strayed: There is no repression in El Salvador; things are getting better; Salvadorans just come here to find work or to go on welfare.[14]

These themes were not only untrue, it was impossible that they could all be true. If there was no repression in El Salvador, why must things be getting better? If Salvadoran refugees came here to find work, they wouldn't need welfare; but if they came here to go on welfare—for which refugees and undocumented people are ineligible—they wouldn't need work.

It's true that Salvadorans worked. "Everyone has to work," said Alberto. Alberto worked twelve hours a night in a bakery. He was exhausted the morning he talked to me in a church basement in Adams Morgan. He had just come off his shift and planned to work a few hours with CRECEN before going to sleep. "I think this betters my life," he said, "to be with friends, working to better the life of the community. We collect money and food for other refugees. There's always work to do."[15]

Like most Salvadoran refugees, Alberto is Catholic. He had been a catechist in Chirilagua until November 18, 1980, when the army abducted him from the plaza and tortured him from 1 P.M. until 5 A.M. the next day.

> They tortured me and asked where the other guerrilla were: Where their camps were, their guns, all this. Well, I knew nothing of this. I realized that there were some *compañeros* organized there, but I knew nothing of where they were. All I did was organize little groups of men and children to study, to celebrate the Word of God. That was why I was captured. I decided in those moments that they were going to kill me, and that it was no matter if one die, if others could live.
>
> In El Salvador I studied in a university that was promoted by your government. There we learned that people have rights, that they can organize themselves in order to learn, to protect their rights. The university was called the *Universidad Campesino de Castaña,* in Chirilagua. When they realized that we were actually being educated, they changed the policies and the name of the university to *Centro Universidad de la Paz.* In 1980, the Third Brigade of San Miguel captured and destroyed the university. They destroyed everything, the books, the walls, the blackboards, the chalk. They carried off all the equipment. The leaders of the university had to leave the country. Some are in Nicaragua, others in Spain. They closed the university in 1979 after the coup[16] and destroyed it in 1980.

Alberto fled Chirilagua to San Salvador, where he got a job working construction. "What I can't remember is if it was November or December when the leader of the union was murdered," he said, as we drank tepid coffee from white Styrofoam cups. As death squads murdered more union members, Alberto fled to the United States. He was arrested by the Border Patrol in Hidalgo, Texas, and sent to the *corralón.* He was out on bond when I talked with him, waiting for his political asylum trial.

> I was passing out literature at our *fiesta* last week, and a *gringo* asked me, "Why do you oppose the United States government and not the government of the Soviet Union?"
>
> I told him, "Look, *amigo,* I learned that I have rights from your government. I give you *gringos* thanks for that. I'm not talking theoretically, like you are, but of what I have witnessed in my own flesh. My ideas come from the United States, not from the Soviet Union. I learned these things from you, not from the Soviet Union. That's why I blame your government."
>
> I don't want to help the guerrilla. I want to help the poor people, the people hurt by the war, the poor ones in Honduras in the refugee camps. I'm not smart. I'm just a poor, sad *campesino.* But I know that the solution to problems of health and illiteracy and poverty is not rifles and helicopters. I am illegal here, and subject to your laws. If I am deported, then I am de-

ported. But wherever I am, I will always be Salvadoran. I will always fight for my *pueblo*.[17]

Public Secrets

Just as baffling as the dissonance between the lives of Salvadorans and the politics of Washington was the ease with which one could find government documents that proved U.S. complicity in torture and murder. It took me just a few weeks to collect the U.S. embassy documents that confirmed the murders of Salvadoran deportees, the FBI and CIA cables that revealed the INS and FBI intention to turn over Ana Guevara to the Salvadoran National Guard, and the INS document that spelled out precisely how the Justice Department violated the law and its own regulations to discriminate against Salvadoran refugees and deport them.[18] I was not a journalist or a government employee or an academic. I just walked into offices, told people what I knew about the border, and they gave me the documents. It took longer to get the information printed in newspapers than it did to collect the documents that provided it.

The limp diplomatic pressure the U.S. exerted on El Salvador and the attendant news coverage stemmed from the murders of six Americans and of Archbishop Romero, not from the 30,000 Salvadorans dead from civil war. Regardless of the horror of each refugee's story and the cumulative weight of them, for the average North American, including news editors, Central America was still remote, small, and unimportant.

By late 1984 the hot story in Washington was Nicaragua. In a dramatic statement on network television the night Reagan was reelected, the White House announced that Soviet MIG fighter planes were about to be delivered to Nicaragua.[19] The MIGs supposedly were in boxes on a Soviet ship. Though the MIGs never materialized, it was apparent by election night in 1984 that war with Nicaragua was a real possibility. For the next three years, Washington policy battles and the news would focus on Nicaragua. The Reagan administration had pushed the political dialogue so far to the right that to oppose Contra aid meant one had to acquiesce to the destruction of El Salvador.

This was nowhere clearer than at an April 1985 press conference in the Capitol called by Senator Dennis DeConcini and U.S. Representative Joseph Moakley. The congressmen explained why they were reintroducing the Moakley-DeConcini Bill, which proposed to stop deportations of Salvadorans until the civil war ended or the Salvadoran government demonstrated it was willing to abide by internationally recognized standards of human rights. Also speaking were Senator Patrick Leahy of Vermont, cochairman of the Senate Intelligence Committee; U.S. Representative Ralph Regula of Ohio; Harriet Nelson of the National Council of Churches; and the Reverend John Fife.

Except for Fife, the speakers were models of timidity. The congressmen assured us that their bill to offer humanitarian relief to Salvadoran refugees did not mean they opposed President Reagan's Central American policy. DeConcini said Salvadorans would not be eligible to receive state or federal money and that the bill would not encourage immigration because it would not apply to Salvadorans who entered the country after the bill was passed. Moakley said the bill had 140 cosponsors. Leahy recalled that the home where he grew up had been part of the Underground Railroad during the Civil War. Then Fife spoke.[20]

He said he was "sick and tired" of seeing refugee children cry and hide under tables at his church every time a helicopter flew by. He said, "Not a single church, human rights group, or refugee agency has taken the administration's side" on the issue of Salvadoran refugees. "We've been accused by the commissioner of INS of being anarchists, by the right-wing press of being communists, by the administration of being criminals, because we care for refugees." DeConcini, Fife's senator, looked intensely uncomfortable at Fife's immoderation, but he stood there and listened.

After Fife spoke, DeConcini acknowledged, "I don't think there's any question we have an uphill fight on our hands ... because of the administration's embarrassment that El Salvador cannot provide for the safety and security of its own citizens."[21]

The View from the Salvadoran Consulate

As Fife and DeConcini spoke, the INS was opening a new prison in Laredo, Texas, to detain women and children. Patrick Hughes, one of Proyecto Libertad's first attorneys, was opening a law office specifically to defend refugee children. I decided to go to Laredo to work for him whether he paid me or not. I planned to work in all the border prisons to document that the abuses in the *corralón* were not isolated cases.

The daily struggle for human rights in the United States in the 1980s was on the southern border. Washington policymakers had little real interest in human rights unless the abuses were committed in a Soviet or Chinese satellite and could be used to score ideological points.[22] Refugees were not a visible presence in Washington, as they were from Brownsville to Tijuana. Washington policy debates on refugee issues and immigration were conducted on a stage that had little relation to reality.

Two scenes typify the contradictions of refugee issues in Washington under the Reagan administration. On a cold night in January 1985, I went to a party in a townhouse a few blocks from the U.S. Supreme Court building. Officials in all the important refugee groups were there: people from the State Department, Amnesty International, the United Nations High Commission on Refugees, the U.S. Committee for Refugees, the Refugee

Policy Group, and others. There were imported beers, white wine, champagne, caviar, and baked Brie with walnuts. The average annual salary of the people at the party was certainly more than $50,000. Canapés and champagne were carried around the room on silver trays by two servants dressed in white linen. The servants were Cambodian refugees.

The second scene is my interview with Marco Antonio Salazar, the Salvadoran consul in Washington. I lied my way into his office by saying I worked for a newspaper in Arizona. The first thing I saw inside the Salvadoran embassy was a blue-and-white bumper sticker in Spanish: "Journalists, Tell the Truth!" This was Roberto D'Aubuisson's 1984 campaign slogan.

Salazar received me in his second-floor office in the embassy on California Street. It was furnished with dark polished wood, a plush couch and chairs, a low coffee table, and a huge, beautiful, gleaming desk. There was no paper on the desk—not a pen, not a scratch, not a speck of dust. Behind it was the Salvadoran flag. The consul and I sat on opposite sides of the coffee table, and I told him that I had interviewed hundreds of Salvadoran refugees in cities all across the United States.

"Interesting," Salazar said.[23]

Many of the people I interviewed had been tortured by the army, the National Police, or the National Guard. I had seen the scars. I asked Mr. Salazar whether he had a comment on that.

"As a system, there is no torture," Salazar said. "But in some cases, perhaps, yes. I cannot deny that there is torture at times, but as a system, no."

Students are especially targeted for assassination. The National University has been closed for years. Why are students selected as targets of the army and the death squads, I asked.

It's not true. The National University served for many years as a training and recruitment center for the guerrilla. All of the assailants and robbers in the city, all the thieves would run to the university after committing their crimes because the university was absolutely autonomous, and the authorities could not enter.

In 1980 there was a fight with the guerrilla near the university and the army entered the university in pursuit of the guerrilla and found them there. It was a base of recruitment and training for the guerrilla. Many of the students and professors were guerrilla and communists. Joaquin Villalobos was a student there.[24] There were classes of guerrilla. I was a student there. All of the walls were covered with communist slogans and murals. It was like another world.

And the University at San Miguel?
"The same reason. There was an army encounter with the guerrilla; they chased the guerrilla to the university and destroyed the university in pursuit of the guerrilla."

And the *Universidad Campesino de Castaña?*

"For the same reason. There was an encounter, and ..." Salazar's voice trailed off. His hands unwound a ball of something that wasn't there. It was simple.

I had more questions for Salazar: questions about professors on death-squad lists, about elementary students being shot, about women being raped in army barracks. I didn't ask the questions. I suffered my first attack of journalist syndrome. *This guy doesn't need to talk to me. I might need to talk to him again. What if he won't talk to me?* I did not expect myself to fall into line so quickly when faced with an official title and a big desk, but I did. I was silenced by my own cowardice and ambition. I asked Salazar instead that if it were true the universities were infiltrated by communists, how did the communists infiltrate El Salvador? What is a communist?

"I couldn't tell you how," he said. "I don't know anything about communists. Ask those other people you talk to."

Notes

1. Salvadoran priest, interview with the author on Northwest V Street, Washington D.C., December 11, 1984.

2. Salvadoran priest, interview with the author in Adams Morgan, Washington, D.C., December 17, 1984.

3. Attorney Patrick Hughes, interview with the author, December 17, 1984. William Van Wyke, interview with the author, March 25, 1985.

4. Police officers acknowledged that Salvadorans victimized by crimes were afraid to file police reports. Police officers of the Third District Police Community Center, Eighteenth and Columbia Streets, Washington, D.C., interviews with the author, December 11, 1984.

5. B. Drummond Ayres Jr., "Street Unrest Flares Again in Capitol," *New York Times,* May 7, 1991; Robert L. Jackson, "Washington Mayor Imposes Curfew," *Los Angeles Times,* May 8, 1991.

6. Ibid.

7. Members of the Mayor's Committee on Latino Economic Development, Washington, D.C., interviews with the author, July 31, December 10 and 11, 1984.

8. The no-work provisions of the Simpson-Mazzoli Bill, later known as Simpson-Rodino, were incorporated into the Immigration Reform and Control Act, which President Reagan signed into law on November 6, 1986.

9. Victor, Salvadoran community organizer, Casa El Salvador, interview with the author, December 11, 1984.

10. Lynn Conway, staff member for U.S. Representative Roman Mazzoli, interview with the author, August 2, 1984.

11. Lee Johnson, director of State Department's Office of Asylum Affairs, Bureau of Human Rights and Humanitarian Affairs, interview with the author, August 3, 1984.

12. Ibid.

13. Paula Kuzmich, interview with the author, August 2, 1984.

14. Author interviews with Salvadoran consul Marco Antonio Salazar, August 1, 1984; Lee Johnson, director of asylum affairs in the U.S. Department of State's Bureau of Human Rights and Humanitarian Affairs, August 3, 1984; Paula Kuzmich, assistant to Laura Jordan Dietrich, assistant to Elliott Abrams, director of the State Department Bureau of Human Rights, August 2, 1984; INS spokesmen Duke Austin and Verne Jervis, repeated interviews throughout the 1980s; spokeswoman for U.S. Representative Roman Mazzoli, August 2, 1984; all interviews in Washington, D.C.

15. Alberto, interview with the author, July 31, 1984.

16. The coup of October 15, 1979, overthrew General Carlos Romero and established a five-member junta with two military representatives and three civilians. The "revolutionary junta" issued a proclamation that called for an investigation of the status of political prisoners and the disappeared, land reform, and the nationalization of foreign trade in coffee and sugar. The failed attempt to institute progressive government unleashed the military and right-wing death squads. Death-squad murders and military repression increased and the junta's progressive intentions were blocked. After repeated demonstrations that civilian members of the junta had no control over the military, all civilian members of the junta resigned on January 3, 1980, as did most civilian members of the cabinet and most civilian subministers. The best history of political developments after the coup of 1979 is Tommie Sue Montgomery, *Revolution in El Salvador* (Boulder, Colo.: Westview Press, 1994).

17. *Pueblo* is a complex, emotion-laden word in Spanish. It can mean a town, a village, a neighborhood, a nation, or one's people.

18. For FBI and CIA cables and the murder of Salvadoran deportees see "Murder by Remote Control." For the INS violating the law and its own regulations see "Murder by Remote Control" and Stipulated Settlement Agreement, *American Baptist Churches v. Richard Thornburgh, Gene McNary, and James Baker III,* U.S. District Court, Northern District of California, December 14, 1989.

19. The tale of the disappearing MIGs was reported in the *New York Times* the day after Election Day: "Nicaragua Said to Get Soviet Attack Copters," November 7, 1984. The next day's headlines read, "Nicaragua Says No Jet Fighters Are Being Sent," and "U.S. Warns Soviet It Won't Tolerate MIG's in Nicaragua (-) Planes Suspected on Vessel Now in Harbor There—Confirmation Lacking," *New York Times,* November 8, 1984. Friday's headline declared, "Shultz Indicates Soviet Has Denied Shipping Fighters," *New York Times,* November 9, 1984. On Saturday, the headlines stated, "Officials Doubt Soviet Freighter Contains MIG's—But U.S. Is Ready to Act if Nicaragua Gets Jets," and "Nicaragua Held Unlikely to Get Advanced Jets," *New York Times,* November 10, 1984. The progression of stories indicates the extent to which the Reagan administration was able to control the story line of events in Central America.

20. News conference in Room 5207, U.S. Capitol, Washington, D.C., April 3, 1985.

21. U.S. Representative Joseph Moakley and Senator Dennis DeConcini first introduced their bill to protect Salvadoran refugees in November 1983. The bill was incorporated into the 1990 Immigration Act, which gave temporary protected status to Salvadorans who entered the country before September 19, 1990, if they reg-

istered with the INS by June 30, 1991, which was later extended to October 31, 1991. President George Bush signed the act into law on November 29, 1990.

22. Bill Frelick, policy analyst for the U.S. Committee for Refugees, aptly summed up the Reagan administration's human rights policy: "While Salvadoran refugees were an embarrassment for the administration, Nicaraguan refugees were trophies." Personal communication with the author.

23. Salvadoran consul Marco Antonio Salazar, interview with the author, August 1, 1984.

24. Joaquin Villalobos was a leader of the guerrilla coalition, the Farabundo Martí National Liberation Front, or FMLN, and is generally credited as being the guerrillas' chief military tactician.

LAREDO

These children are here with horrible stories, true stories. Isn't it enough what they had to suffer in El Salvador? Do we have to strip-search refugee children in the United States?

—Attorney Patrick Hughes, Refugee Legal Services, Laredo, Texas

As CHERRY TREES BLOOMED on the Capitol Mall, the secret arms-for-hostages deals later known as the Iran-Contra scandal were under way. On April 11, 1985, Oliver North wrote to National Security Adviser Bud McFarlane that "$17,145,594 has been expended for arms, munitions, combat operations, and support activities" for the Contra war against Nicaragua.[1] That summer, North and arms dealers Richard Secord, John Singlaub, and others would collect more than $4.5 million in "assets," including six airplanes, warehouses, ships, boats, land vehicles, communications equipment, and a 6,520-foot runway in Costa Rica with which to supply the Contras.[2]

Congress had cut military funding to the Contras on October 3, 1984,[3] but North would later defend himself by saying that although government officials were prohibited from using federal money to finance the Contra war, it was all right for government officials to raise funds "privately." Funding was needed because the Sandinista army was finishing up a six-week offensive that had driven most of the Contras into Honduras. The Sandinista army was in control of the national territory.[4] Though the arms deals were not known to the public, profits from them kept the war going, which had an impact on the southern U.S. border. The second wave of refugees was coming. The prisons were overflowing with Salvadorans and Guatemalans; now more Nicaraguans and Hondurans were joining them. More Salvadoran army veterans were coming too, fleeing from the guerrilla.

As the National Security Council privatized the war against Nicaragua, the Justice Department began to privatize immigration prisons. Across a dry wash in the desert just east of the Laredo city limits, the INS opened a 208-bed prison in March 1985 on a private contract with the Corrections Corporation of America (CCA). It was the first U.S. immigration prison specifically designed to imprison children and babies. Privatization was supposed to cut administrative costs. The INS paid CCA about $30 per inmate per day. CCA ran the prison for profit.[5]

Prison guards strip-searched children and adults before and after they met with a legal adviser. The searches included the body cavities of all detainees, including babies. Children at Laredo were held with no bond, and the INS would not release them except to be deported or into the custody of a close relative. If the relative could not produce documents, the child would not be released and the relative would be incarcerated. The average bond for adults was $7,500—the highest immigration bond in the country.[6]

The INS had no standards or regulations for the detention of children in 1985. It has none now. The 1952 Immigration and Nationality Act set no standards at all for immigration detention centers, nor did it mandate special protection for children. Neither did the 1980 Refugee Act, the 1987 Immigration Reform and Control Act, or the 1991 Immigration Act. The INS still has not promulgated any regulations on standards of detention for children or adults.[7]

Patrick Hughes moved to Laredo to represent the children when the prison opened. I arrived in Hughes's downtown law office, Refugee Legal Services, at noon on Tuesday, April 30, and told him I was going to work for him. Hughes was angry at the detention of children and outraged at the strip searches, which he considered "not only unreasonable, they may be criminal, and they are certainly unnecessary."

> This is not a search and seizure in order to gather evidence. It is a form of intimidation and punishment: to detain whole families, and babies, for the despicable act of trying to escape from a war. And to strip-search them, to psychologically coerce and make people refrain from exercising their right to talk with an attorney, and that it is done selectively, on the basis of one's interview with an attorney, is an outrageous interference with the right to counsel.[8]

Hughes was the most aggressive, uncompromising, and effective lawyer I ever worked with. With immigration prisons filled beyond capacity all along the border, he believed the simplest solution for the INS would be to release all his clients, and he spent endless hours persuading INS officers to see it his way.

The INS/CCA immigration prison in Laredo violated prison standards for detention of juveniles and violated state and federal laws, INS regulations, U.S. district court and Supreme Court orders, and immigration case law—all as a matter of policy.[9] Children were put into long-term detention with adults, were denied access to education, denied access to sunlight, put into solitary confinement without a hearing, punished with three days of solitary confinement if they stood too close to a barred, bulletproof window, repeatedly strip-searched for seeking legal counsel, denied the right to post bond, sexually threatened and pressured by an adult guard, and given "trials" in their cells by prison guards who impersonated immigration judges and made them sign legal forms waiving the right to seek asylum and requesting deportation. Adult prisoners were transferred to other prisons or deported with no notice given to their attorney.[10]

The prison windows are bulletproof glass reinforced with chicken wire and with iron bars on the outside. A semicircle with a radius of about one meter had been drawn on the floor under each window. Any child who stood within that semicircle to look out the window could be punished with solitary confinement, and many were. In the solitary confinement cells, all personal objects were taken from the children, including their shoes. The children were given nothing to do for three days—no paper, no pencils, no books—because they had looked out a window. The light in the cell was never turned off.[11]

"Commingling juveniles with unrelated adults violates every known standard for juveniles," states the only contemporary legal assessment of the problem. "Nonetheless, at most INS facilities, minors are commingled with unrelated adults throughout the day."[12]

The INS had never promulgated standards for juvenile prisons because the agency had never incarcerated undocumented children and babies in great numbers until the Central American wars of the 1980s. Standards for children's detention were left to the discretion of INS district directors.

On my first full day in Laredo—Wednesday, May 1, 1985—President Reagan ordered the total economic embargo of Nicaragua, and Hughes sent me to the prison to interview two clients.[13] As I stood in the tiny prison lobby, INS deportation officer Ken Hickel told me through bullet-proof glass that I could not come in, that one of my clients had been sent to Los Fresnos and the other was already in Guatemala. I held two blue G-28 forms signed by Hughes and dated by the INS and showed them to Hickel. "You can hold that all day," Hickel said. "I don't have any record of it."

From Hughes's office I called INS and CCA officials in Laredo and San Antonio, identified myself as a journalist, and asked if INS had policies on detention or strip-searching of children. INS San Antonio District Director Ricardo Casillas said, "I don't know whether they do or not. Is this sup-posed to be something really sacred? Dealing with aliens? If they have di-rect contact with a lawyer, I don't blame them. Listen, don't try to nail me. You're trying to create a controversy. I know your type ... you damn turkey!"[14]

Casillas's assistant district director, Scott Robertson, apparently took the phone away from him at that point. I asked Robertson whose policy it was to strip-search children for asking to see an attorney, INS or CCA?

"They do have a policy manual that they go by," Robertson said. "It's a CCA policy manual. However, their policy, by contract, has to be in accord with INS policies."

But INS had no policies on detention of children except that minors not be detained with adults. The only rule was broken so that children could stay with their mothers. So there were no rules.

Privatization of the immigration prison did not create the abuse—privatization made responsibility for the abuse indeterminate. Nobody had to answer for it.

The strip searches at Laredo were punitive and occasionally perverse. A sixteen-year-old Salvadoran girl cried with embarrassment when she was strip-searched by a large female guard who then led her to her cell. A few minutes later, the guard returned to the cell, called the girl by name, and said, "I have to examine you again."[15] A thirteen-year-old Nicaraguan girl having her first menstrual period was strip-searched and forced to show the guard the soiled sanitary napkin. She cried from shame and humiliation.[16] Hughes referred both girls to another attorney, who sued the INS and won cash settlements for the girls.

Refugees' rights were violated regularly and systematically at Laredo. A prison guard, masquerading as an immigration judge, told a sixteen-year-old Salvadoran boy that he had decided the boy would not be allowed to post bond unless he had a wife, brother, or sister who was a U.S. citizen.

"I was very sad," the boy told me in one of the two tiny neon-lit interview rooms in the air-conditioned prison. "Then he told me that I might just as well sign a paper he had with him so that I could be deported as soon as possible. I signed the paper. Later, I called my attorney to thank him for trying to help me but that the immigration judge had decided against me."[17]

Hughes was mystified because there was no immigration court at the prison. Detainees were taken to court in San Antonio or to a courtroom at the international bridge in Laredo. But the boy had never been to court. We found that prison guards were impersonating judges, telling children to sign immigration form I-274, which waives the right to seek asylum and requests "voluntary repatriation." Hughes asked sixteen-year-old José if any other children had signed those forms. José brought us two fourteen-year-old Salvadorans. All three boys wanted political asylum; all had been duped into signing an I-274 by a prison guard.[18] As a regular part of our intake interviews we had to ask children to bring us their I-274 so that we could withdraw it.

Prison guards and deportation officers systematically violated the federal court orders in *Orantes-Hernandez v. Meese* and *Nuñez v. Boldin*. In the 1982 *Orantes-Hernandez* injunction, Judge Kenyon ordered the INS to prepare a Notice of Rights to Salvadorans and to give the notice to every Salvadoran arrested on immigration charges. The notice lists four rights: the right to be represented by an attorney, the right to a deportation hearing, the right to request political asylum, and the right to request voluntary repatriation. Most Salvadoran children told us that when they were arrested they were given the notice of rights, then told they had to choose one of the four. Two Salvadoran boys who were arrested together showed me their notice of rights with number 2 circled—the right to a deportation hearing. Both said the INS interrogator had chosen that right for them.[19]

Twenty-year-old Catalina Cayetano and her one-year-old baby were ordered deported to El Salvador, though they were citizens of Mexico. Catalina was arrested on April 24, 1985, at a checkpoint near San Clemente, California. She said the INS interrogator, a young blonde woman, "did not speak Spanish very well. I could barely understand her Spanish." Yet, "Many times, this woman told me that I spoke like a Salvadoran. She told me this about six times."[20]

Catalina showed me the deportation orders for her and her son. Both were scheduled to be deported to El Salvador, though they were residents of Jalisco, Mexico.

"I am scared of being deported to El Salvador, both for myself and my son," Catalina said. "I know no one in El Salvador. I have never been to El Salvador. I know practically nothing of El Salvador, only that there is war there."

With the help of the Mexican consul in Laredo, we got Catalina and her baby deported to Mexico.

A timid seventeen-year-old Salvadoran girl suffered a complete breakdown in Laredo prison brought on by the murder of her family in El Salvador, by being repeatedly strip-searched in prison, and by the manner in which she was taken to a simple bond reduction hearing. At 4 A.M. on May 10, prison officials awakened Dolores and eleven other detainees and put them on a bus, with no explanation. Families were separated. Every one of them thought at all times that he or she was being deported.

They were driven to San Antonio. The men were handcuffed and the children were put into a cell with the adults for six hours with no food or water. While they were in the holding tank, an INS officer told them that their lawyer, Patrick Hughes, was a communist subversive. He advised them to have nothing to do with him and to change lawyers. Many were not allowed to speak to Hughes after the bond hearing and had no idea what had happened until we called them the next day in Laredo.[21]

I saw seventeen-year-old Dolores before and after her bond hearing. From that night on she could not sleep, until she had a mental breakdown. Her skin became paler each day; she became disoriented. "My heart hurts," she said. "I have trouble breathing."[22]

"You must understand," one of Dolores's friends said, "when one is taken from one's bed in the middle of the night in El Salvador, one is never seen again." When Dolores broke down in uncontrolled weeping, she was sedated and then returned to her cell.[23]

Our client Leon celebrated his sixteenth birthday in solitary confinement in Laredo, and he was a U.S. citizen. A CCA officer told Leon to clean the toilets on April 30, and he did clean them. Later that day he was told to clean the toilets again. Leon said he had already cleaned them. For that insubordination, he was taken to "trial" in the prison on May 1. His legal representative and translator was the CCA guard who had told him to clean the toilets: the man who wanted to put him in solitary confinement.[24]

The guards took Leon's shoes and he spent May 1–4 in solitary confinement. He was a U.S. citizen, the son of a Guatemalan mother and whose father was a U.S. citizen. When we telephoned his father, the man was elated and immediately posted bail. The day he got out of prison Leon told me, "I felt sad inside solitary, thinking that I would spend my birthday there. I became sixteen years old in solitary confinement in *el pozo* (the hole), in the INS/CCA facility in Laredo, Texas."

Other children were put into solitary confinement for horsing around, laughing, playing roughly, or for standing too close to a window.[25]

The INS violated virtually every term of Judge Kenyon's order in *Orantes-Hernandez v. Meese*. To feign compliance with the injunction, the INS sometimes gave Salvadorans a list of lawyers who might represent them. About half of our clients had been arrested in California and transferred to Laredo; half had been arrested between Laredo and Houston. None of the prisoners who had been arrested in California was given a list of attorneys. The few prisoners who did have a list had been arrested in Texas, and they all had the same list: law firms in Albuquerque and El Paso that did not do asylum work and would not accept collect phone calls, which are the only phone calls detainees can make from an immigration prison.[26]

Repression Increases

Hughes and I were working sixteen-hour days, from 7 A.M. to 11 P.M., including Saturdays. The mood in the prison was changing, and the guards knew it. We told dispirited, dejected refugees that they had rights, that their rights were being violated, and that we were going to put a stop to it. Some of them believed us. We took depositions describing the strip searches, the sexual threats, and the physical violence.

A Border Patrolman had held a knife to the face of a seventeen-year-old Guatemalan boy when he arrested him:

I was arrested by the Border Patrol on the night of January 31, 1985, and taken from the jail in Zapata to the offices of the Border Patrol in Freer, Texas. In the offices of the Border Patrol in Freer, I was interrogated by an INS official named F. San Ramon. His name was on a metal plate on his shirt. The interrogation began about 11:30 that night. Mr. San Ramon asked me if I had any scars or distinguishing physical marks. I said, "No." Another INS official, dressed in green, then placed a knife upon my right cheek, and grabbed my face with his other hand. In Spanish, he asked me, "And wouldn't you like me to make you a scar right now?" I told him, "No." He removed the knife from my cheek then.[27]

INS officials separated children from their parents and interrogated the children to elicit information about their parents.[28] One of our clients was a five-year-old boy who had been separated from his mother and interrogated about her.[29]

A prison guard threatened to "knock in the head" with a walkie-talkie a sixteen-year-old Salvadoran boy after I asked him to return to his cell and bring me his I-274 so we could retract it. While strip-searching him, the guard asked the boy what his legal advisers had told him.[30]

Every day, Hughes and I told INS and CCA officials they were violating federal court orders, that the strip searches were illegal and unconstitutional interference with the right to counsel. The prison officials laughed. But as the refugees gained confidence, the guards became nervous. When they strip-searched the children and asked what their lawyers had told them—an unconstitutional invasion of privacy—the guards learned we were taking notarized statements describing the strip searches.[31] Hughes notarized the statements in the prison's little interview rooms.

On May 4, CCA restricted our access to clients. The CCA prison director, Terry Sparbel, handed me a memo that stated legal visits would be prohibited after 5 P.M.—a violation of the *Orantes-Hernandez* injunction, which set the hours for legal visits with Salvadoran asylum seekers as 9 A.M. to 9:30 P.M.[32] Until that day, prison officials had let Hughes see clients as late as 10 P.M.

On that day I took Leon's statement about his three days in solitary confinement and discovered he was a U.S. citizen. A guard took Leon back to his cell, then brought two Salvadoran women to us in the two tiny interview rooms off a little hall in the prison. One of the women was beautiful and defiant.

Before she said a word, I knew she had been beaten and that if she went back to El Salvador, she would refuse to bow her head, and she would be beaten again. She was simple and direct, with the high cheekbones of a Maya. She was twenty-five, from Mejicanos, the daughter of *campesinos*.

"My family is very poor," she said. As she described the life that had driven her from El Salvador, she put her head down and cried. "Should I be saying this? I am so scared. I am the only hope of my family."

I assured her there were churches in the United States that helped refugees and that I could get her out of jail if a church congregation would pay her bond. "But do they let you out of the church?" she asked, crying. "Are you allowed out of the church?"[33]

I spent Sunday on the telephone, trying to find $3,000 for her bond. On Monday I was barred from the prison. INS Deputy District Director Scott Robertson drove down from San Antonio to inform me that I was not a legal assistant but a journalist. Therefore, I could no longer enter the prison.[34]

I had never worked for a newspaper. Four of my articles about refugees had been published—by the *Baltimore Sun,* the *National Catholic Reporter,* Pacific News Service, and the Washington, D.C., *City Paper.* I was denied the right to work as a legal assistant because I had written a few articles about refugees.

I told Robertson that to deny me entrance would violate the federal court orders in *Nuñez v. Boldin* and *Orantes-Hernandez v. Meese.* He told me to get out of there.

The prison was filled nearly to capacity. Most detainees were Guatemalan and Salvadoran asylum seekers who were being repeatedly strip-searched for consulting their only access to legal services, Refugee Legal Services. I was the organization's only paralegal.[35]

On Tuesday morning I went back to the prison. I was met there by two men in dark suits and sunglasses and by CCA head of camp Terry Sparbel, INS San Antonio District Assistant Director Scott Robertson, and INS prison director Emilio Saenz. Saenz told me I could not enter, by order of the INS district director in San Antonio. I read a short statement that denying me entrance would violate federal court orders in *Orantes-Hernandez v. Meese* and *Nuñez v. Boldin.* The men in suits laughed and Robertson ordered me to leave the prison. Of the five men, only Saenz seemed concerned that he did not know the law. As I left the prison, he took me aside and said he would look it up.[36]

Hughes wrote a long letter that night to the INS Southern Region commissioner in Dallas describing the strip searches, the limited hours of legal visits, and the violations of *Orantes-Hernandez* and *Nuñez v. Boldin.* He expressed great concern that "Mr. Robertson claimed that he had not even heard of these two cases."[37]

I returned to the prison the next day, and after an hour's wait Saenz ordered CCA to let me in. The guards ruthlessly intensified the strip searches and made us wait forty-five minutes to an hour between each client. Until that day, guards had occasionally let children return to their cells after stripping to their underwear. Now they conducted thorough body-cavity searches. The week before, CCA guards would bring us a family of parents and children or groups of three or four within minutes after we'd asked to see them. Now they began bringing us one client at a time after long delays.

The guards were tense. They brought me only five clients between 10 A.M. and 3 P.M. Sparbel called me to his office at 3:10 and accused me of "threatening" him by telling a CCA guard I was taking notes about what was happening in the prison.[38] I returned to Hughes's office and discovered the reason for the tension. Early that morning a Salvadoran boy had climbed the twelve-foot-high chain-link fence surrounding the prison, cut himself on the razor wire, and escaped. Prison guards were telling the other children the boy had been seriously hurt and was in a hospital. Hughes had called all the hospitals and clinics in Laredo; none had received a bleeding refugee. Saenz told us later that the child escaped.

A Small Victory

I was falling in love with the beautiful, defiant Salvadoran. She had planned to come to the United States with her older brother, an auto mechanic who had been arrested and tortured after he worked on a Volkswagen that the police claimed belonged to the guerrilla. They didn't have enough money for both to come north, so he told her to go and he would follow. She had been arrested with another Salvadoran woman, who called us late Wednesday afternoon to tell us she had heard from relatives in Houston that her friend's brother had just been killed by a death squad.

I drove back to prison to see her and asked the guard not to strip-search her. By then the whole prison knew what had happened, and he agreed. The next morning she told me she couldn't stand the strip searches anymore. She knew she would not win asylum, and she wanted to find out who had killed her brother. She would rather be deported than stay in prison. I told her not to go back to El Salvador but to marry me. She gave me a stunned look that changed from unbelieving to believing, said yes, and left the cell in a daze. She had a bond-reduction hearing in San Antonio the next day.

I went to the office, told Hughes I was going to marry his client, and started typing an affidavit for him to submit in requesting a bond reduction.

At 4 A.M. the next morning, my fiancée and eleven others were rousted from their beds and put on a bus to San Antonio. I went to the office early and called everyone I had met in Washington. I asked them to call their congressman or senator and ask why the INS was strip-searching refugee children in Laredo. I called every refugee and human rights office I had visited, every church, think tank, and attorney, and described the conditions at Laredo. No newspaper would accept an article from me because I was involved in the story. None thought it worth sending a reporter to Laredo. Neither of Laredo's two daily papers had written a word about the strip searches. The INS is one of the city's biggest employers, with hundreds of Border Patrol officers, detention officers, immigration officers, antismuggling units, clerks, and secretaries. The prison was a new business in town. For the Laredo Morning Times and the Laredo News, it was hands off the INS and hands off CCA.

I called the Washington office of Texas Senator Lloyd Bentsen and told Bentsen's legislative assistant Felix Sanchez that I was not calling as a journalist but as a constituent whose fiancée was being repeatedly strip-searched because she sought legal advice. Sanchez said he knew "just who to call," and that he would call back. He did, in ten minutes. He reported that INS Commissioner Alan Nelson had told him strip searching is a "blanket policy" in immigration prisons.

I said the commissioner had lied to him. I had worked at Los Fresnos prison for months, and they had never strip-searched after attorney visits. The prisons at Houston and El Paso didn't strip-search, either; nor did any other prison legally detain children. "These are children we're talking about," I said. "Where does it say the INS has the right to contract the power to strip-search children?"

Sanchez said nothing for several seconds, then he said he would call back.

In San Antonio, our seventeen-year-old client, Dolores, who would soon suffer a nervous breakdown, was called to her bond hearing. Hughes asked her to tell the immigration judge what had happened to her in El Salvador and Laredo. She hung her head and wept.

Hughes argued that Dolores didn't deserve to be in jail at all. She had found the lower half of her brother's body on the street in her village in El Salvador. Now she was being repeatedly strip-searched in Laredo prison, she was confined with adults, and she had a bond of $7,500. Hughes requested that she be released on her own recognizance.[39]

The judge asked the INS attorney, who had no idea what was going on in Laredo, why Dolores was being strip-searched. He then lowered Dolores's bond to $1,000 and called the case of an eighteen-year-old Salvadoran girl. Hughes told the judge that her father had been murdered and the Salvadoran army had surrounded her village with tanks.

The INS attorney objected that this had nothing to do with her request for a bond reduction. Hughes retorted that it had everything to do with it: The girl was a refugee; she was being imprisoned with a prohibitively high bond; and the precedent-setting case for immigration bonds, *Matter of Patel,* ruled that immigration detainees should be released unless they pose a threat to the national security of the United States.

The judge lowered the bond to $1,000, and the INS attorney asked to speak to Hughes privately. He complained that Patrick was raising issues that were inappropriate for bond hearings. "I don't care," Hughes said. "I'm going to run each case like a trial on the merits [for asylum]. It'll take all afternoon and you won't be able to deport anyone."[40] As long as the judge was tied up with Hughes's clients' bond hearings, he couldn't order deportations. Hughes was also giving the judge an earful about conditions at Laredo, and the INS attorney could not refute his statements. The INS attorney finally caved in. He agreed to lower most of the bonds to $1,000.

In Laredo, I had spoken with correspondents for the *New York Times,* the *Los Angeles Times,* the *Chicago Tribune,* and the *San Jose Mercury-News.* After preliminary interviews with INS officials in Washington and Texas, reporters from the *Tribune* and the *Mercury-News* were persuaded there were enough issues at stake that they wanted to go to Laredo. Late in the afternoon, Felix Sanchez called back. He said "a high INS official" had ordered that strip searches stop after legal visits, though strip searches would continue after family visits. "The whole policy is being reviewed."

In San Antonio, the INS guards would not let our clients see Hughes after the bond hearings ended. They were handcuffed and put back on the bus. They thought they had been ordered deported and were being driven to a waiting aircraft.[41] As they were being led away, Hughes called from a pay phone in the courthouse with the news that the judge had lowered my fiancée's bond to $500. I didn't let him finish. "We stopped the strip searches," I said. "Bentsen stopped them."

Hughes relayed the message to the INS attorney. I heard the man tell Patrick he didn't know what he was talking about. Hughes couldn't resist rubbing it in. "Senator Bentsen ordered you to stop," he said. "You lost."

At the prison on Saturday afternoon the guards led Hughes and me to a big conference room they had never allowed us to use before. They brought us five clients immediately. Hughes told them to bring three more. The guards, with a respectful "Yes, sir," brought them immediately.

We told our clients that most of them had gotten low bonds and that the strip searches would stop. Just then, an announcement came over the prison's public address system: "There will be no strip searching under any circumstances. New policy." We translated the message for our clients, who were mostly women, and we all felt about as happy as you can in prison. A middle-aged Salvadoran woman mentioned that she had seen the names of people who applied for political asylum printed in Salvadoran newspapers as traitors and defamers of their country, but she didn't care; she was going to apply. Hughes told the women they had won a great victory for all Salvadorans. At 9:30 P.M. a CCA guard knocked on the door: "With all due respect, counselors, it's nine-thirty."

On Sunday, CCA Vice President Richard Crane called Hughes from corporate headquarters in Nashville, Tennessee, to say that he felt sure they could come to an agreement without litigation. The guards in Laredo knew that heat was coming down. Some were afraid they might lose their jobs. While Hughes and Crane discussed how the Corrections Corporation of America could assure that detained Salvadorans would be granted access to legal counsel, a CCA guard at the prison informed me I could not see an eleven-year-old boy who had called our office. I looked at the guard's metal name tag and wrote his name in my notebook. The guard remarked through bulletproof glass, "If something happens to me, then something's going to happen to you."

I asked what he meant by that. He repeated his threat.[42]

Chaos on the Border

Our small legal victory had no effect on the inexorable forces that were driving the border toward chaos. The wars continued in Central America, and the influx of Nicaraguans was starting to divide refugee workers just as U.S. sponsorship of the Central American wars was dividing Congress and the country. While Hughes and I struggled to ameliorate conditions for the 208 detainees at Laredo, U.S. military and economic pressure on Central America continued, further destabilizing the region and exacerbating the conditions in immigration prisons and along the U.S.-Mexican border.

On May 7, 1985, the day the economic embargo of Nicaragua took effect, former U.N. Ambassador Jeane Kirkpatrick announced that she had accepted $100,000 to form a nonprofit organization to funnel money for non-lethal aid to the Contras in Honduras and Nicaragua.[43] Arnaud de Borchgrave, editor of the *Washington Times,* publicized the gift in a front-page editorial that day. The funds came from News World Communications, Inc., the *Times's* parent company, which is affiliated with the Reverend Sun Myung Moon's World Unification Church. The corporation would be called the Nicaraguan Freedom Fund.

The Contra war intensified pressure on Nicaraguans to abandon their country and join the thousands of Salvadorans and Guatemalans fleeing north. As the refugee tide mounted, repression increased along the U.S. border. On May 8, Mexicans in San Ysidro, California, across the border from Tijuana, passed out leaflets warning that U.S. citizens in Mexico might be shot in retaliation for the April 28 shooting of twelve-year-old Humberto Carrillo Estrada by Border Patrol Agent Edward Cole.[44] The U.S. Justice Department investigated the incident and found the shooting to be a reasonable act. But the protesters demanded compensation for Carrillo's family and punishment for Cole. "If our demands are not met within 72 hours," the pamphlet warned, "any North American male found in Mexico will be in the same situation to undergo what happened to our Humberto Carrillo."[45]

The only glimmer of hope in U.S. immigration policy was that Cuba had agreed to accept 2,746 deportees from the United States, most of whom were incarcerated at the federal penitentiary in Atlanta.[46] Until the United States and Cuba reached the deportation accord, Fidel Castro had refused to accept deportees from the United States because the United States refused to recognize the government of Cuba.

The United States needed the deportation agreement to free up space Cubans were occupying in federal prisons. The agreement was the closest approach to diplomatic relations between the United States and Cuba in more than twenty years and was the first diplomatic step the Reagan administration had taken that might reduce pressure on immigration prisons.

But on May 20 the agreement fell apart. On that day, 125 employees of the federally funded Radio Martí had begun broadcasting U.S. government programs to Cuba on a 50,000-watt transmitter—in President Reagan's words, to "help defuse the war hysteria" spread by Fidel Castro.[47] Castro had warned Reagan that he would retaliate if Radio Martí went on the air. The day broadcasts began, Castro canceled the immigration agreement—leaving 1,800 potential Cuban deportees in Atlanta Federal Penitentiary and more than 6,000 Cubans in other U.S. prisons.[48] The United States could not deport Cuban criminals and would not release them to the streets. They continued to take up prison space.

The Reagan administration addressed the Central American immigration problem by building Oakdale prison in the swamps and pine forest of southwest Louisiana. Seventeen million dollars had already been spent on the prison in fiscal year 1983; another $10.5 million would be spent to finish the buildings in fiscal year 1986. It would be the largest immigration prison ever built in the United States, with 1,000 beds, emergency capacity for 10,000, and its own airstrip for deportations. Eight immigration judges and sixteen INS attorneys would be assigned there. The INS contract this time would be with the U.S. Bureau of Prisons.[49]

As Radio Martí hit the airwaves and the Cuban agreement fell apart, I married Cecy, and we left Laredo. There was still work to do in the prison, but I now had financial obligations and couldn't work pro bono. It would take my wife thirteen months to become a legal U.S. resident; then we could arrange for her three young children to join us.

We didn't know as we drove west toward Tucson that one year later we would be driving east toward Oakdale, where Central American refugees would be stripped, beaten, kicked, drugged, tortured, sexually molested, robbed by professional con men, arrested for "loitering" while waiting for a bus, and ordered to get out of town by sundown. We didn't know about all the lawsuits ahead that would cause the INS to move Central Americans out of Oakdale and turn it into a prison for Cubans, who would burn it down in 1987, along with the prison at Atlanta. And as we drove toward another nonpaying job in another immigration prison, we didn't know that Cuban detainees were about to burn it down as well.

Notes

1. John Tower, Edmund Muskie, and Brent Scowcroft, *The Tower Commission Report* (New York: Times Books, 1987), 458.

2. Ibid., 469–471.

3. The passage of the Boland Amendment prohibited the CIA and Department of Defense from supplying equipment, training, or advice "for the purpose of overthrowing the government of Nicaragua or provoking a military exchange between Nicaragua and Honduras."

4. "The [Contra] rebels have not been able to take and hold a single Nicaraguan town," the *New York Times* reported on March 19, 1985, in an article headlined "Little in Nicaragua Escapes War's Onslaught." The Contras never mounted a successful sustained military operation against the Sandinista army, the *Times* reported one year later: "Most Contras Reported to Pull Out of Nicaragua," *New York Times,* January 30, 1986; "Anti-Sandinista Adviser Lists Aid Needs of Rebels," *New York Times,* February 21, 1986; and "Contra Forces Now Viewed as a Much-Reduced Threat," *New York Times,* March 6, 1986. These three articles reported that the Sandinista army had driven the Contras from Nicaraguan territory into Honduras, that the Sandinista army was in its strongest position in six years, and that the Contra army was in its worst shape in two years. For a history of the Contras, see Sam Dillon, *Comandos: The CIA and Nicaragua's Contra Rebels* (New York: Henry Holt, 1991); and Christopher Dickey, *With the Contras* (New York: Simon & Schuster, 1985).

5. The estimate of $30 paid by the INS to CCA per detainee per day was provided by two high-ranking INS officials at the Laredo prison. The U.S. government offered to pay $29 per detainee per day for the first year, $31 per detainee per day in the second year, and $23.46 per detainee per day in the three years after that: "Solicitation, Offer and Award," March 7, 1984, 9. ("Solicitation, Offer and Award" is the government document that includes specifications for the contract to build and operate the prison, the bidder's offer, and the U.S. government's awarding of the contract.) The Corrections Corporation of America got the contract by bidding $28.76 per detainee per day for the first five years, "Amendment of Solicitation," June 15, 1984. Security guards at the Laredo prison were paid $3.91 an hour, less than the highest-paid nonclassified employee, maintenance workers, who got $4.87 an hour, "Solicitation, Offer and Award," March 7, 1984, 48. In an article about the INS/CCA immigration prison at Houston, Texas, the *New York Times* reported, "The Federal Government spends $26.45 a day for each resident at its own immigration detention centers. C.C.A. charges the Government $23.84." The cost of salaries and training also was lower at privately run prisons: "Jails Run by Private Company Force It to Face Question of Accountability," *New York Times,* February 19, 1985.

6. Attorney Patrick Hughes kept records of immigration bonds for detainees at Laredo. Hughes was the only attorney in Laredo who regularly represented detained asylum seekers for no charge.

7. A standard textbook, David Weissbrodt's *Immigration Law* (St. Paul: West Publishing, 1991), does not even mention standards of detention because the INS has no regulations on it. The problem surfaced again in June 1995 when detainees rioted at an immigration detention center in Elizabeth, New Jersey, privately run for the INS by Esmor Corporation. Though detainees complained before the riot about being shackled during the day and being fed spoiled and inadequate food, the INS had no standards by which to judge the Esmor facility because it has no standards for conditions of detention in immigration prisons.

8. Patrick Hughes, interview with the author, April 30, 1985. Hughes thought the strip searches may have been criminal because of the opportunity they presented for sexual abuse of children. In fact, two children did file successful lawsuits that year charging sexual abuse by prison guards at Laredo, as mentioned in this chapter.

9. The Laredo prison violated INS regulations and state law by incarcerating children with adults; it violated state and federal law and the 1982 U.S. Supreme Court order in *Plyler v. Doe* by denying children access to education; it violated federal court orders in *Orantes-Hernandez v. Meese* and *Nuñez v. Boldin* by denying Salvadorans access to legal counsel and misinforming them of political asylum law; it violated the precedent-setting decision in immigration case law, *Matter of Patel,* which states that noncriminal immigration detainees should be released unless they pose a threat to national security. More than sixteen children and adult detainees signed notarized affidavits inside Laredo prison testifying to these abuses in May 1985. Photocopies of documents are in the author's possession.

10. Child and adult detainees inside Laredo INS/CCA prison, interviews with the author, May 4–11, 1985; Affidavit of Leon H., signed and sworn before attorney Patrick Hughes, May 11, 1985, INS/CCA prison, Laredo, Texas. All affidavits cited in this chapter were signed and sworn by affiants and notarized by Hughes.

11. Description of solitary confinement cell in Laredo prison provided by child and adult detainees in interviews with the author, May 4–11, 1985; Affidavit of José G., May 4, 1985, INS/CCA prison, Laredo; Affidavit of José C., May 11, 1985, INS/CCA prison, Laredo; and letters from detainees to the author.

12. Carlos Holguin, "Children in INS Prisons: An Educational Assessment," unpublished manuscript, 1985. Holguin, a staff attorney for the National Center for Immigrants' Rights in Los Angeles, prepared the report for the Boston-based National Coalition of Advocates for Students.

13. "Reagan Reported Planning Nicaragua Trade Embargo, Retaining Diplomatic Links (-) Decision Imminent," *New York Times,* May 1, 1985; "Statement by Principal Deputy Press Secretary Speaks on Economic Sanctions Against Nicaragua," *Presidential Papers: Administration of Ronald Reagan, 1985,* 549–550. Notice of the embargo was filed with the Office of the Federal Register on May 1, 1985; the embargo took effect May 7.

14. INS San Antonio District Director Ricardo Casillas, telephone interview with the author, May 1, 1985.

15. Affidavit of Ana Maria M., May 12, 1985, INS/CCA prison, Laredo.

16. Affidavits of "Jane Doe" [thirteen years old] and her mother, "Jane Smith," May 12, 1985, INS/CCA prison, Laredo.

17. Affidavit of José B., May 4, 1985, INS/CCA prison, Laredo.

18. Affidavit of José B. and Affidavit of José L., May 4, 1985, INS/CCA prison, Laredo; three child detainees inside INS/CCA prison, Laredo, interview with the author, May 9, 1985.

19. First reported in interviews of two child detainees with the author inside INS/CCA prison on May 8, 1985, Laredo. In the weeks that followed, several more child detainees showed the author the INS form Notice and Request for Disposition with their first "right" circled in pen or pencil—the right to a deportation hearing. All the children said a Border Patrol officer had chosen their "right" for them.

20. Affidavit of Catalina Cayetano, INS/CCA prison, May 11, 1985, Laredo.

21. Eight child and adult detainees in INS/CCA prison, interviews with the author, May 11, 1985; and Deposition of Robert Kahn, 109–110, in *Orantes-Hernandez v. Smith.*

22. Dolores and three friends, interviews with the author, May 11, 1985, INS/CCA prison, Laredo.

23. Patrick Hughes, telephone interview with the author, June 13, 1985.

24. Leon H., interview with the author, May 4, 1985; Affidavit of Leon H., May 11, 1985, INS/CCA prison, Laredo.

25. Affidavit of José C., May 4, 1985, INS/CCA prison, Laredo; Affidavit of Leon H., May 11, 1985, INS/CCA prison, Laredo; and interviews with other children inside the prison.

26. Numerous child and adult detainees showed the author the list of attorneys' offices provided by the INS—seven attorneys were in New Mexico and three in El Paso. None accepted collect phone calls or did pro bono political asylum work. Detainee interviews with the author, May 2–17, 1985.

27. Affidavit of "I.S.," May 4, 1985, INS/CCA prison, Laredo.

28. Affidavit of "Maria," May 11, 1985, INS/CCA prison, Laredo.

29. Affidavit of "Fernando," May 11, 1985, INS/CCA prison, Laredo: "I am five years old. I am from Guatemala. I was arrested by some men from the immigration in a hotel in San Diego. They would not let us leave the room. Then they took us in a car. I was scared. In a room, one official made me lower my pants, and he made me raise my shirt and he looked at me. An official grabbed my nose and he grabbed my head, and he said, 'Look, where are you from?' and I said, 'From Guatemala.' I was scared. The official who grabbed me had blue eyes."

30. Rene, interview with the author, May 9, 1985.

31. Author interviews with two child detainees, May 2 and 9, 1984, who said prison guards asked them, "What did the lawyer tell you?" as the guards strip-searched them.

32. Permanent Injunction, *Crosby Wilfredo Orantes-Hernandez et al. v. Edwin Meese III et al.*, U.S. District Court, Central District of California, April 29, 1988, 61. Judge David V. Kenyon's final order made permanent the terms of the injunction he issued in 1982.

33. In early 1980, Archbishop Oscar Arnulfo Romero opened the seminary of San José de la Montaña in San Salvador as a sanctuary for Salvadorans displaced by the war. Tommie Sue Montgomery, then professor of political science at Dickinson College in Carlisle, Pennsylvania, and author of *Revolution in El Salvador* (Boulder, Colo.: Westview Press, 1994), described conditions at the church refuge in a September 21, 1984, deposition in the case of *United States of America v. John Elder:* "These people whom I interviewed in March of 1980 came to, in a de facto way, create the first of a number of refugee centers that the church in El Salvador has set up. This particular refugee center is still today in existence four and a half years later. Some of the people who came in March of 1980 I saw as recently as May of 1984 in that same refugee center. ... I have talked with people who literally have not been out of that center in four years ... an area approximately the size of three football fields ... because some of the people who lived there have gone outside for various reasons, such as to buy medicine, to buy food, and have either disappeared, or

have turned up dead in a matter of days. So people do not go out unless they absolutely have to."

34. INS San Antonio District Deputy Director Scott Robertson, interview with the author, May 6, 1985.

35. On the day the author was barred from the Laredo immigration prison, José Conejo, a former prison guard at the INS prison at Los Fresnos, pleaded guilty in Brownsville Federal Court to selling INS documents to a Colombian for $2,000. Two charges of bribery and a charge of destroying INS documents were dismissed in exchange for the guilty plea. He was sentenced to four years in jail.

36. Agency spokesmen refused to tell the author whether the men in suits and sunglasses were from the INS Internal Affairs Division or the FBI. Robertson said in 1992 that he had no recollection of the incident.

37. Patrick Hughes, letter to INS Southern Region commissioner, May 6, 1985. A copy of the letter is in the author's possession.

38. Kahn notebooks, vol. VII, 18.

39. Hughes described the bond-reduction hearings in an interview with the author, May 10, 1985.

40. Ibid.

41. Eight child and adult detainees, interviews with the author, May 11, 1985; Deposition of Robert Kahn, 109–111, in *Orantes-Hernandez v. Smith*.

42. Kahn notebooks, vol. VII, 22–23; and Deposition of Robert Kahn, 111–114, in *Orantes-Hernandez v. Smith*.

43. "Paper to Aid Nicaraguan Rebels," *New York Times,* May 7, 1985.

44. Associated Press dispatches, April 29, 1985, and May 8, 1985.

45. Associated Press dispatch, May 8, 1985.

46. On December 14, 1984, Cuba agreed to accept the deportation of 2,746 *Marielitos* who had been excluded from the United States. The 120,000 Cubans who entered the United States in 1980 are known as *Marielitos* because many of them left Cuba at the port of Mariel. Most of the *Marielitos* whose deportation Castro agreed to accept were incarcerated in the federal penitentiary at Atlanta, Georgia. The United States planned to deport about 100 a month beginning in January 1985. "U.S. and Cuba Gain an Accord on Repatriation," *New York Times,* December 15, 1984. The agreement, however, conflicted with an October 15, 1984, order by U.S. District Judge Marvin Shoob in Atlanta. Shoob's order barred the United States from deporting Cubans unless they first were given the opportunity to apply for political asylum. Shoob rejected federal entreaties to rescind his order. See "Judge Reasserts Right of Cubans to Get Hearing—Rejects U.S. Complaint on Pact with Havana," *New York Times,* January 1, 1985.

A federal appeals court overturned Shoob's order on January 16, 1985, allowing the deportations to proceed. See "Bar to Deporting of Cubans Stayed—Appellate Court Acts After a Judge Frees 34 in Prison," *New York Times,* January 17, 1985. The first Cuban deportees were sent to Havana on February 21, 1985. See "First Group of Cuban Aliens Sent Back as Undesirables," *New York Times,* February 22, 1985. The United States deported 201 Cubans before the agreement with Cuba collapsed. See "Detaining Cubans Exacts Rising Toll," *New York Times,* March 10, 1986.

47. "In a brief statement read by a Radio Martí announcer, President Reagan said he hoped the new service would 'help defuse the war hysteria on which much of current Cuban Government policy is predicated'": "Radio Martí Goes on Air and Cuba Retaliates by Ending Pact," *New York Times*, May 21, 1985.

48. "Return of Cubans from U.S. Is 'Going Well,'" *New York Times*, May 20, 1985; and "Radio Martí Goes on Air."

49. *Congressional Quarterly* (February 16, 1985): 325–327; and "Louisianans Wait for Alien Center," *New York Times*, October 7, 1984.

FLORENCE PRISON

They are waiting for the end of the world.

—*Attorney Dave Meyers, on the legal status of
Cubans in U.S. immigration prisons.*

MY 1,000 INTERVIEWS with Salvadorans and Guatemalans had not yet taught me what it's like to live as a refugee in the United States. Now I would see constant humiliations, insults, and lewd behavior forced upon my wife because she was foreign and did not speak English—because people could get away with it. A common argument in today's furious debate about immigration is that immigrants come here to "take advantage of the system."[1] One hears little about how the system makes it easy for citizens to take advantage of immigrants.

We rented an apartment in Tucson and my wife looked for work in Mexican restaurants in the *barrio* on Sixth Avenue. After a half dozen rejections one hot afternoon in June, she came out of a restaurant smiling, holding a sheet of paper in her hand. "The bartender told me to fill out this application and bring it back to him at midnight," Cecy said proudly, handing me the form. It was an English-language application for a Social Security card.

"This isn't a job application," I said.

Cecy was furious that the bartender had mocked her and tore up the paper. I wondered what the bartender would do if she did return at midnight. At another restaurant she stayed inside for a long time. When Cecy got in the car she was trembling and close to tears. "Let's go," she said. "I can't do this anymore."

The restaurant owner had told her he might have an opening; she would have to come back at 9 P.M. But as she left through the kitchen, a middle-aged Mexican woman warned her, "He'll make you have sex with him if you want the job. If you don't have sex with him when he wants it, he'll fire you." The other women in the kitchen confirmed it. Cecy was scared and revolted. I was furious. But there was nothing to be done. The owner hadn't made an illegal proposition yet. If we reported him, the Mexican women would lose their jobs.

Cecy finally found a job in a sewing sweatshop, altering and repairing industrial uniforms from 5 A.M. to 3:30 P.M. The factory had no air-conditioning, and the manager yelled at the women for "wasting time" when they drank from the one water fountain. On Cecy's first day at work, a middle-aged woman died of cardiac arrest at a sewing machine. Cecy put up with the terrible conditions so she could send money home for her children.

Waiting for the End of the World

Seventy miles north of Tucson, on a flat, dusty plain in the desert, is the INS prison at Florence. The only attorney who worked regularly at the prison was Dave Myers, a Catholic priest from Guadalupe, a Yaqui Indian *barrio* near Phoenix. Myers was a burned-out case. He had been driving the hundred-mile round-trip across the desert two or three times a week for more than a year. He had 220 active cases and didn't make a dime from any of them. I called him from Tucson, and he gave me the names of five Salvadorans to call for intake interviews. There were twenty more inside the prison who needed to fill out asylum applications. Myers was also the prison priest, so he had the run of the place.

"Jails are intrinsically inhuman, and these guys are nothing but political prisoners," Myers said.[2] "I ate their food and got deathly sick on it once. They treat them like cattle. Stick them out in the morning and let them graze for a while; take them in and feed them; stick them out and graze them again."

The Department of Justice was turning Florence into a Cuban prison, transferring Cuban convicts to it as they were released from state and federal prisons. Myers had just lost eleven Salvadoran clients who were transferred to an old federal prison in Anthony, New Mexico, that had once held John Dillinger.[3] There was no way Myers could represent them there, and they were deported. Fights were becoming more frequent inside Florence prison as Cuban convicts took advantage of young Salvadorans.

Florence and El Centro are the most physically brutal immigration prisons: They are on desert plains where summertime temperatures regularly reach 110 degrees. Florence is the older, more primitive prison. It was built in the early 1940s to imprison Japanese Americans displaced by the Japanese Relocation Act of 1942.[4] It is a stereotypical western jail, with concrete floors and three big, barred cells, each one about as big as a quarter of a basketball court, and a dusty yard for "recreation." Immigration court was held in a portable trailer inside the prison compound. Despite the nineteenth-century setting, prisoners at Florence were spared the abuses of El Centro and the *corralón* because Florence had an intelligent and humane prison director, Manuel Cornejo.

"The operating capacity of the jail is 160, but we have had as many as 190 as late as May 1," Cornejo told me in his prison office on July 2.[5] He had read in INS publications that Florence prison had a capacity of 223 but didn't know how the INS had come up with that figure. Myers said the prison had 213 beds and 212 mattresses.

I identified myself as a paralegal working with Myers and as a journalist. He did not object to that. He answered all my questions, citing immigration law from memory by section, subsection, and paragraph, and the citations were always relevant to the question. Cornejo let prisoners take English classes on Saturday evenings—though an official at Los Fresnos had been reprimanded for suggesting English classes there. Cornejo let prisoners photocopy his law books, and he had the prison guards under control.

"I've never seen it like this," a Cuban felon told me. He had been bounced around the U.S. prison system for years. "The guards call you 'Sir' here. 'Good morning, Sir,' they say. I've never seen it like this."[6]

Many guards were miners who had lost their jobs in Globe or Superior when copper prices plummeted in the 1970s. They were middle-aged men, the sons or grandsons of Mexican immigrants, and they knew what it was like to suffer and to be out of work.[7] The Cubans who rioted and destroyed Florence immigration prison that summer did not riot because of brutality or unfair treatment from prison guards. They rioted because Cubans in U.S. immigration prisons are in an intolerable situation.

Every Cuban in a U.S. immigration prison is the hero of his own Kafka novel: held under no charge, given no hearing, with no hearing scheduled. They are guilty of being Cuban and can be held in prison forever and never go before a judge. As Myers put it, "They're waiting for the end of the world."

The Exclusion Process

More than 120,000 Cubans entered the United States near Miami from May to August 1980 in the Mariel boatlift. As thousands of Cubans left the port of Mariel, Castro opened his prisons and released hundreds or thousands of habitual violent criminals along with the rest. Because the Cubans were fleeing a Marxist government the United States had refused to recognize for twenty years, most of the *Marielitos* were given special parole to enter the United States. Immigration parole is a peculiar legal status.

First, the Cubans were excluded—a procedure applied to people who are arrested before they enter the United States, as with the Haitian boat people. People in exclusion proceedings have limited constitutional rights because they are not considered to have entered the United States. They have no right to an attorney, to a speedy trial, or to appeal a judge's decision. The only "right" they have is the right to an exclusion hearing. If a judge excludes someone from the United States, the legal process is over.

All the *Marielitos* were excluded, and then all but about 1,700 were given special parole to enter the country. Those who were not paroled had admitted to immigration inspectors that they had committed crimes in Cuba that would be felonies in the United States. They were excluded and immediately imprisoned. But the other 120,000 *Marielitos* were not home free. The U.S. attorney general can revoke parole for a misdemeanor or for no reason at all, and a parolee who has lived legally in the United States for years can be imprisoned even if he or she is found innocent. He or she can be held indefinitely without being given a hearing because he or she has been excluded from the United States.

Many of the 6,000 *Marielitos* in U.S. prisons in 1985 had committed violent crimes in the United States—murder, rape, arson, armed robbery. An INS officer who followed the *Marielitos* from Miami to an internment camp in Fort Jeffrey, Arkansas, to Oakdale, Louisiana, knew one *Marielito* who went back to jail after he threw a hand grenade into the living room of his former girlfriend. "Not nice people," was his description.[8] Other *Marielitos* were poor kids who were arrested for stealing food.

Máximo, an honest Cuban with a wife who was a legal U.S. resident and a daughter who was a U.S. citizen, spent two years in Los Fresnos prison because he left the United States to go to the dentist. Máximo came to the United States on the Mariel boatlift. He was excluded, paroled, and sent to the relocation camp at Fort Jeffrey, which he left in June 1980 to go to Las Cruces, New Mexico, and later moved to the lower Rio Grande Valley. He had never been accused of a crime in Cuba or the United States.

"I left one Thursday to go to a dentist in Mexico," Máximo said, while waiting for his wife to visit him in the *corralón*.[9]

> He worked on me and I presented my parole papers at customs. I had no problems coming back. The next Monday I went to the dentist again, and on returning, the same official who had let me in Thursday had me arrested as an illegal. I told him that he had let me through Thursday, and now he was arresting me. I asked what was the difference between Thursday and Monday?
>
> I'd crossed the border a lot of times with those papers. I was working with a fruit company in Weslaco when they arrested me. The head of the company sent the *migra* a letter telling of my good conduct.
>
> As I understand it, in this country, almost all the people have the right to a bond: drug smugglers, robbers, everyone. Then why not me? Because I'm Cuban? Because I went to the dentist?[10]

Máximo's fellow Cuban detainee, Herman, was in a similar situation. Herman was a born-again Christian sailor who'd jumped ship in Mexico and entered the United States at Laredo in 1983. He was arrested and interrogated by the FBI.

> They wanted to know what I did in Cuba. I said I was a simple sailor. I said the communist government of Cuba was no good for me. My own idea, born from my own body, is that the government of Cuba is worth nothing. The government practically destroys the people. For me, the government of Cuba does not exist.[11]

Probably because he is black, four INS prison guards took him to a bathroom one night and beat and kicked him while he was handcuffed. They put him into solitary confinement, then sent him to the Wharton County Jail for three months.

> That's a bad place, even worse than here [Los Fresnos immigration prison]. It's a prison, completely enclosed. It's bad. It's bad. After three months I was brought back here. I never had a hearing, neither before nor after this. I don't know why I was sent to Wharton, or why I was sent back.[12]

Herman probably was sent to Wharton so his attorney, Clare Cherkasky, could not see his bruises. Herman and Máximo are free today because Clare and Jeff Larsen of Proyecto Libertad insistently badgered an immigration judge into giving them asylum trials. People who have been excluded do not have the right to request asylum, but the judge agreed to hear their cases in the *corralón*. He denied them asylum and ordered them deported—which is what the attorneys wanted.

Under INS regulations, after an immigration judge orders a prisoner deported, the INS has six months to carry out the deportation; otherwise, the prisoner must be released. Cuba wouldn't accept Herman or Máximo, so the INS eventually released them to the same uncertain status in which they had lived before they were imprisoned.

When the INS realized it had slipped up by giving Máximo and Herman asylum hearings, the agency refused to grant any more asylum hearings to detained Cubans until the agreements that ended the Oakdale and Atlanta prison riots in 1987.

Refugees and Felons Together

Not all *Marielitos* are as innocent as Máximo and Herman. One man had tried to rape a young Salvadoran boy in Florence prison the day before I got there. Some Salvadoran men had had to "talk strongly" to the Cuban.[13] Tension increased in the prison as the Cubans moved in. Cornejo said six to ten Cuban felons were entering the prison each week. Every month, about thirty Cubans finished serving time in state and federal prisons and were turned over to the INS for detention.[14]

The immigration prisons were filled to capacity with Salvadorans, Guatemalans, and Nicaraguans. In just six months, Cuban felons who had served their sentences could fill Florence; in seven months they could fill Laredo; in fifteen months they could fill the biggest immigration prison, at Los Fresnos. So Florence was chosen to become a Cuban prison. Salvadorans and Guatemalans were being moved out by deportation or transfer as the Cubans were moved in.

The first day I entered Florence prison, Cornejo's guards brought me my five clients right away: three Salvadoran teenagers, a twenty-year-old Salvadoran army veteran, and a middle-aged health-care worker. The Salvadoran army had killed more than six members of the health-care worker's family and was looking for him. I had to interview them all together in the shallow interview room overlooked by prison guards.

It's impossible to interview asylum seekers in that situation. The health-care worker's family had been killed by the Salvadoran army, and the Salvadoran army veteran watched him as he talked. The three teenage draft dodgers knew that a veteran was watching them. And the veteran feared retaliation from the guerrilla. I took enough information from each of them to get a feeling for who they were and drove back home. During the interviews I learned that the Border Patrol had stolen a camera, a cassette tape player, luggage, books, clothes, and toiletries from the Salvadorans when they arrested them.[15]

I returned to the prison on Friday for the men's court hearings. The population was down to 120, sixty of whom were Cubans.[16] I saw four new Salvadoran clients in the morning, then went to court with the ones I had interviewed on my first day. Myers was late. I told our clients to say nothing until their attorney got there. Neither they nor I had ever met him in person. At 1:25 P.M., Judge William F. Nail announced he would go ahead without a lawyer, and Wilfredo admitted that he had entered the United States without documents. Nail gave Wilfredo three days to file for political asylum.

The next client, Antonio, also admitted he had entered the country without documents. He was afraid to ask for asylum. "Sincerely, I wish to stay here in the United States," he told the judge in Spanish, but asylum was his only relief from deportation. Nail ordered him deported. Antonio asked if he could appeal. Nail gave him ten days and noted it would cost $50.

When our third client asked if he could appeal, Nail responded, "Do you have the $50?"

The next client was the health-care worker whose family had been tortured and murdered. I blustered and protested, trying to delay the case until Myers arrived. He came in swinging. "You're not still playing your double-purpose continuance game, are you?" he asked the judge.

Under INS regulations and federal court orders, immigration judges have to give detained Salvadorans time to find an attorney and time to file for asylum. Nail combined the two steps: He gave Salvadorans three days to find an attorney and to file for asylum. Nail also refused to change venue for Salvadorans who bonded out of Florence. He ordered penniless refugees to return to Florence once a month, for no particular reason, and he wouldn't allow them to change venue to the INS district where they lived. Myers eventually won this point in *Campos v. Nail*, because Nail had accepted a change of venue for a Salvadoran case from Washington, D.C., then refused to grant a change of venue to San Francisco, where the Salvadoran lived.[17]

Myers and Nail were openly hostile to each other. I had never seen such antagonism, even in Los Fresnos. Nail told Myers, "I feel I'm not hearing asylum claims of aliens: I'm hearing asylum claims of lawyers and representatives." Nail rewound his tape machine and played a tape of a June 28 hearing at which he'd told our client that he would give him one week to find a lawyer and apply for political asylum. Nail switched the tape to record and told the health-care worker in English, "The government of the United States says that you ought to leave. I am not going to accept your application for political asylum if you try to submit it later, so it's either today or not at all."

I had a worthless asylum application I could give him. But if I didn't submit it, he would be deported.

Myers accused Nail of trying to intimidate people from seeking asylum "by your infamous dual-purpose continuance." Nail switched off the tape recorder. Myers reminded the judge he had already beat him on appeal. Nail responded that he didn't care what the Bureau of Immigration Appeals said. He said Salvadorans and Guatemalans did not really want to apply for asylum; it was their attorneys and representatives who wanted to do it.

"An alien ought to be able to articulate if he's going to apply for asylum," Nail said. He claimed lawyers told Salvadorans to apply for asylum just so they could be released on bond and get a change of venue.

Nail was half right. In 1985, no Salvadoran had ever won political asylum while detained in an immigration prison. Salvadorans had to travel north to get a fair hearing, preferably into the Ninth Circuit in San Francisco or to Washington, D.C., where immigration courts were most lenient. The day-to-day legal struggle in the prisons had nothing to do with justice: It focused on bonding people out.

Myers was suing Nail in federal court, seeking an injunction to bar him from hearing any asylum cases at Florence because of his "blanket policy of denial." The case was made moot when Florence became a Cuban prison and Nail was transferred to Seattle.[18] "Aren't you glad, though, you won't have me to kick around anymore?" Nail said off the record, relishing the thought of escaping from Florence. With a prison full of *Marielitos*, there's no need for an immigration judge—or an attorney.

We saved one client from deportation that day.

The Riot

Eight days later, on July 13, the Cubans began a hunger strike. "It started with twenty-three people," prison director Cornejo said.[19] "There's dissension even among themselves." Cornejo sympathized with the Cubans: He was out in the yard talking to them every day, but there was nothing he could do. By the second day there were fifteen hunger strikers. There was no public reaction to a prison protest by Cuban felons. Cornejo counted only three hunger strikers by the third day. The Tucson newspaper reported the hunger strike ended on the fourth day.[20] But when I got to the prison on July 23, a *Marielito* told me the hunger strike was still going on. A guard said there had just been "almost a riot. Something about wanting to be released right away, 'cause Castro won't take them."[21]

José Pupó, eighteen, told me about the hunger strike and about himself in fluent Brooklynese. He came to the United States on the boatlift when he was thirteen. Rejected by relatives in New York, he lived on the streets for three years, "hanging out, sleeping on the subway. I ate whatever I could find, drinking a lot of water, you know, piece of bread on the floor."[22]

He found a home with the family of classmates at Kennedy High School in the Bronx. "I met this guy, Raymond. ... One day he told his ma, 'Listen, I think Pupó here doesn't have any family, 'cause I always see him in the same clothes.' So she talked to me and said that they would be my family. So I accepted. I was with them about three or four months."

Then Pupó, along with Raymond and his brother, robbed a man in the subway, holding a hammer handle in his pocket as though it were a gun. "We got about $40. So the next time we did it we got caught. There were about six of us. I wasn't caught, but I went to the officer and said, 'Look, I'm involved in this. I did a robbery before. I can't live with this.'"

He was sixteen years old. Pupó was sentenced to two to seven years for armed robbery. He served two years in New York state prisons at Elmira, Taconic, Coxsackie, and Sing Sing. On June 20, 1985, he was released from prison and turned over to the INS. They sent him to the Paterson County Jail in New Jersey, to the Brooklyn Navy Yard, to the INS prison at Varick Street in New York City, back to Paterson, back to Varick Street, then to Florence.

Since I've been in jail I've learned English. I got a high school diploma. I did a crime. I went to prison. But I got something out of it. I've made something of myself.

I'm still young. I'm eighteen. I read the papers. I hear that a federal judge in Atlanta wants to let us on the street, but the immigration don't want to let us on the street. I hear in Atlanta there's 2,000 Cubans. They call them criminals. They had a year in jail in Cuba: Maybe they stole a chicken. I know a guy in Varick Street that spent a year in jail in Cuba for stealing a chicken, cause you have to steal in Cuba to eat, to give your family clothes. You'd steal too if you had to, to give your family something to eat.

What are we going to think of this country? We think this country is the best in the world. A lot of us, we had a dream: to work, to live like a decent person. My release date was June 20, 1985. Since then, I've had no hearings, no lawyer, nothing. I've just been run around.[23]

There was nothing I could do for Pupó. Though he had earned a high school equivalency diploma in a New York prison, legally, he had never been in the United States.

Pupó had been imprisoned under no charge for five weeks. Some of his fellow detainees had been in that situation for years. By July 30, there were 128 detainees at Florence, eighty-one of them Cubans.[24] Cornejo said, "Out of eighty-one that I have here, I don't think there's one of them that's had a hearing."

There were 1,400 Cubans in the Atlanta Federal Penitentiary. Nine Cubans had been murdered in the prison and seven had committed suicide there since 1981.[25] They were facing no charges in the United States. They had no hearings scheduled.

On the night of August 21 until lunchtime the next day, Cubans rioted, destroying Florence prison. Chanting "We want freedom!" and "*Libertad!*" they tore out and smashed all the plumbing, burned mattresses, and piled up the junk to barricade the doors of two cells. Prisoners in the third cell did not take part in the riot. The twelve INS guards on duty did not try to stop it.[26]

The Florence Police, the Pinal County Sheriff's Department, and the Arizona Highway Patrol surrounded the building. Cornejo got there at about 1:30 A.M. on August 22 and talked to the rioters through a bullhorn. He said he was "concerned about them getting hurt and about us getting hurt." The protest quieted down about 4 A.M. The two cells of rioters surrendered that afternoon.[27]

The destruction of the Florence detention center cost the INS prison system 8 percent of its holding capacity. The Cubans were sent to whatever prisons had space to hold them. Their situation had not changed, only their location. Rioting would be repeated nine months later at Miami, at Oakdale and Atlanta in 1987, and at Talladega, Alabama, in 1991. The situation has not changed for Cubans in U.S. prisons today.

"When you have a stagnant population, pressure tends to build up," Cornejo said.

Notes

1. In May 1995, U.S. Representative Ron Packard, a conservative Republican from Oceanside, California, suggested that immigrants are drawn to the United States by the prospect that they could benefit from being in an earthquake. Packard had introduced a bill that would deny most forms of disaster relief to undocumented immigrants. The bill would allow undocumented immigrants to receive emergency medical treatment after earthquakes and other natural disasters but would deny them other forms of help, such as emergency housing. "I know just what a magnet these kinds of benefits are to people who cross our borders illegally,"

Packard said. "I want to do everything I can to discourage people from breaking our immigration laws." Packard's comments were reported by Todd Henneman, "Packard Bill Cuts Disaster Aid to Aliens," *The Californian*, May 17, 1995.

2. Dave Myers, telephone interview with the author, June 29, 1985.

3. Dave Myers, telephone interview with the author, June 29, 1985; confirmed by Florence prison director Manuel Cornejo, telephone interview with the author, July 30, 1985.

4. President Franklin D. Roosevelt signed the Japanese Relocation Act into law on February 18, 1942. Japanese Americans were rounded up and sent to internment camps at Gila River, Arizona; Jerome, Arkansas; Minidoka, Idaho; Heart Mountain, Wyoming; and Manzanar, California. They lost their homes and all the possessions they could not take with them.

5. Manuel Cornejo, interview with the author, July 2, 1985.

6. Cuban detainee at Florence INS prison, interview with the author, July 21, 1985.

7. Prison guards at Florence INS prison, interviews with the author, July 2, 5, 21, 23, 1985.

8. High-ranking INS officer inside Oakdale prison, interview with the author, October 23, 1986.

9. Máximo, interview with the author, October 1, 1984.

10. Máximo's story of his arrest and two and one-half years in detention in the *corralón* was confirmed in interviews with his attorneys, Clare Cherkasky and Jeff Larsen of Proyecto Libertad, and with a high-ranking INS officer in the prison.

11. Herman, interview with the author, October 1, 1984.

12. Details of Herman's story were confirmed in interviews with attorney Clare Cherkasky.

13. Salvadoran detainees at Florence INS prison, interviews with the author, July 2, 1985. Prison director Manuel Cornejo was aware of the incident.

14. Manuel Cornejo, interview with the author, July 2, 1985.

15. Five detainees at Florence INS prison, interviews with the author, July 2, 1985.

16. Manuel Cornejo, interview with the author, July 5, 1985.

17. Personal communication from attorney Dave Myers, fall 1986.

18. Nail was transferred to Seattle on October 1, 1985. Personal communication from attorney Dave Myers, fall 1986.

19. Manuel Cornejo, telephone interview with the author, July 30, 1985.

20. "Cubans End Protest at INS Center," *Arizona Daily Star*, July 17, 1985.

21. Cuban detainee and INS prison guard at Florence INS prison, interviews with the author, July 23, 1985.

22. José Pupó, interview with the author, July 23, 1985.

23. Ibid.

24. Manuel Cornejo, telephone interview with the author, July 30, 1985.

25. "Since they rioted 16 months ago in the Atlanta penitentiary, which has been turned over almost entirely to the detention of Cubans, most of the Cubans there have been locked for 23 hours a day in cells that hold up to eight inmates each.

"Representative Robert W. Kastenmeier, who toured the maximum-security prison last month, said in an interview that the 'intolerable' conditions were putting severe stress on inmates and staff.

"'There are tensions that don't exist in any other federal prisons,' said Mr. Kastenmeier, the Wisconsin Democrat who is chairman of the House Judiciary Subcommittee on Courts, Civil Liberties and the Administration of Justice. 'To maintain people in conditions like these is beneath us as a society.'

"According to reports furnished to Mr. Kastenmeier, there have been nine homicides, seven suicides, 400 serious but unsuccessful suicide attempts and more than 2,000 serious incidents of self-mutilation since 1981 among Cubans detained in the prison."

See "Detaining Cubans Exacts Rising Toll," *New York Times,* March 10, 1986.

26. "Cubans Moved from Florence Following Riot," *Arizona Daily Star,* August 23, 1985.

27. Ibid.

Hundreds of Central American refugees camped in fields by Casa Romero, a refugee shelter on the outskirts of Brownsville, in January 1989. Photos by Brad Doherty.

Three hundred or more Salvadoran and Guatemalan refugees who were not allowed to travel in the winter of 1988–1989 camped out in the Amber Motel, an abandoned, condemned two-story structure on Central Boulevard in Brownsville. This photo was taken January 6, 1989, just before the city of Brownsville evicted the refugees and sealed shut the Amber Motel.

A refugee looks over his political asylum application on February 15, 1989, sitting in the brush near the INS detention center in Bayview, Texas.

Jimmy Alejandro Melgar, 22, from El Salvador, spends a week in an abandoned windshield wiper factory in Brownsville, as the Red Cross looks for a more permanent shelter for refugees. Photo taken January 19, 1989.

An INS officer escorts an asylum applicant at the *corralón* on the second day of the detention policy, February 22, 1989.

Outside the Bayview detention center, Fernando Ruiz, left, charges five dollars for a set of fingerprints, to be submitted with the application for political asylum. Other entrepreneurs drove to the *corralón* to sell food and drinks to the refugees who lined up outside the immigration prison in mid-February 1989.

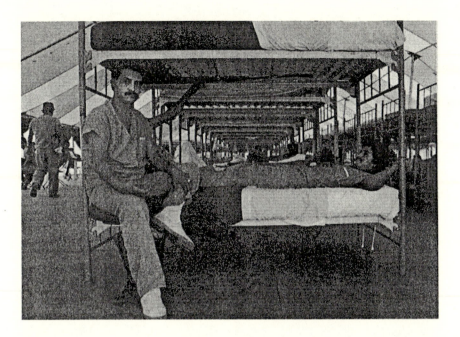

During the South Texas detention project, the entire process of applying for political asylum took just three hours. Those who were rejected, such as these men, were incarcerated immediately under tents set up at the Bayview immigration prison.

Before the detention policy began on February 21, 1989, Border Patrol agents would bus asylum applicants back from the Bayview detention center to Harlingen at the end of the day.

Denied, detained, deported. Central American women are taken to detention at the *corralón*.

A Border Patrol agent looks toward the Rio Grande from Brownsville.

Refugees had to move from the fields by Casa Romero after Cameron County Sheriff Alex F. Perez posted "No Trespassing" signs on January 8, 1989.

Oakdale

All of those persons who have been detained will lose their asylum cases. All of them.

—INS general counsel Maurice C. Inman, June 26, 1986

THE IMMIGRATION PRISON AT OAKDALE, Louisiana, received its first prisoners on April 7, 1986—forty-six people who were transferred from El Centro, California.[1] The Reagan administration had planned to open such a prison since the Department of Justice began incarcerating refugees as a matter of policy in 1981.[2] The $27.5 million appropriated for Oakdale was sufficient to build the prison and operate it for its first ten months.[3]

Oakdale is the largest of eight towns in Allen Parish, in the moss-covered pine forest on the edge of Cajun country in southwest Louisiana. Nineteen to 30 percent of the parish's 7,200 people were unemployed when the federal government finished building the prison.[4] The prison was a popular project in Oakdale: It created 325 jobs.[5] Many of them went to Bureau of Prisons (BOP) employees who were transferred from out of state, but dozens of Oakdale residents were also employed there. The Justice Department expected immigration judges to hold 200 hearings a day in the eight immigration courts inside Oakdale prison, and the INS and the Bureau of Prisons planned to "process" 35,000 detainees a year—to turn over the prison population every eleven days.[6] Most of the prison's annual operating budget of $13 million came from the U.S. Bureau of Prisons, so resources did not have to be taken away from the seven other INS border prisons.[7]

Oakdale prison had three two-story dormitories: two dorms for men and one for women. A 200-bed section to hold felons was still under construction in the summer of 1986. The felons—U.S. citizen trusties on the way to a halfway house—tended the yard and kept the prison clean and painted. One hundred acres of federal land behind the prison was available to hold 5,000 tents as a "contingency site" in case of an "immigration emergency."[8] The contingency site was a marshy area of tangled brush with a dirt road hacked out around it.

Oakdale's mayor, George Mowad, was an enthusiastic backer of the prison and had traveled to Washington several times to lobby for it. Mowad said the prison would lead to the "economic rebirth" of Oakdale and Allen Parish. Immigration prisons, Mowad said, are "a recession-proof industry," because if the U.S. economy suffers, the world economy will follow, which will lead to more undocumented aliens coming to the United

States, and thus more employment for Oakdale.[9] After the prison opened, Mowad was indicted for contract fraud, for assigning city work crews to improve a housing project outside of town in which he held an interest. Mowad said the housing project was developed primarily to house prison officials.[10] The mayor was acquitted of one charge, and one charge was dropped before trial.

The first lawsuit challenging conditions at Oakdale was filed even before the prison opened. The lawsuit filed in July 1984 by Arthur Helton of the Lawyers Committee for International Human Rights claimed that "putting a detention center in rural southern Louisiana essentially deprives detainees of the right to counsel because there are so few lawyers around Oakdale."[11] The suit was dismissed because the issues raised were not ripe for review— no one had been incarcerated in Oakdale yet.

As the prison was being built, an attorney in Lake Charles, Louisiana, conducted an informal survey of 650 lawyers in the Lake Charles–Oakdale–Alexandria area, asking if they could provide free legal services for refuge seekers detained at the prison. Three lawyers indicated they might be able to take a few pro bono cases. Only one actually did.[12]

There were five people in our law office in Oakdale: Sister Suzanne Lasseigne, of the Society of the Sacred Heart, a native Louisianan from DeRidder; Jorge Costa, a skinny, hyperkinetic Cuban American bundle of nerves who was the only native Spanish speaker; Nancy Kelly, an attorney from Boston who had a fine appreciation of the absurd—a good thing to have in Oakdale; the office manager, Vicki Sanford from Southern California, who dyed her hair purple that summer; and me. None of them had experience in immigration law. The National Lawyers Guild recruited immigration lawyers from the north to work brief stints, but in early June it was barely a law office at all: It was five people with little or no experience in immigration law trying to represent refugees in the biggest immigration prison in the country.

The office was in an old, downtown furniture store that had once been a whorehouse.[13] A false wall at the back had been removed; behind it had been the beds, which had been removed, and a large, open safe with drawers in it labeled "White" and "Colored." Now the old whorehouse was a sixty-foot-long room with rows of empty desks along the walls, a dozen telephones, and a few used filing cabinets. The first major case the office handled concerned a mass transfer of detainees from the immigration prison at Krome Avenue in Miami.[14]

The Krome Avenue Case

On May 28, 1986, Cuban detainees burned down a dormitory at the Krome Avenue detention center. The INS sent the Cubans to other federal prisons and transferred 226 other detainees, mostly Central Americans, to

Oakdale. The new prisoners brought the prison population at Oakdale to 712.[15] The INS was serving the 226 people with changes of venue and preparing to try them in Oakdale. Niels Frenzen, an attorney with Miami's Haitian Refugee Center, came to Oakdale to work on a request for a restraining order to stop deportation hearings for asylum applicants who had been removed from their lawyers and witnesses in Miami.[16]

When the Bureau of Prisons was notified that the INS was about to be sued in Miami in a challenge to the forced changes of venue for prisoners, guards at Oakdale called all the prisoners together, one dorm at a time, and told them that lawyers were trying to stop them from obtaining hearings. They persuaded them that their hearings would be delayed for months if the prisoners did not object.[17] Spanish-speaking guards asked prisoners to sign statements written in English by a prison official demanding a hearing immediately in Oakdale. Guards posted the name and Miami telephone number of Ira Kurzban—the president of the American Immigration Lawyers Association who was helping the Haitian Refugee Center with the case—and urged prisoners to call Kurzban collect to tell him they didn't want him as a lawyer. Dozens of them did.[18]

In a curious legal twist, refugees were aided by convicted alien felons who had been sent to Oakdale to await deportation. Many of the felons were legal U.S. residents, fluent in English, bilingual, and wise to the legal system. They alerted me to what the guards were doing, and the Central Americans confirmed it. Every Salvadoran and Guatemalan I talked to in my first week at Oakdale related that guards had asked detainees to sign a "petition of protest" and had claimed that our office was trying to deny them the right to a hearing.

In addition to removing refugees from their attorneys en masse, the Bureau of Prisons made it exceedingly difficult for an individual prisoner to defend himself or herself from deportation. A Salvadoran asylum applicant who had been transferred from Krome asked to see the personal papers that had been confiscated from him when he was arrested. He had forgotten the phone number of the family of his wife, who was a legal U.S. resident. The guard told him to write a note in English making the request.[19] I had to write the note for him.

Our staff attorney, Nancy Kelly, notified officials with the INS and the Bureau of Prisons that they could not legally deny Salvadoran asylum seekers access to the personal documents that were needed to prepare their requests for asylum. We explained to the prisoners who Ira Kurzban was and why the Haitian Refugee Center had filed a restraining order. When they realized the guards had duped them, dozens asked to withdraw their signatures from the petition. Tension grew between the prisoners and the guards and between the guards and our office. Guards charged that our legal work was interfering with their "mission." A bilingual prisoner who had been using the prison's law library was denied access to it and threatened with transfer to the county jail.[20]

On Friday, June 6, the INS informed detainees that paperwork had arrived for everyone who had been transferred from Krome and that deportation hearings would begin Monday.[21] Niels Frenzen flew to Miami to file a request for a restraining order. Jorge, Suzanne, and I were receiving requests for legal assistance from sixty to seventy people a day.

While Niels presented his case to a federal judge in Miami, the Bureau of Prisons cracked down on our law project. On Wednesday, June 10, BOP officials refused to let Jorge enter the prison with a camera to take photos of the scars from a Guatemalan client's torture wounds, to be submitted with his application for political asylum. Nancy Kelly obtained a signed order from Oakdale's chief immigration judge Edwin Hughes to allow her into the prison with a camera for that purpose. The BOP refused. "I think the lawyer has a problem with the Bureau of Prisons, not with the INS," said Duke Austin, the chief INS spokesman in Washington. "We're going to defer to the Bureau of Prisons."[22]

That day I waited for two hours to see seven clients, none of whom was brought to me. It was Laredo all over again, with one difference. The Corrections Corporation of America is a private company that eventually responded to congressional pressure. The Bureau of Prisons is a government agency. Few citizens or members of Congress are troubled when an incarcerated felon claims he has been mistreated in a federal prison. Nearly every day a convicted felon somewhere in the United States tries to file a lawsuit against the Bureau of Prisons.[23] Most prisoners at Oakdale were not felons, but they weren't citizens either.

The First Class Action Lawsuits

On June 13, U.S. District Judge Kenneth Ryskamp in Miami issued a temporary restraining order prohibiting the INS from holding deportation hearings for prisoners who had been transferred from Krome to Oakdale.[24] Ryskamp allowed the INS to hold bond hearings but warned it not to order the former Krome prisoners deported from Louisiana. He gave the refugees' attorneys five days to prepare additional arguments. After hearing them, Ryskamp would decide whether to make the injunction permanent.

The prison population was up to 850.[25] We had a backlog of dozens of people to see, and now we had to gather depositions for a federal lawsuit. At 10:40 that night, Peter Upton, an attorney with the American Friends Service Committee in Miami, walked into our office, and I assigned myself to the case of the Krome Avenue prisoners.

Lawyers receive better treatment in immigration prisons than paralegals do. Guards brought us Peter's clients Saturday morning without much delay. We took depositions all morning, drove to the office to translate and type them, then returned to prison to retranslate the statements for the clients to sign. We repeated the routine all day, working until 3 A.M. We worked another twenty-hour shift the following day. Peter left at noon Monday, and Niels filed the depositions Tuesday in Miami.

On Wednesday, Judge Ryskamp vacated all the changes of venue and all the deportation hearings held in Oakdale for the former Krome prisoners. He ordered the INS to resubmit all their motions, this time giving detainees' attorneys "meaningful notice" and time to respond.[26] We felt we had won a victory for due process. But as Judge Ryskamp made his ruling in Miami, forty-seven Central Americans, mostly Salvadorans, arrived in Oakdale from Long Island. They had been arrested in factory raids, and though many of them had political asylum cases pending in New York with attorneys there, the INS had changed venue for all of them while they were in transit. It was the same situation all over again. We would have to gather more depositions to argue the same points to another federal judge.[27]

The INS was transferring Central Americans to Oakdale from all over the country, removing them from their attorneys. Each time they made a mass transfer we would have to take the refugees' depositions and locate a lawyer where they had come from to file the case in federal court. And we couldn't even keep up with intake.

At this point our law office sponsor, Ecumenical Immigration Services (EIS), backed out. With 850 people in prison, one federal lawsuit behind us and another one expected, and a backlog of dozens of calls from prison, our corporate directors asked us to stop accepting clients: We were taking on too much work. EIS, a church-sponsored project in New Orleans, had collected tens of thousands of dollars in contributions from other churches and refugee support groups when it announced it would sponsor the Oakdale law project. But the two EIS lawyers, Ted Keating and Kathy Lampard, seldom made the five-hour drive to Oakdale, and they hadn't expected the huge caseload—120 clients in two months. Keating and Lampard withdrew from the project on June 17 and notified the INS that they were no longer associated with our office.[28]

Without an attorney to sign a G-28 or appear in court, we could not accept clients—we could no longer operate as a law office. Nancy Kelly, who had planned to leave Oakdale at the end of June, tore up her plane ticket. We reorganized the office under a new name, Oakdale Legal Assistance, with help from the directors of the National Lawyers Guild Immigrant Rights Project in Boston, Proyecto Libertad in Harlingen, and the Central American Refugee Center in Houston.[29] We continued taking calls, explained to detainees their legal rights, and "informally" helped them fill out applications for political asylum. When an asylum trial was called, Nancy filed a G-28 as a private attorney. National Lawyers Guild attorneys took turns flying south to assist her, but our office was paralyzed during the seven weeks it took to regain our tax-exempt status. The corporate affiliation made it possible for an attorney to accept clients without being obligated to remain in Oakdale until all the cases were resolved.

Refugees in Oakdale

Our clients at Oakdale were just as desperate as refugees in the *corralón*, Florence, and Laredo had been. In El Salvador, the strength of the FMLN had grown, and more army veterans were coming north to escape the vengeance of the guerrilla. In Los Fresnos in 1984, perhaps one in ten Salvadorans I interviewed was an army veteran. By late 1986 in Oakdale, the ratio was about one in four.[30] With army veterans, guerrilla supporters, and neutral civilians locked up together, relationships inside the prison were tense. The first client I adopted in Oakdale had fled the army and the guerrilla and was threatened by Salvadoran soldiers in the prison because he had requested political asylum. The other detainees called him *el flaco*— "the skinny one."

Orlando walked to the United States from El Salvador. His father had been tortured and murdered by the army. Soldiers had pistol-whipped Orlando twice as part of their recruiting procedure. After he deserted, the guerrilla forced him to go with them, felling trees across roads. "I respected the guerrilla, but I couldn't stand the hunger," Orlando told me under the antiseptic white fluorescent lights of an interview room in Oakdale prison.[31]

Orlando deserted the guerrilla one night with three other recruits. The guerrilla shot at them as they fled. One died. Later Orlando received a letter telling him to leave the country or die. So he walked north, with no money and nothing in his pockets. He ate when people gave him food. In Mexico City, the immigration police paid a taxi driver to take him to his cousin's apartment—the only act of kindness a Mexican policeman performed for a Salvadoran refugee that I ever heard about.

"They were good to me," Orlando said. "It was probably because of my condition. In truth, there was nothing left of my shoes. And my feet, well, there was more blood than skin."

His cousins in Mexico City were barely surviving. They couldn't help him. Not being able to find work, Orlando walked north to Los Angeles, where his luck continued—he was run over by a car. Upon release from the hospital, he was turned over to the INS and sent to Oakdale.

His journey showed in his eyes, in the skin stretched tight over the bones of his face. As a deserter from both sides, Orlando tried to stay away from everyone inside Oakdale prison. But one night he heard Salvadoran veterans bragging about how many guerrillas they had killed. "You know what?" he told them. "Those weren't guerrillas you killed. They were farmers. And for every real guerrilla you killed, the guerrilla killed ten of you."[32]

The veterans challenged him to fight. They threatened to report his political opinions and his location to the army when they were deported. They never beat Orlando inside Oakdale prison because he was protected by another of our clients, a Guatemalan deserter. Luis was enormous for a Guatemalan—more than six feet tall, with the physique of a wrestler. He had been forcibly recruited by the Guatemalan army—beaten, pistol-whipped, and thrown onto a truck. After basic training, he was sent to the mountains to fight the guerrilla. Luis showed me a picture of himself standing in front of a Guatemalan army barracks in his camouflage uniform, proudly holding a machine gun. He said he had deserted "because I couldn't bear to torture the people."[33]

When Luis's platoon entered an Indian village, they forced the men and boys to lie down in the square, then ran over them with their boots on. Sometimes they hung men in a tree and hit them with rifles or put them in *la bartolina*—a metal box too small to stand or sit in. Men were left in the box under the sun until they died of thirst and hunger. Sometimes officers urinated on them as they were dying.

"It made me sick," Luis said. "They weren't guerrilla; they were farmers." After he deserted, the army sent soldiers to his home to look for him, so he moved to Guatemala City and got a job selling fish. When he was out on his route one day, soldiers came for him at his shop. So Luis left Guatemala. This is the story revealed to immigration judge Edwin Hughes in Oakdale.

"I don't believe you were in the army at all," Hughes said, while he held the photograph of Luis in army uniform.[34] He found Luis's stories of torture "incredible," denied him asylum, and raised his bond to $5,000.

Luis is alive today because Sister Suzanne raised the money to pay his bond. After months of pleading phone calls, I found someone to pay the bond for Orlando, too. After spending four months in Oakdale prison, Luis and Orlando were granted political asylum in Canada. Their stories are typical of our clients, but Luis and Orlando were far luckier than most.

The Bureau of Prisons Cracks Down

The prison population rose to more than 900 on Thursday, June 19.[35] That day prison guard Kirk Bullock informed us we could see only five people a day on weekdays and five people an afternoon on weekends. I asked him if that was a BOP or INS regulation. Bullock glanced at a sheet of paper in his hand and said, "That's what's handed here to me."[36]

Restricting legal visits violated the federal court orders in *Orantes-Hernandez v. Meese* and *Nuñez v. Boldin*. It also made it harder to prepare class action lawsuits. Each deposition requires at least two visits with a prisoner: one to call him or her to take a statement and another to read back the statement and have it signed. Peter Upton and I had each interviewed more than a dozen people on the weekend in which we prepared the Miami lawsuit. Now, in a similar situation we would be limited to seeing two people a day. A prison rule ostensibly imposed to increase security limited refugees' access to the legal system and violated the orders of two federal judges.

It wasn't Bullock's fault that he was breaking the law. He was only following orders. Bullock was a good guard. He was a cocky young man in his early twenties who was on front-desk duty when I got to Oakdale. He was transferred into a dorm for a few weeks, and when he came back to the front desk his attitude had changed. Detainees who could speak English had told him why some of the refugees had come here. Bullock was no longer impressed with his own power and had become interested in the people he was guarding. He even wanted to go to Central America on vacation.[37]

Bullock was an exception. Being a prison guard—having virtually absolute power over others—brings out the worst in some people. Many Oakdale guards had been unemployed before they went to work in the prison.[38] I saw over the weeks and months how some became impressed with themselves, more abusive to prisoners and to us. One guard set off a "riot" in the prison by his abusive behavior, to which a detainee finally responded by conking him on the head with a billiard ball.[39]

The Bureau of Prisons had offered its employees raises and promotions to leave the prisons where they worked and put in a tour of duty in Oakdale.[40] The worst torturers in Oakdale were career prison guards. Most of the ones who beat, kicked, and drugged refugees on the steel bed in the solitary confinement room were captains and lieutenants.[41] It was Bureau of Prisons policy to treat noncriminal immigration detainees and refugees the same way they treat the murderers, rapists, and arsonists in other prisons.

Fortunately, some guards understood that this wasn't necessary. One had transferred to Oakdale from Marion prison in Illinois, the highest-security prison in the country. In Marion he had collected the signatures of famous mass murderers. He spoke Spanish and knew the difference between dangerous criminals and the detainees at Oakdale. He treated prisoners like human beings. "These people aren't dangerous," he said.[42] Most of the guards at Oakdale, however, could not speak Spanish; they couldn't even communicate with the people they were guarding.

A Typical Day at Oakdale

The work load at Oakdale was worse than it had been at either the *corralón* or Laredo. The guards were more abusive, and the increasing numbers of Salvadoran army veterans made life miserable for the civilians imprisoned with them. Two Salvadoran army officers, a lieutenant and a sergeant, walked into an interview room together to see me. They had taken two-week leaves and flown north to look for work. "If you can find the money to pay our bonds and find us a job within two weeks, then we'd like to stay," the lieutenant said. "If not, please have us deported as quickly as possible."[43] They wanted to get back before their leave was up.

I considered my reply while I looked at these men, who were accustomed to giving orders. There was no way they would be deported before their two-week passes ended. Then they'd have to deal with the Salvadoran army—after that with the guerrilla. I thought of a few things I wanted to tell them, but they had enough problems. I gave them the name of a private attorney and called for another client.

She was a beautiful young Salvadoran woman with a good education and sparkly eyes. The Salvadoran air force had broken her collarbone because she'd refused to lure her employer into a trap where he would be kidnapped to be held for ransom.[44] The boss she had refused to betray was a veteran of the U.S. Army. Susana had relatives living legally in the United States. I called her aunt in Los Angeles, who wept with joy and gladly agreed to pay her niece's $2,000 bond if I explained how. I told her to take a cashier's check or cash to the INS office in Los Angeles and specified her niece's control number. The aunt called me that night, still weeping. She had taken $2,000 out of the bank and was knocked down and robbed on the way to the INS office. What should she do now?

Add another half dozen stories or more, and that was a typical day at Oakdale. Five minutes after meeting someone, I was deeply involved in the intimate details of his or her life. I was polite to people I despised and politely distant to victims of rape and torture, who needed more than anything, besides their $2,000 bond, some affection and at least six months of intensive therapy. But Oakdale had been set up to deal with criminals, not refugees. And as at the *corralón* and Laredo, the medical care was woefully inadequate.

A Death in the Prison

On Friday evening, June 20, a prison guard called a twenty-four-year-old woman from her dorm to translate for a doctor. The woman was a legal resident of the United States who had lived in New York City since she was three. She had been convicted of drug possession, and after she served her time, the Bureau of Prisons turned her over to the INS, which was trying to take away her green card and deport her. Elena stated in a sworn deposition: "I remember it was Friday evening because I had rollers in my hair, and I was called just after I got out of a shower. I went to translate for the doctor with a towel wrapped around my head."[45]

In the prison clinic she saw a Guatemalan man from Allen 2 dormitory, "who had wires hooked up to his chest, legs, and arms, and the wires were connected to a machine that had buttons and numbers on it." The doctor studied the man and the machine, then told Elena to tell the man he was all right.

> I asked the doctor if the man was all right. I said, "Is he?" The doctor said, "No, he's not. He needs surgery. He's got a bad heart."
>
> I asked the doctor why he couldn't send the man out to have surgery. The doctor said that he couldn't. He said that they wouldn't allow it. He did not say who "they" were.
>
> I told the doctor that that was wrong, to tell the patient that he was OK when he was not. I told him that that was lying. The doctor said, "Well, why worry the guy?" He said that he was not going to die. He said he was not going to have a heart attack. He said that he'd get along. I told the patient not to worry, to relax, and that maybe the pain would go away.[46]

Early Tuesday morning, June 24, a thirty-year-old Guatemalan man, Juan Diego Sebastian, died in Allen 2 dorm.[47] Elena called from the prison that day and asked to see me. She did not say why. I took her statement that evening. Next morning I got a call from an Argentinian housed in Allen 2. He said the dead Guatemalan had been scheduled to be deported June 26 with his brother, who also was in prison. The body could not be deported without health certificates that would take days to arrange. The dead man's brother wanted his own deportation delayed so he could go home with his brother's body.

I drove to the prison and called for the Argentinian and the dead man's brother at 10:20 A.M. I never saw them that day. At 10:30, BOP Lieutenant Charles Marmolejo ordered me to leave because I was violating the prison dress code. I was wearing white cotton pants and a white button-down dress shirt, both of which I had worn to the prison before. I asked what the problem was. Marmolejo responded that prison rules prohibited T-shirts. I was wearing a T-shirt under my dress shirt.

"Oh, come on," I said. "A guy just died and his brother wants to see me."[48] I offered to go into the bathroom and take off the T-shirt. Marmolejo called Captain Larry Craven and Associate Warden Homer Sherrod. They entered the little interview room at 10:35 and told me to leave the prison.

"I'll take the T-shirt off," I offered. Craven slammed the door shut before I could leave, then put his hand on my chest and kept me away from the door. I asked if they were denying me access to clients because I was wearing a T-shirt.

Without answering, they left the room, locking me in it. I took notes. At 10:40 they cleared everyone out of the interview rooms, each of which has a window facing the central waiting room, but kept me locked up. I tapped on the glass at 10:42 and Craven cracked open the door. I asked again if he was denying me access to clients because of the T-shirt. He closed the door without answering. They reentered the room at 10:46 and threatened to call the Oakdale Police if I didn't leave.

I drove home and put on black pants, removed my T-shirt, and drove back to prison. When I signed in again at 11 A.M., Marmolejo, Sherrod, and Craven took me into a small room, and Sherrod told me that my shirt was "not an ordinary T-shirt." He said it could have had "subversive writing" on it.[49] It was a yellow T-shirt that had "BHS Physical Ed. 102" stamped on it in blue. I was not allowed to talk with the Guatemalan whose brother had died, so I drove back to the office. We were unsuccessful in holding up the brother's deportation.

The Paper Chase Begins

As Nancy pleaded fruitlessly with the warden, my wife and I drove to the Houston airport to catch a plane to Los Angeles. Cecy had to renew her Salvadoran passport there, then interview at the U.S. consulate in Tijuana to become a legal U.S. resident. When she got her green card, she would fly home to get the children.

After three days of bureaucratic purgatory, my wife flew home to El Salvador and I returned to Oakdale, where I found a letter from Warden Steve Schwalb addressed to me at our office. In the letter, dated June 26, Schwalb wrote that I

> chose to ignore the commonly accepted community standard for individuals associated with professional occupations. ... Despite the fact that you were told your attire did not meet our standards and were requested to leave, you initially refused to do so. When we summoned the local police, you finally chose to leave voluntarily, but not before hurling verbal profanities at several of our staff.

He threatened to bar me from the prison if I were "disruptive" again.[50]

I replied in writing, denying that I had committed "'disruptive behavior, verbal abuse or profanity.' What I did was wear a T-shirt, Mr. Schwalb."[51] I enumerated how he and his officers had denied our clients access to counsel by banning law books at the prison, by lying to detainees about U.S. law, by violating the mail, by failing to call clients to legal visits, by denying medical treatment and access to writing materials, by confiscating legal materials and personal correspondence, by tapping phone calls to attorneys, and by prohibiting attorneys from giving written material to clients. I reminded him that these and other policies at Oakdale violated federal court orders, immigration regulations, and the legal rights of detained Salvadorans. I sent the letter to Schwalb and gave a copy to our office director.

A similar incident occurred in August, with more serious consequences, after I received a telephone call from a detainee who had seen guards beat a handcuffed prisoner. The Salvadoran informant told me that he had written a description of the incident, which a prison guard had taken from him. When I went to the prison to hear his story, guards declared me disruptive again, and I was barred from the prison for two months.[52]

Abuses Continue

Schwalb had received a subpoena to testify in the *Orantes-Hernandez* case. He was not familiar with immigration law, and he and the Justice Department were trying to make the case that immigration regulations did not apply in Oakdale because it was run by the Bureau of Prisons.[53] Judge Kenyon was skeptical. But while the *Orantes-Hernandez* trial dragged on in Los Angeles, the INS continued to deport 250 people a week from Oakdale: one-third of their target rate of 35,000 people a year.[54] The federal lawsuits in Miami and Long Island and the *Orantes-Hernandez* and *Nuñez v. Boldin* injunctions had slowed deportations, and every time a refugee decided to see an asylum application through to the end, no matter how many appeals it took, it removed one more bed from the deportation mill.

The INS and the Bureau of Prisons were correct that access to legal services slowed deportations and clogged their prisons. Denying detainees access to legal services freed up prison space and made their job easier. But the policies they adopted to pursue this goal, and the goal itself, were illegal.

On July 10 a Salvadoran who had been transferred to Oakdale from Long Island was released on bond from Oakdale prison. He had called us when he'd arrived three weeks before and indicated he wanted to talk to the press. Reporters from the New Orleans *Times-Picayune* and the Alexandria *Town Talk* went to the prison, asking for José by name. Prison guards told them José had refused to sign a release—that he wasn't interested in talking to reporters. The reporters left without a story. The night José bonded out, I asked him why he had changed his mind.

"What do you mean?" he said in Spanish. "I wanted to talk. No one ever called me."[55] Prison officials had never asked him to sign a release. He had never been told reporters had come to talk to him.

Later that night, two Salvadorans described to me how INS guards tortured prisoners at the INS jail at Chula Vista, California.[56] Two guards had made everyone in their dorm stand on one foot and hold both arms in the air for more than half an hour. Anyone who put a foot down or lowered his arms was kicked in the shins and beaten.[57]

This is mild torture compared to what goes on in El Salvador, but it's torture nonetheless, inflicted for no other reason than that guards can get away with it. As usual, the Salvadorans didn't want to lodge a complaint. Had they done so, they could have been held in jail as material witnesses. They would have drawn INS attention to their cases. They told us to forget it.

Kafkaesque Policies

On July 15, U.S. District Judge Jack B. Weinstein issued a temporary restraining order in Brooklyn, New York, that stopped deportation hearings for the forty-seven people transferred to Oakdale after the factory raids in Long Island.[58] The Long Island detainees, most of them Salvadorans, bonded out one by one and went home to New York. The owner of the factory had kept their jobs open for them and spent thousands of dollars to help his workers return.

As we got the news that we had won that case, the Bureau of Prisons imposed a new rule—clients could see us only once a day. This made it still harder to collect depositions for class action lawsuits and violated the court orders in *Orantes-Hernandez* and *Nuñez v. Boldin*. In response, I sent yet another letter to the warden listing various violations of rights that regularly occurred in Oakdale.

That weekend, three Central Americans who had bonded out of Oakdale prison were arrested for "loitering" in the Alexandria bus station while waiting for a bus. They had their tickets, but the Alexandria police couldn't communicate with them, so they arrested them. The three spent the night in jail.[59]

On July 24 an immigration judge raised the bond of a detained Salvadoran from $3,000 to $4,500 because the man had "failed to appear" at his court hearing in the prison. Prison guards said they "couldn't find him," so the judge ruled that he had "absconded."[60] That judicial order was attorney Jane Rocamora's introduction to Oakdale. "How can someone abscond from a hearing when he is already in prison?" Rocamora asked. Another Salvadoran's bond was raised for the same reason on August 1, and a third Salvadoran was ordered deported a few days later for "absconding" from a deportation hearing, though he was locked up in prison at the time.[61]

A Deserter from the Death Squad

It was a steamy Louisiana summer. Traffic was sparse on State Highway 165, the only north-south road through town. Through the plate-glass windows in our office we could see an occasional car roll down Main Street. School was out, so there was no rhythmic bustle of people or traffic in the mornings or afternoons. The busiest place in Oakdale was our office early in the morning when the workers and volunteers arrived, and again in the evening after prisoners bonded out and we had to finish their paperwork. The only other busy place was the Greyhound bus station, down the block and around the corner, where I translated ticket requests for Mr. Johnson, the kind, patient Greyhound agent.

As a modern air-conditioned prison, Oakdale was physically more comfortable for detainees than the *corralón* and luxurious compared to Florence, but the prisoners were tougher, with a higher percentage of felons. The greatest change in the prison population was that more Salvadoran soldiers were coming north for fear of the guerrilla. "My sergeant told me to either join the National Guard, leave the country, or die," more than one Salvadoran veteran told me.

Ex-soldiers were prime recruits for the guerrilla and were under suspicion by both sides in the war. They knew how to use a gun, they were in good physical condition, they knew something about warfare, and they had information about the army. The potentially lethal mixture of incarcerated felons, army veterans, FMLN supporters, and neutral civilians created a charged atmosphere: There are no secrets in prison. Orlando was not my only Salvadoran client whose family had been murdered by the army or who had been tortured himself and was threatened inside Oakdale prison by army veterans.

Salvadoran enlisted men were difficult cases. Most had not voluntarily joined the army, yet a person who persecutes someone in his own country is statutorily ineligible for political asylum in the United States.[62] One of our clients had risen to the rank of sergeant and deserted after being assigned to a death squad. The death squad injected suspected "subversives" with LSD, then subjected them to mock executions; they tortured them with electroshock during interrogations; they executed prisoners.[63] This man had fled El Salvador for reasons of conscience and faced near-certain persecution from both sides if he were deported, but he was ineligible for asylum. It destroyed him physically and psychologically to admit what he had done. There was no chance for him either here or in El Salvador.

The Torture Report

Salvadorans, particularly those who sympathized with the political opposition to the government, faced the possibility of torture after deportation. In El Salvador that summer, Lisa Brodyaga was translating a report compiled by the leaders of the Non-Governmental Human Rights Commission of El Salvador (CDHES), all of whom were political prisoners in Mariona prison. The 165-page document, "Torture in El Salvador," was written after the CDHES members interviewed 433 of the 434 political prisoners sent to Mariona from January to August 1986.[64] The five CDHES leaders—Herbert Anaya, Reynaldo Blanco, Joaquin Caceres, Miguel Rogel, and Rafael Terezon—all had been arrested and tortured and sent to Mariona: Caceres in November 1985, the rest in May 1986.

Of the 433 prisoners interviewed, 432 confirmed they had been tortured during the fifteen days of detention permitted under Decree 50 before they were brought before a military tribunal.[65] All had been imprisoned on the basis of extrajudicial confessions extracted under torture, which were permitted under Decree 50. Of the 433 prisoners, 47 percent said they were strangled in the course of their interrogation; 63 percent were forced to listen to others being tortured; 47 percent were drugged; 71 percent were submitted to mock executions; 94 percent received death threats to family and loved ones; 99 percent were tied, blindfolded, and beaten.[66]

Two prisoners reported interrogation by U.S. military advisers during torture sessions. One said he was given electroshock in the ears by "a major of the North American army. ... He was about two meters tall, thin, and wore glasses with corrective lenses."[67]

The document lists forty types of torture, with illustrations, to which political prisoners were subjected, the military or police unit that performed the abduction and torture, the professions of the political prisoners, and the signature and thumbprint of all 433 torture victims/political prisoners, with a list of all the tortures to which each had been subjected. The report was completed on September 24, 1986. Lisa Brodyaga and Jonathan T. Jones smuggled it out of Mariona prison. Lisa then translated it and presented it to the U.S. embassy in San Salvador in late September. The torture report received virtually no press coverage, in the United States or El Salvador. On October 26, 1987, Herbert Anaya, the principal author of the report, was shot to death in front of his home.[68]

Stealing from the Desperate

On August 1, two men entered the prison at Oakdale dressed in flashy suits and gold chains, carrying leather briefcases. Bruce Shirley, Fernando Luna, and associates took more than $15,000 from the families of Oakdale detainees that summer. They worked a racket from Houston with a partner named Larry Shea for which they later were indicted.[69] Luna spoke Spanish and lied to detainees that Shirley was a lawyer.[70] On his first day inside Oakdale prison, Shirley informed Nancy Kelly that he had a "network of 150 lawyers" across the nation. He claimed to have worked with Proyecto Libertad and Linda Yañez, an immigration lawyer in Brownsville.[71]

I called Yañez, whom I had met in the *corralón*. She had never heard of Shirley.[72] I called Danny Katz at Proyecto Libertad. He reached Shirley at the Sunset Motel in Oakdale "and told him very clearly not to use our name, and that we were contemplating criminal action, and that if he goes around trying to get clients by using our name, then he could be sued for solicitation."[73]

A high-ranking INS officer at Oakdale agreed that the men were frauds.[74] But the INS was being sued in every federal district on the southern U.S. border for limiting refugees' access to legal counsel. The more attorneys or "attorney's representatives" the INS and Bureau of Prisons allowed into prisons, the easier it would be to convince Judge Kenyon, who was hearing the *Orantes-Hernandez* case, that there were plenty of lawyers helping Salvadorans. So the INS and Bureau of Prisons permitted Shirley and Luna to keep working the camp. They handed out business cards from *Oficina de Relaciones Latinas,* with "Ricardo Garcia, Esq.," "Bruce Shirley, Representative," and "Fred Luna, Representative" handwritten on them.[75]

I called Garcia in Houston and asked in rapid Spanish if he was the lawyer for *Oficina de Relaciones Latinas.* He said he was.[76] But when I switched to English, he refused to answer any questions about his relationship with Shirley or Luna and hung up. I called back half a dozen times, until he talked. Garcia claimed he had heard that "a lot of people" had paid money to a man named Miguel Gutierrez and had received nothing for their money, so he sent Shirley to Oakdale to "help these people out." He'd sent Shirley to Oakdale as a paralegal "because that's the only way he can get in."[77]

Shirley and his partner Larry Shea had stolen money from refugees in every immigration prison in Texas, always under the guise of social service organizations: *Servicios a Latinos, Ayuda Latina,* and *Servicios para Inmigrantes.* Iselda Sanchez, a paralegal for Catholic Social Services in Laredo, remembered she had met Shirley in his Laredo office, *Servicios a Latinos,* in the summer of 1985 and that Shirley was soon appearing inside the INS/CCA prison there, claiming to work for Catholic Social Services.

"The refugees thought that I was working for him," Sanchez said. "Then my boss [the Bishop of Laredo] heard and thought I was working on the side. ... I almost lost my job."[78]

Patrick Hughes knew Shirley and Julian Esparza, another cohort. "Esparza and Shirley are the same thing," Hughes said. "They're crooks. They're criminals. They tell people they're lawyers. They'll tell them anything, anything that makes the people forget about getting an attorney. They take the money and wait until the people are deported and then they waltz with it. It's a real crooked operation."[79]

On a hunch, I called the only immigration lawyer I knew in El Paso, Bertha Zunigar Galindez. She had "just finished writing an irate letter to Elida Shea [Larry Shea's wife]. One of our clients paid them [*Ayuda Latina*]

$500 for a bond reduction and they left with the money. Their phone number is no longer in service. They're a bunch of frauds."[80]

Esparza had worked the same scam in Los Fresnos immigration prison, Jeff Larsen, legal director of Proyecto Libertad, told me. "He offers incompetent legal advice. People would come into a hearing saying, 'I have a lawyer. His name is Julian Esparza.' People would think they had a lawyer and they didn't have a lawyer, and so they were deported."[81]

I phoned Esparza in Houston, where he was working the INS/CCA prison. He did not deny a word of it. His wife was sick, and he needed the money.[82]

I turned over the story to an investigator for the Texas attorney general's office, and in June 1987, Shirley, Luna, and Larry Shea were sued for conspiring to rob undocumented people by falsely advertising Fernando Luna as a lawyer.[83]

Shirley, Shea, and Luna were put under permanent injunction to stop advertising Luna as an attorney and another front, *Servicios para Inmigrantes,* as an agency offering legal services. They were barred from "soliciting or accepting money or any other consideration in exchange for immigration services without disclosing at the time of the solicitation and before accepting anything of value the following: Defendants Lawrence N. Shea and SPI accepted money from immigrants seeking amnesty status without filing amnesty applications as promised."[84] Luna, Shea, and the corporation were each fined $1,000 and investigative costs, and were ordered to pay 75 percent of the court costs—a fraction of the money they had stolen from refugees.

Refugees in Oakdale were bilked of money by telephone from as far away as California. Miguel Gutierrez, in Ontario, California, collected at least $7,625 from our clients' families.[85] When I contacted him, he said he had met Shirley and Luna in Houston, and they had gone to Oakdale to refer cases to him. "I'm a bondsman," Gutierrez stated. He claimed to work for National Bail Bonds—the Harlingen bond company that had gone out of business in 1984.[86]

At least four Gutierrez victims, some of whom were our clients, reported that Luna and Shirley had called them in prison, introduced themselves as lawyers, and promised to have their bonds reduced for $600 apiece. We took statements from twelve clients whose families had paid more than $6,000 to Shirley, Luna, or Gutierrez during the first week they worked Oakdale prison and statements from another half dozen who had been solicited by them.[87] So blatant were the thefts that on August 9 Gutierrez promised Jane Rocamora he would return $4,825 to family members of four of our clients.[88] He never did.

Shirley and Luna left Oakdale and sent Raul Hoyos to continue the scams. Soon all three were working with Hugo Morales. Morales had graduated from a law school in Mexico but was not certified as an attorney in the United States.[89] When the Oakdale prison had opened, Morales took a job as a paralegal for New Orleans attorney Riguer Silva, one of two private attorneys who regularly represented detainees in Oakdale. Silva fired Morales in July when he discovered that Morales was soliciting clients for himself in the prison, identifying himself as a lawyer.[90] Morales then returned to work in the prison as a paralegal for Oakdale municipal judge John Navarre.[91] He also started an unlicensed taxi service, charging detainees who bonded out of prison $25 for a ride to the Oakdale bus station, one and one-half miles away from the prison gates.[92]

With five of our clients we signed formal complaints that were submitted to the FBI and the Louisiana State Bar.[93] Silva wrote that he had fired Morales for "falsely representing himself as an attorney."[94] A Salvadoran woman signed a complaint that she had given her attorney, Hugo Morales, "$200 that he does not wish to return to me. Even though I had court [date], I went and he did absolutely nothing in my behalf."[95] A Salvadoran man's complaint read:

> At the beginning, I had the lawyer Hugo Morales. He was going to represent me in court as long as I would pay him three hundred dollars. ... He telephoned my family, telling them that Mr. Fernando Luna was a lawyer and bonding company, and he was going to help me get out of here. My family sent him the money believing that he was going to pay my bond, and he has not paid the bond.[96]

The Bureau of Prisons made it easy for Morales to run his scams. Each time an attorney or paralegal signed in to prison, we had to write in a registry book the names of all the clients we wanted to see. Morales copied the names of our clients from the registry and called them after we left. Two paralegals who had worked with Morales said he had shown them this trick.[97]

Because Oakdale is a federal prison, I contacted the FBI in St. Charles. FBI Special Agent Roger Rubrecht's reaction to our reporting Morales to the state bar was, "Reporting a lawyer to the Louisiana Bar is like reporting a whore to a whorehouse."[98]

The victims of these con men were Salvadoran war widows and rape victims—vulnerable and poor. One Salvadoran widow who had left four children with her mother in a war zone in Usulután sent $650 to Gutierrez, with which he promised to bond her out of prison. Then Shirley and Luna showed up. "They said that for $600 they could get my money back from Mr. Gutierrez. But that will only leave me $50. My bond is $3,000. I am worried about my children in El Salvador, and now all this has happened. Imagine how I feel."[99]

On the afternoon of February 12, 1987, Raul Hoyos burst into the office of *Servicios para Inmigrantes* in Houston carrying a baseball bat. Shirley and Larry Shea were both in the office. One of them shot Hoyos to death. The Houston Police Department called it justifiable homicide.[100]

A Change of Mission

Budget restraints, thousands of Central Americans on the streets of South Texas, and more than 6,000 Cubans in state and federal prisons were straining the INS's holding capacity. At noon on October 17, an INS officer called me from prison and suggested I go to City Hall. Mayor Mowad had called a press conference.

I took a seat on a wooden bench as Mowad announced a "short-term change of mission" for Oakdale prison: All the Central Americans would be moved out and Cuban felons would be moved in.[101]

"This has nothing to do with any of the lawsuits or the pressures of any groups that did not want us here," INS head of camp Dave Johnston said. "The process will begin next week and will take place over the next two months."

I was stunned. I sat in disbelief as Mowad lied to his constituents: "This is a temporary change until the Cubans can be processed out to halfway houses or Cuba," he said, though there were no halfway houses for Cubans and Castro would not accept them. The "bad Cubans" would stay in Atlanta, Mowad said. "Atlanta will be for the black-hatted Cubans, and Oakdale will be for the white-hatted Cubans." Cubans would be told they would be released sooner if they behaved well, which Mowad said would control violence. I asked how the INS planned to release exclusion cases. Mowad had no idea what I was talking about. Warden J. R. Johnson shouldered him away from the microphone and stated that he would increase security at the prison perimeter. "I don't perceive any problems at all," arising from the fact that the incoming Cubans would be convicted felons.

A man in the crowd asked if the Cubans would be released "into our community, to take our jobs, and go on our welfare rolls."

"Don't you worry about that," I said softly as I left city hall.

I felt no jubilation, as I had when we'd stopped the strip searches at Laredo. I felt only relief. The U.S. Supreme Court had just ended a five-year legal battle by refusing to hear an appeal on behalf of 1,800 Cubans in Atlanta Federal Penitentiary who had sought and failed to get limited constitutional rights. U.S. courts had effectively ruled that the INS could hold Cubans forever.[102]

They moved our clients out fast. Some went to Laredo, some were deported, most went to the *corralón*. The INS found places for everyone except our last four clients—Salvadoran and Guatemalan women. Judge R.

Kevin McHugh called them to a hearing in November, and Nancy Kelly and I were with them in the prison courtroom. Three of them were young, one middle-aged. None wanted to go back to the war, the threats, the rape, and hunger of Central America.

Judge McHugh questioned each woman briefly.[103] They all wanted political asylum. Nancy asked that they be released on their own recognizance; the INS senior trial attorney, Charlie Wiegand, did not object. Judge McHugh had nowhere to send them, and he couldn't keep them in Oakdale. "Well," he said, "I'm going to let you go."

None of the women understood English. The translator said, "*Que se puedan ir*" ("You may go") and the women burst into tears. They thanked the judge in Spanish and asked God to bless him. Judge McHugh smiled.

One year later the Cubans at Oakdale rioted, destroying and burning the prison administration building. They burned the prison at Atlanta and took guards hostage in both places. The riot got Oakdale prison more news coverage in one day than it had received in the entire nine months it had held Central American prisoners. When the Cubans ended the riots and released the hostages unharmed, the INS agreed to review Cubans' cases individually, to parole some to the streets and return some to Cuba, under a new agreement with Fidel Castro.[104]

It took four prison riots to persuade the INS to judge Cubans individually, on the merits of their cases. But what to do with the Cubans was a minor problem compared to Central Americans. There were 6,000 Cubans in U.S. prisons when the Oakdale and Atlanta prisoners rioted. By November 1988, more than 2,000 Central Americans were entering the United States each week near Brownsville, and they all wanted political asylum.[105]

Notes

1. "Prison for Aliens Opens in Louisiana," *New York Times,* April 9, 1986.

2. "Oakdale will be nearly twice as large as any existing detention facility for illegal aliens. Plans for such a center were first proposed late in 1981, after the administration announced its detention policy": "Administration Presses Policy of Incarcerating Illegal Aliens," *Congressional Quarterly* (February 16, 1985): 327.

3. Ibid., 325; and "Louisianans Wait for Alien Center—People of Remote City Fought for the Detention Unit as a Source of Employment," *New York Times,* October 7, 1984.

4. "Unemployment [in the town of Oakdale] has been higher than 30 percent during some months," "Administration Presses Policy," 327. The *New York Times* reported "high unemployment, which at one time reached 31 percent": "Louisianans Wait for Alien Center," October 7, 1984. Oakdale Mayor George Mowad told the author in June 1986 the town unemployment rate was 19 percent. The discrepancy in figures probably is attributable to the fact that a lumber mill had just closed,

throwing numerous Oakdale residents out of work; then the prison opened, offering a new source of employment.

5. "Louisianans Wait for Alien Center."

6. A Bureau of Prisons newsletter distributed to BOP employees in 1986 stated that the goal of Oakdale prison was to process 35,000 detainees a year. An Oakdale prison guard allowed the author to read the newsletter but not to copy it. Associate Warden Homer Sherrod wrote in the August newsletter: "I think it is very interesting to note that 4,579 inmates have been processed in and out of this institution since its opening in early April. This has been done without being fully staffed. The question remains, 'What can we do when we have all the staff and resources we need?'"

7. Ibid. The major immigration prisons on the southern U.S. border are at El Centro, California; Florence, Arizona; El Paso, Laredo, Los Fresnos, and Houston, Texas; Oakdale, Louisiana; and Krome Avenue, Miami, Florida.

8. A high-ranking INS officer at Oakdale told the author on October 23, 1986, that the "contingency site" could hold 1,000 tents that could be built with some of the $30 million in "immigration emergency funds" available under the Simpson-Rodino immigration bill.

9. George Mowad, interview with the author, June 1986. Robert Kahn, "Inside Louisiana's New INS Holding Pen—Imprisoned Aliens Stuck in Legal Limbo," Pacific News Service, June 12, 1986.

10. Mowad, interview. Robert Kahn, "The Jail an Indicted Mayor Helped Build," *Hartford Courant,* July 27, 1986.

11. "Administration Presses Policy," 327.

12. Personal communication from two attorneys in Louisiana, June 1986. Attorney Mark Oliver, of Alexandria, Louisiana, accepted pro bono every case and every appeal the author referred to him.

13. Several Oakdale natives, including a clergyman, related stories of the days when the office of Oakdale Legal Assistance had been a house of prostitution.

14. Inmates at Oakdale were strip-searched after attorney visits until June 2. Oakdale prison warden Steve Schwalb ordered the strip searches halted after he received a subpoena to testify in the *Orantes-Hernandez* lawsuit in Los Angeles. Attorneys Nancy Kelly and Sheila Neville, interviews with the author, June 1986. Neville was co-counsel in *Orantes-Hernandez v. Meese.*

15. Bureau of Prisons guards provided daily counts of the prison population at the request of the author and of Oakdale Legal Assistance office manager Vicki Sanford.

16. Attorney Niels Frenzen, interview with the author, June 3, 1986.

17. Detainees from El Salvador, England, Chile, Guatemala, and Haiti in Oakdale prison, interviews with the author, June 2, 3, 4, 5, 6, 9, 10, 11, 12, 13, 24, 1986.

18. Detainees at Oakdale prison, interviews with the author, June 1986; and Ira Kurzban, telephone interviews with the author, June 1986.

19. Mario, Salvadoran detainee in Oakdale prison, interview with the author, June 24, 1986.

20. English detainee in Oakdale prison, interview with the author, June 24, 1986.

21. Detainees from El Salvador, Guatemala, Chile, and England in Oakdale prison, interviews with the author, June 6, 1986.

22. Immigration judge Edwin Hughes, attorney Nancy Kelly, and paralegal Jorge Costa, interviews with the author, June 10, 1986; and INS spokesman Duke Austin, telephone interview with the author, June 10, 1986. The author saw Judge Hughes's signed order to admit Kelly into the prison with a camera.

23. FBI Special Agent Roger Rubrecht, of the bureau's Lake Charles, Louisiana, office, explained the profusion of prisoners' lawsuits in a September 9, 1986, interview with the author at the office of Oakdale Legal Assistance.

24. *Velasquez v. Nelson,* U.S. District Court, Southern District of Florida, 86-1262, June 13, 1986.

25. Bureau of Prisons guards provided the author and Oakdale Legal Assistance office manager Vicki Sanford reports of the prison population upon request.

26. *Velasquez v. Nelson.* Judge Ryskamp issued his ruling the day after Niels Frenzen filed the depositions gathered by Peter Upton and the author in Oakdale.

27. The INS policy on change of venue at Oakdale was the opposite of change-of-venue policy at the Florence prison. In Florence, Judge William Nail refused to grant changes of venue out of the district even at the request of an attorney. At Oakdale, the INS changed venue into the district and notified refugees' attorneys of the INS "request" for change of venue after it had been granted.

28. Ecumenical Immigration Services formally withdrew from the Oakdale prison project in a meeting at their office on 821 General Pershing Street, New Orleans, June 17, 1986. The author was present. Information on office finances was obtained in interviews with Victoria Sanford, manager of the law office under both its names—Ecumenical Immigration Services and Oakdale Legal Assistance—from interviews with board members of both nonprofit corporations, and from the author's personal observations. Sanford handled office finances, including payroll and fundraising.

29. Dan Kesselbrenner, with the National Lawyers Guild Immigrants Rights Project in Boston, Danny Katz, with Proyecto Libertad in Harlingen, and Salvador Colon, with the Houston office of CARECEN, helped reorganize our office as Oakdale Legal Assistance and joined our new board of directors.

30. The ratio is calculated from the author's interviews with more than 1,000 Central American detainees at Los Fresnos and Oakdale prisons in 1984 and 1986. The exile of Salvadoran veterans continued until the Salvadoran civil war ended. In July 1987, Laredo immigration attorney Patrick Hughes reported, "Nine of the last ten political asylums I did were based on the theory of guerrilla persecution": Robert Kahn, "The Changing Face and Fears of the Illegal Alien," *Newsday,* July 27, 1987.

31. Orlando, interview with the author, June 1986.

32. Orlando related this conversation after he had been released from the prison on bond in an interview with the author at the office of Oakdale Legal Assistance, August 1986.

33. Luis, interviews with the author, June–July 1986.

34. The author witnessed Luis's asylum trial in Judge Edwin Hughes's courtroom in Oakdale prison, July 1986.

35. A Bureau of Prisons guard told the author on June 19, 1986, that ninety-one detainees had arrived the night before, bringing the prison population to more than 900.

36. Bureau of Prisons guard Kirk Bullock, interview with the author, June 19, 1986.

37. Kirk Bullock, interview with the author, July 1986.

38. Oakdale prison guards, interviews with the author, June–November 1986.

39. The prison "riot" at Oakdale on October 6–7, 1986, was described by more than a dozen detainees and trusties in the week after the incident. All said the trouble started after the 4 P.M. count on October 6, when a particularly abusive guard seized a man to take him to solitary confinement for no apparent reason. Another detainee hit the guard on the head with a billiard ball or a rock. Sporadic problems recurred through the night, and on the morning of October 7, the prison called in a riot squad equipped with protective gear, visored helmets, and clubs. Thirty-three detainees, mostly black, were transferred to the Lafayette jail. The author witnessed the transfer. The author and other legal workers at Oakdale Legal Assistance received repeated phone calls from the prisoners at Lafayette, at least six of them Salvadoran political asylum applicants. Some detainees apparently were chosen at random to be transferred. One Salvadoran asylum applicant was asleep during the "riot" but was transferred to Lafayette as a "trouble-maker." Trusties, detainees, INS officials, Bureau of Prisons guards at Oakdale prison, and detainees at Lafayette jail, interviews with the author, October 7, 8, 9, 1986.

40. Interviews with guards inside Oakdale prison and at the Oakdale apartment complex where the author and many prison guards were neighbors.

41. Detainees and U.S. citizen trusties in Oakdale prison, interviews with the author, July 27; August 5; September 3, 12, 23, 24; October 10, 1986. In many cases, detainees' identification of the guard who tortured them was confirmed by their statement that the torturer signed the administrative detention order to place them in solitary confinement. The author has photocopies of some of these orders.

42. Prison guard in Oakdale prison, interview with the author, July 1986.

43. Salvadoran veterans in Oakdale prison, interview with the author, June 1986.

44. Detainee in Oakdale prison, interview with the author, June 1986. The woman's story was confirmed in telephone interviews with her aunt and sister in Los Angeles. A kidnapping ring led by military death squads was "broken up" in 1986, the RAND Corporation reported in 1991: "Those implicated included Lieutenant Sibr[i]an, who subsequently evaded justice for his role in the Sheraton murders ... and reputed death squad leader Colonel Mauricio Staben, the suspected mastermind of the kidnapping group, who was released without ever having to submit to a formal investigation after his military colleagues, including [future Chief of Staff Mauricio] Ponce, his fellow *Tandona* member, demanded that he be returned to active duty. Staben resumed—and retained for two years—the command of the elite U.S.-trained Arce Battalion. Two other officers accused of involvement in the kidnapping ring were warned by fellow officers and allowed to flee the country. ... In 1986 three key witnesses were killed, two while in security forces custody and a third in a suspicious shootout with the armed forces. In 1987 the house of Judge Miriam Artiaga, who was handling the case, was machine-gunned twice in a span of three weeks, forcing her to quit the case. Her successor, Judge Jorge Alberti Serrano, was killed by three gunmen a year later." Benjamin C. Schwartz, "American Counterinsurgency Doctrine and El Salvador" (report prepared for the undersecretary of defense for policy, RAND Corporation, Santa Monica, California, 1991), 28–29.

A *tandona* is a graduating class of the Salvadoran military academy. Graduates of the large class of 1966 wield extraordinary power in El Salvador. Because classmates are promoted together, a *tandona* "often shows more loyalty to its members than to the rule of law or even to the [Salvadoran] President," the RAND Corporation reported (ibid., 29), quoting "Barriers to Reform: A Profile of El Salvador's Military Leaders," a May 21, 1990, report of the Arms Control and Foreign Policy Caucus, Washington, D.C.

45. Deposition of "Elena," July 17, 1986, Oakdale prison.

46. Ibid.

47. The death of Juan Diego Sebastian was reported to the author by two detainees and confirmed by attorney Nancy Kelly in interviews with Warden Steve Schwalb and INS officials.

48. The author recorded this incident as it occurred: Kahn notebooks, vol. IX, 18–19.

49. Assistant Warden Homer Sherrod, Bureau of Prisons Lieutenant Charles Marmolejo, and Captain Larry Craven of Oakdale prison, interview with the author, June 25, 1986.

50. Steve Schwalb, letter to Oakdale Legal Assistance, June 26, 1986. A photocopy of the letter is in the author's possession.

51. Robert Kahn, letter to Steve Schwalb, July 5, 1986. A photocopy of the letter is in the author's possession.

52. The author sued the Bureau of Prisons in August 1986 after the warden at Oakdale barred the author from the prison for two months. *Oakdale Legal Assistance et al. v. Steven Schwalb et al.*, U.S. District Court, Lake Charles, Louisiana, August 27, 1986. The lawsuit requested a temporary injunction prohibiting the Bureau of Prisons from excluding the author from the immigration prison at Oakdale. Schwalb barred the author from the prison for two months after a fabricated incident with a guard. On August 29, Judge Edwin Hunter ordered the Bureau of Prisons to reinstate the author's work privilege after a suspension of thirty days. The next day, the Bureau of Prisons transferred warden Steve Schwalb away from the prison at Oakdale.

53. In his July 8, 1986, deposition, Oakdale warden Steve Schwalb acknowledged he had no training in or knowledge of INS guidelines on detention or detainees, or of INS detainees' rights, or of court injunctions regarding conditions of detention for INS detainees, or of the injunctions in *Orantes-Hernandez v. Meese* or *Nuñez v. Boldin*. He stated that the INS limit of seventy-two hours' solitary confinement did not apply to Oakdale prison. Deposition of Steven Schwalb, passim.

54. See note 6. Excerpts from the Bureau of Prisons newsletter stating the bureau's ambitious goals were reprinted in "Central American Refugee Defense Fund Newsletter," National Immigration Project of the National Lawyers Guild, Boston, Massachusetts, September 1986, 1.

55. José, interview with the author, July 10, 1986. At Los Fresnos prison, INS officials threatened detainees with solitary confinement and loss of meal privileges if they spoke to reporters who occasionally visited the detention center on prearranged conducted tours. Two Salvadoran detainees, interview with the author, July 3, 1984, and several interviews thereafter.

56. The immigration detention center at Chula Vista, just north of Tijuana, is not used for long-term detention. It is a short-term holding facility near the border crossing most heavily used by undocumented immigrants.

57. Two Salvadoran asylum seekers, interview with the author, July 10, 1986.

58. Temporary Restraining Order, *Herrera-Bonilla v. Alan Nelson,* U.S. District Court, Eastern District of New York, 86-2353, July 15, 1986. The attorneys in the case were Joe Azar and Ann Pillsbury.

59. Two INS officers inside Oakdale prison, personal communication with the author, July 21, 1986. The arrests were common knowledge among INS officials at Oakdale.

60. Attorney Jane Rocamora, interview with the author, July 25, 1986.

61. Sister Suzanne Lasseigne attended a hearing in Oakdale prison on July 24, 1986, at which the immigration judge raised a detained prisoner's bond because the detainee "absconded." The second case was reported to the office of Oakdale Legal Assistance on August 1, 1986, by an attorney for the Father Moriarty Center in San Francisco, who represented a Salvadoran detainee by telephone inside Oakdale prison. A Salvadoran was ordered deported in early August for "absconding" from his prison hearing because he was in the prison clinic, not his dormitory, when a guard came to take him to court. This case was reported by the detainee's family members on August 7. They had paid the man's bond "a few days" before that and wondered why he had not been released. Attorney Jane Rocamora found that the man's bond had been paid on July 2, yet he had never been released. On August 7 Rocamora asked the INS to release the man because his bond had been paid. The INS refused, saying the man had been ordered deported.

62. "The term 'refugee' does not include any person who ordered, incited, assisted or otherwise participated in the persecution of any person on account of race, religion, nationality ... social group or political opinion." U.S. Code of Regulations, vol. 8, Immigration, sec. 110a, 42. A similar exclusion is written into the 1980 Refugee Act.

63. Nancy Kelly (the Salvadoran sergeant's attorney), interview with the author, August 1986.

64. "Torture in El Salvador," compiled in Mariona prison, Ayutuxtepeque, El Salvador, by members of the Non-Governmental Human Rights Commission of El Salvador (*Comisión de Derechos Humanos de El Salvador*), September 24, 1986. Translated into English by Lisa Brodyaga.

65. The Salvadoran Assembly enacted Decree 50 on February 24, 1984, to replace Decree 507 of December 3, 1980. Decree 507 had been subjected to blistering analysis by human rights, religious, and legal organizations because it made extra-judicial confessions extracted under torture a legal basis on which to convict the subject and arrest others; it permitted arrest and long-term detention without warrant; it gave special military courts the power to try civilians, including children; and it permitted the military to interrogate suspects for up to fifteen days before bringing them before a judge. Confessions extracted under torture could be used to hold the suspect for another 120 days in "administrative detention," during which time "neither the accused, nor the prosecution shall have the right to participate in the proceedings." American Civil Liberties Union, cited in *Report on Human Rights*

in El Salvador (New York: Vintage Books, 1982), 91–105. Amnesty International called Decree 507 "an invitation to torture."

Decree 50 replicated all the repressive elements of Decree 507, but limited the "administrative detention" without access to an attorney to eighteen days; in other words, the torture had to be applied more quickly. Americas Watch, "Free Fire: A Report on Human Rights in El Salvador," August 1984, 65–67.

66. "Summary of Statistical Data Presented," "Torture in El Salvador," 77–83.

67. Ibid., 126. Another political prisoner described the involvement of a U.S. officer in a torture session, 101.

68. Lisa Brodyaga and Jonathan T. Jones, interviews with the author. The only mention of the torture report the author has found in the U.S. press is his own article, "Salvadoran Group Finds Torture of Detainees Widespread," *National Catholic Reporter,* December 19, 1986.

On the evening of October 26, 1987, Herbert Anaya, head of the CDHES, left his office at the usual time. Attorney Patrick Hughes was working with Anaya and living at his house, on the premise that the Salvadoran army would be less likely to assassinate Salvadoran human rights workers in the presence of North Americans. Hughes stayed in the CDHES office that night to watch the seventh game of the World Series. Hughes is a native of Minneapolis, and the Twins were playing. "You *gringos* with your baseball," Anaya told him. Early the next morning, Anaya was shot to death in the presence of his children in front of his home. The Salvadoran government arrested an FMLN sympathizer and tortured him until he confessed to the murder, which he later recanted. Anaya's widow asked the government to free the man. Patrick Hughes, personal communication with the author.

69. Final Judgment and Agreed Permanent Injunction, *State of Texas v. Bruce A. Shirley, Lawrence N. Shea and Fernando Luna, Sr. d/b/a Oficina de Relaciones Latinas and Servicios para Inmigrantes and Servicios para Inmigrantes, Inc.,* Harris County District Court (Houston, Texas), January 28, 1988.

70. Interviews and signed affidavits from more than a dozen detainees inside Oakdale prison, August 1986.

71. Nancy Kelly, Bruce Shirley, and Fernando Luna, interviews with the author, August 1–5, 1986.

72. Linda Yañez, telephone interview with the author, August 5, 1986. Yañez is now a state judge in Texas.

73. Danny Katz, interview with the author, August 5, 1986.

74. INS officer in Oakdale prison, confidential interview with the author, August 5, 1986.

75. The author gave photocopies of the cards to FBI Special Agent Roger Rubrecht on September 9, 1986, and to INS agents Sam Brown and Felix Torres on September 5, 1986, in interviews in the office of Oakdale Legal Assistance.

76. Ricardo Garcia, telephone interview with the author, August 5, 1986.

77. Ibid.

78. Iselda Sanchez, telephone interview with the author, August 5, 1986.

79. Patrick Hughes, telephone interview with the author, August 5, 1986.

80. Bertha Zunigar Galindez, telephone interview with the author, August 5, 1986.

81. Jeff Larsen, telephone interview with the author, August 5, 1986.

82. Julian Esparza, telephone interview with the author, August 5, 1986.

83. Plaintiff's Original Petition, *State of Texas v. Bruce A. Shirley.*

84. Final Judgment and Agreed Permanent Injunction, *State of Texas v. Bruce A. Shirley.*

85. Seven sworn affidavits from Central American detainees at Oakdale prison, August 8, 1986. The author gave copies of the affidavits to agents for the FBI and INS Internal Affairs. Copies of the affidavits are in the author's possession.

86. Miguel Gutierrez, telephone interviews with the author, August 5 and 8, 1986.

87. Copies of the affidavits were given to the FBI and INS.

88. Jane Rocamora, interview with the author, August 9, 1985.

89. Hugo Morales, interview with the author, June 10, 1986.

90. Affidavit of Riguer J. Silva, December 5, 1986, New Orleans, Louisiana.

91. Hugo Morales, interview with the author, September 30, 1986. The author saw Morales working with Navarre inside Oakdale on several occasions in September and October 1986.

92. Hugo Morales, interview with the author, September 30, 1986; immigrants who bonded out of Oakdale prison and paid for Morales's taxi service, interviews with the author, August–October 1986; Oakdale police officers who were investigating Morales's unlicensed business, interviews with the author, October 1986.

93. Fifteen depositions were sent to the Texas Bar Association's Unauthorized Practice of Law Committee in December 1986, after Morales moved to Brownsville. Copies of all documents are in author's possession. The local chairwoman of the committee was attorney Linda Yañez.

94. Silva, affidavit.

95. Affidavit of Amparo A., October 24, 1986, Oakdale, Louisiana.

96. Affidavit of Eligio L., October 6, 1986, Oakdale prison.

97. Paralegals Shana Thompson and Mario Cierra, interviews with the author, August 1986.

98. FBI Special Agent Roger Rubrecht, interview with the author, September 9, 1986.

99. Affidavit of Elena, August 8, 1986, Oakdale prison.

100. Office of the Texas Attorney General, personal communication with the author. The fatal shooting of Raul Hoyos was reported in the February 13, 1987, *Houston Post.* The *Post* did not name the "office manager" who shot Luna. An investigator for the attorney general's office confirmed that Shirley and Shea were in the office when Hoyos was shot.

101. Press conference of October 17, 1986, Oakdale City Hall. Mayor George Mowad, Bureau of Prisons Warden J. R. Johnson, and INS head of camp Dave Johnston spoke to a sparse crowd of Oakdale residents. Robert Kahn, "Cuban Felons Get Their Own Prison," *National Catholic Reporter,* October 31, 1986.

102. *Garcia-Mir v. Smith,* 766 F2d 1478 (11th Cir., 1985). *Cert. denied sub nom. Marques-Melding,* 106 Sup. Ct. 1213, 1986. A federal appeals court in Atlanta ruled in April 1986 that the prolonged detention of Cubans in the federal penitentiary in Atlanta did not violate the Cubans' limited constitutional rights. The U.S. Supreme Court refused to review the issue in October.

103. The author attended the November 12, 1986, hearing in Judge R. Kevin McHugh's courtroom in Oakdale prison.

104. The *New York Times* reported on the 1987 Oakdale prison riot on November 23, 24, 25, 26, 27, 28, 29, and 30 and on December 1, 4, 6, and 27, 1986. The *New York Times* printed one news story about Oakdale while the prison held Central Americans, "Prison for Aliens Opens in Louisiana," on April 9, 1986.

105. "Asylum claims in Harlingen, Texas, have risen from 400 per month in spring of 1988 to over 400 a day since January 15." U.S. Immigration and Naturalization Service, "Enhancement Plan for the Southern Border," memorandum, February 16, 1989, 1.

Children of the Contras

The anti-war movement has actually arrived
before the horror has come to the United
States: The Refugees have brought it. My only
regret is that we did not have Vietnamese
refugees in the United States in 1959.

—Attorney Patrick Hughes

IN NOVEMBER 1986, TWO DAYS after President Ronald Reagan signed into law the only major immigration bill of his presidency, Reagan's Central American policy began unraveling as details of the Iran-Contra arms-for-hostages deals became public. After years of pressure upon El Salvador, Nicaragua, and the U.S.-Mexican border, the pressure suddenly shifted to Washington, as journalists and Congress directed their attention to the Contra support network operating out of the National Security Council. The president who had complained that the border was out of control suddenly lost control of his Central American policy.

On November 6, 1986, President Reagan signed the Immigration Reform and Control Act, which made it illegal for undocumented people to work in the United States. This repressive measure was paired with an amnesty under which undocumented people who had entered the United States before January 1, 1982, could prove they had lived here since, and had not been convicted of a felony or more than three misdemeanors, had one year to apply for temporary resident status. Farm workers could qualify if they proved they had worked in the fields for ninety days in the year ending November 1, 1986. Amnesty applicants who qualified would get permission to work and could apply for permanent resident status if they learned English and the essentials of U.S. history and government within two and one-half years.[1]

Two days later, the *New York Times* and *Washington Post* reported the secret arms-for-hostages deals with Iran that would soon be known as the Iran-Contra scandal.[2]

On November 12, immigration judge R. Kevin McHugh released the last four Central American prisoners at Oakdale prison on their own recognizance.[3]

On November 15, Eugene Hasenfus was sentenced to thirty years in prison by a Sandinista tribunal. He would be released before Christmas.[4]

On November 19, citizens of Brownsville began to protest when news spread that the Catholic Diocese had applied for a sewer permit for a house on Minnesota Avenue. The application showed the diocese planned to move its Casa Romero refugee shelter from San Benito to Brownsville.[5]

On November 25, President Reagan called a press conference at which U.S. Attorney General Edwin Meese announced that almost $30 million from the Iranian arms deals had been diverted to weapons shipments for the Contras. National Security Council Adviser John Poindexter and his aide Lieutenant Colonel Oliver North were fired.[6]

The Iran-Contra scandal effectively ended the Contra war. But uneasy peace in Nicaragua did not stop the immigration pressure on the southern U.S. border. The economic embargo of Nicaragua remained in effect, and Meese's Justice Department was still offering work permits and protection from deportation to any Nicaraguan who applied for political asylum in the United States. Thousands of deserters from the Contras, their families, and disaffected or ambitious Nicaraguans fled from Honduras and Nicaragua and headed for the United States. The closest point of land entry was Brownsville, Texas.

Now the U.S. Justice Department faced the same ideological problem with Nicaraguans that it faced with Cubans: Could we abandon our fight against communism and deport people to a country with a Marxist government, even if that country were at peace? And if not, how should we treat people who were fleeing from our avowed enemies? Give them political asylum or keep them in immigration prisons indefinitely?

As the Iran-Contra network was laid bare on national television, Patrick Hughes had four-year-old clients, children of the Contras, held under $7,500 bonds with their mothers in Laredo prison. The children's fathers were with the Contras in Honduras or were looking for work in Miami. One of Hughes's Nicaraguan clients in Laredo had filed a complaint with the INS that a CCA prison guard had sexually assaulted her while she was naked in a prison shower.[7]

Hughes had moved to a house on a bluff overlooking a bend in the Rio Grande. At dusk, the Border Patrol parked its green-and-white van in a copse of bushes nearby and scanned the opposite shore with binoculars, looking for Patrick's future clients. Hughes and I sat under the trees in his backyard and watched the Border Patrol. On December 1, 1986, Patrick introduced me to the children of the Contras in Laredo prison.

Andrea had been arrested on July 19 with her children, four-year-old Karen, and Sara, three. They were two of about fifteen children in Laredo prison. "I don't even remember when I got here," Andrea said. "I just know I'm about to complete five months in prison."[8]

Andrea's brother, a former member of Somoza's National Guard, was a Contra officer. She had visited him at a Contra camp in July after she left Nicaragua. "He was dressed in the uniform of the Honduran army. He was in a camp by the border called San Marcos, near El Espino, Honduras."

Andrea's brother had driven her in a Jeep to Palmerola Air Force Base, where Americans filled the Jeep with supplies that her brother distributed at El Espino. That had been his job for years. Another brother also worked in Honduras. "The Contras are ex-Somocistas, like my brothers. They were in the National Guard and went to Honduras in 1979. All of us who come to the United States are Contras. We are against the Sandinista system. We want Nicaragua to be free, as it was before, under Somoza.[9]

Another Contra mother, Marina, had been in Laredo prison for more than four months with her eleven-year-old son, Julio. She left Nicaragua because the schools began political indoctrination of children when they were twelve years old.[10]

Maria, in prison with her eleven-year-old son, Omar, and three-year-old daughter, Carla, had a similar story. "At twelve years old they would teach my son about Sandino," Maria said. "I don't want him to know anything about Sandino. He was a communist."[11]

Maria, Omar, and Carla had been arrested along with Maria's husband Carlos, their nine-year-old daughter, and Maria's sixty-five-year-old mother. The adults were each placed under $7,500 bond, which Hughes got lowered to $3,000; a friend in Miami loaned them that amount.

"We had to decide who would leave prison and who would stay," Maria said. Hughes persuaded the INS to allow the father to take his mother-in-law, who had a heart problem, and the nine-year-old girl to Miami.

Carlos was working in Miami, trying to save $3,000 to get the rest of his family out of jail. But time was running out. "The father has gone to a district where there is no deportation of Nicaraguans," Hughes said. "Maria and the kids will have to wait in jail for a few more months to have their political asylum trial in Laredo. Carlos will apply in Miami, and he'll win and she won't."

Maria was afraid that would happen. "Imagine if they deport me, and my husband and mother stay in Miami," she said.

The children were sad, distracted, traumatized. Texas state law and the U.S. Supreme Court mandated they had to be in school, but INS and CCA provided nothing: "No access to books, no tutors, no recreation, nothing," Hughes said.[12]

Hughes and Fernando Tafoya, a San Francisco attorney and advocate for prison reforms, told the author that the INS-CCA contract stated that children would have access to indoor and outdoor recreation areas for free play during waking hours and that supervised recreation also would be provided. Tafoya visited Laredo prison that year. "What was considered recreational facilities was basically a slab of cement with some shade, surrounded by a fourteen-foot fence with barbed wire on top," he reported.[13]

Julio was allowed outside for about forty-five minutes a day, three or four times a week. He was not allowed books. His only recreation was to play Monopoly all day with the other children. "They won't give me crayons, either," Julio said, "so the priest brings some on weekends."[14]

"My girl is so traumatized," Andrea said, trying to hold on to four-year-old Karen, who squirmed away to lie under the table in the interview room.

All she talks about is what the adults talk about: when the *migra* arrested her, how much her bond is. She listens to what the other women here say and she tries to act like they do. She asks me a lot of questions about sex. I have no control over my child's environment here. Sometimes she dials 0 on the telephone just to talk to the operator. I heard her asking the operator for help to pay her bond.[15]

I asked Karen how she spent her time.

"When I get up, I go to eat and to wash myself," she said.

And then?

"Then? What do I do then? I play with the dolls the official gives me. And I fight with the other girls here because they say the toys are theirs, but I say no, and I hit them, because the toys belong to the prison."[16]

Hughes wanted to sue INS and CCA to force them to comply with the 1982 U.S. Supreme Court decision *Plyler v. Doe,* which ordered public schools to accept children of school age regardless of their immigration status. It was a Texas case. But Hughes was an immigration lawyer; he had no financial backing, clerks, or paralegals. The little money he made was from arranging bond reductions for detainees who could afford to pay him. He couldn't sue the U.S. government to make it comply with its own laws unless he gave up his immigration practice.

I asked Patrick why he represented Contra families for free. The women had left Nicaragua because they didn't like the schools—hardly a well-founded fear of persecution. Few if any of them had been tortured or had had innocent family members killed by the Nicaraguan government. Their stories of persecution were milk toast compared to those of Salvadorans. Patrick knew that better than I.

He made a face as if he'd tasted bad medicine and said, "Because they've got kids."

Notes

1. Immigration Reform and Control Act of 1986. Public Law 99-603, 99th Cong., 2d sess..

2. "Reagan Approved Iranian Contacts, Officials Report (-) No Mention of Weapons (-) Secret Approaches Sought to Improve Relations and to Help Free Hostages," *New York Times,* November 8, 1986.

3. The author was present at these trials in Oakdale prison.

4. "Nicaraguan Court Convicts American over Aid to Rebels (-) Hasenfus, Downed on a Flight to Supply Contras, Gets a 30-year Prison Term," *New York*

Times, November 16, 1986; "Hasenfus Freed by Nicaraguans and Heads Home (-) Captured American Is Given Presidential Pardon," *New York Times,* December 18, 1986; "Hasenfus Back in U.S., Ready to Talk," *New York Times,* December 19, 1986.

5. Ed Asher, "Families Circulate Petition to Keep Casa out of City," *Brownsville Herald,* November 21, 1986.

6. Attorney General Edwin Meese's report on the diversion of funds from the Iranian arms deals to the Nicaraguan Contras was reported in two stories in the November 26, 1986, *New York Times:* "Iran Payment Found Diverted to Contras; Reagan Security Adviser and Aide Are Out" and "Statement by Reagan and Key Sections of Remarks by Meese."

7. Attorney Patrick Hughes, telephone interview with the author, September 23, 1986.

8. Andrea and her children, interview with the author, December 1, 1986.

9. For Nicaragua under the Somozas, see Bernard Diederich, *Somoza* (New York: Dutton, 1981).

10. Marina and her son Julio, interview with the author, December 1, 1986.

11. Maria, interview with the author, December 1, 1986.

12. The U.S. Supreme Court ruled in 1982 in *Plyler v. Doe* that public school districts have to admit children who live in the district regardless of their immigration status. Texas state law requires that children attend school until they are sixteen.

13. Fernando Tafoya, telephone interview with the author, September 1986. Tafoya and Hughes told the author their information about provisions for children in the INS-CCA contract came from INS and CCA officials. However, there is no reference to special provisions for children in the seventy-one pages of the ten contracts between the U.S. Immigration and Naturalization Service and the Corrections Corporation of America, beginning with "Solicitation, Offer and Award," DLS-16-84, March 7, 1984, and continuing through nine "Amendment(s) of Solicitation/Modification of Contract," March 9, 14, 19, 30; April 2, 17; May 2; June 15, 1984; and March 10, 1985. The only reference to children states, "The contractor shall furnish the necessary physical structure, equipment, facilities, personnel and services to provide a program of temporary residential care for up to 60 women and children aliens detained by the Immigration and Naturalization Service (INS), Chief Patrol Agent, Laredo, Texas." "Solicitation, Offer and Award," March 7, 1984, 11.

14. Julio, interview with the author, December 1, 1986.

15. Andrea, interview with the author, December 1, 1986.

16. Karen, interview with the author, December 1, 1986.

BROWNSVILLE

To be in detention doesn't mean you have to be behind a fence.

—INS spokesman Duke Austin

As DUSK FELL IN BROWNSVILLE, refugees gathered in the grassy courtyards of hotels on Central Boulevard, less than a mile from the Rio Grande. A Salvadoran approached me at the washing machines at the Plaza Motel and asked if I knew how to get out of Brownsville. Then another Salvadoran showed up, and another. Soon there were nine refugees around me in the courtyard, all wanting to know how to get out of Brownsville. They were gone in the morning. When I came home from work that day, a Nicaraguan approached me. As we spoke, more people appeared out of the weed-grown fields that surrounded the tattered hotel. Refugees were camping out in vacant lots throughout Brownsville, a city of 100,000. It was October 1988—one month before the presidential election.

The collapse of the Contra war had pushed a new wave of refugees to the United States, and it brought them in an election year. Though U.S. citizens were split on the issue of Nicaragua, no one was pleased that the Contras' bullets had been bought with money diverted from the profits of arms sales to Iran.

Nicaraguans were receiving special protection from the Department of Justice, which allowed them to work, travel, and remain in the United States without fear of deportation.[1] But as thousands of Nicaraguans became a public presence on the streets of South Texas, the question arose: If Nicaraguans are not economic migrants but genuine refugees, aren't Salvadorans and Guatemalans refugees as well?[2]

Government massacres and torture in El Salvador and Guatemala had been documented for more than a decade by internationally respected human rights monitors, including Amnesty International, which had received the Nobel Peace Prize for its work. Government torture and disappearances had spread into Honduras, another U.S. ally.[3] But the Sandinistas didn't torture political prisoners: They imprisoned and "reeducated" them. The Sandinistas' greatest offense was that they were ideologically abhorrent to the Reagan administration. The politics of immigration became clear on the streets of Brownsville in the winter of 1988–1989: Nicaraguans were allowed to enter the country freely until the election was won. After that Nicaraguans were jailed with everybody else.

For the average voter who didn't speak Spanish and knew little of Central America, it was hard to tell the difference among Salvadorans, Nicaraguans, Guatemalans, Hondurans, and Mexicans. The Reagan administration's support for the wars in Central America was responsible in great part for the unprecedented numbers of Central Americans entering the United States in search of refuge, but the administration never drew the obvious conclusion that uncontrolled emigration from Central America would end if the wars ended. As the authors of the White House report "Unauthorized Migration" so blithely concluded, "foreign policy decisions ... are driven by considerations often at odds with immigration concerns."[4] Brownsville was where the results of "foreign policy decisions" became "immigration concerns." Just as surely as the Iran-Contra network went down in flames with Eugene Hasenfus's plane, Reagan's refugee policies unraveled when Nicaraguans flooded the streets of South Texas.

Since Attorney General Meese's July 1987 order that allowed Nicaraguans to enter the country to live and work without fear of deportation, Nicaraguan immigration to the United States had quintupled.[5] Nicaraguan political asylum applications increased from 7,111 in fiscal year 1986 to 35,431 in fiscal year 1989.[6] Deportations virtually stopped. In fiscal year 1989 only 36 Nicaraguans were deported while 4,539 Salvadorans were repatriated.[7] Nicaraguans who made it to South Texas were allowed to file an asylum claim and get on a bus to Miami, where they were protected from deportation by the INS district director's fiat; or they could go to any city where they had relatives or shelter. But Salvadorans and Guatemalans were confined to the lower Rio Grande Valley, waiting for their political asylum hearings.[8]

Lisa Brodyaga filed a class action lawsuit against the INS in August 1988 on behalf of seven Salvadoran and Guatemalan clients arrested by the Border Patrol in South Texas.[9] Each had given the INS an address in the northern United States, was released, and ordered to stay in the lower Rio Grande Valley. The INS mailed them notice of asylum hearings in the north—which they never received, since they were not allowed to go there. The INS then ordered them deported in absentia for failing to appear in court. In an August 16 hearing before Federal District Judge Filemon Vela in Brownsville, INS attorney David Ayala conceded this.[10]

Judge Vela found that the INS had violated due process by failing to give refugees proper notice of court hearings. The INS agreed to reopen the seven cases. Ayala argued that made the case moot, but Brodyaga continued to get new plaintiffs. "This is a class action," Brodyaga said, "and the law is very clear that you can't get rid of a class action by buying off the named plaintiffs."[11]

It was no secret that Brodyaga was preparing another lawsuit against the INS that would charge the agency with discriminatory enforcement of law.

As the Bush and Dukakis campaigns entered their final weeks, with neither candidate choosing to make immigration a significant issue, the Justice Department had three choices. One was to continue to give special favors to Nicaraguans—let them work, travel, and stay in the United States—while it kept Salvadorans and Guatemalans confined in South Texas. Then the INS would face a lawsuit it would probably lose, and Judge Vela would determine U.S. policy.

The second was to deny Nicaraguans the right to work and travel and to keep them confined to South Texas with the rest of the Central Americans.

The third choice was to open the gates and allow anyone who applied for asylum in South Texas the right to work and travel.

A Republican campaign slogan was that the Democrats had turned their backs on the Contras. The Republicans wouldn't turn their backs on them until after the election. In September 1988, the Reagan administration opened the gates. Anyone who applied for political asylum in the Harlingen INS District would be given a work permit and permission to travel so long as he or she could provide an address in a city of destination where the INS could send notice of the asylum hearing. But there was a catch. The policy was restricted to affirmative applicants—only those who applied for asylum *before* they were arrested by the Border Patrol.[12]

Central Americans who found their way to the INS office in Harlingen, twenty-six miles from Brownsville, would be given a work permit and permission to travel. Central Americans arrested in a taxi on the way to the INS office were allowed to submit asylum applications, but they were released with no work permit and no permission to travel. People caught violating the travel bond were arrested and sent to an immigration prison with a prohibitively high bond—usually $10,000. They were considered bad bail risks because they had violated an INS order.

It was a generous offer, but it didn't last as policy. The speed with which the INS cracked down after the election shows that its policy was driven by political considerations.

South Texas Becomes a Prison Without Walls

Less than one month after George Bush was elected president, the INS changed policy again by secret memo. The Justice Department ordered the INS to deny all asylum seekers in South Texas the right to work and to confine them all to the Harlingen INS District. A December 5 internal memo, "Nicaraguan Asylum/Harlingen Situation," by INS Deputy Commissioner James Buck, proposed that the INS rescind Meese's July 1987 order, discontinue granting work permits, confine asylum applicants to the districts where they filed their claims, speed up asylum adjudications, and immediately incarcerate applicants whose claims were denied.[13] The memo ordered the INS to "proceed with development of Nicaraguan plan—Phase Two," which included "a Nicaraguan media strategy."[14] INS officers were to "develop quick profile(s) of apprehended Central Americans in the McAllen sector" and "press State Department and INS liaison to secure the assistance of Mexico and Central American countries to slow down the flow of illegal aliens into the United States."[15] Listed first under "Expected results/benefits" was that "the majority of the asylum applicants in Harlingen will remain there."[16]

For South Texas, the crucial policy change was that "all asylum requests should be adjudicated by office of original jurisdiction."[17] Now everyone—Nicaraguans as well as Salvadorans, Guatemalans, and Hondurans—would be confined to the lower Rio Grande Valley, one of the poorest stretches of towns in the United States, with the highest unemployment rate in Texas.[18] The INS had run out of money to imprison refugees, so it dumped them on the cities and counties of South Texas.

By Christmas, thousands of refugees were sleeping on the streets of Brownsville. More than 300 slept under plastic garbage bags or pieces of cardboard and in holes in the ground in a brushy field across a dirt road from Casa Romero. The shelter director, Sister Juliana Garcia, had promised to limit Casa Romero occupancy to 200 people a night, and she kept her word, so overflow refugees slept in the fields nearby.

Three hundred people had moved into the Amber Motel, a condemned and abandoned, two-story, horseshoe-shaped wreck on Central Boulevard. They squatted in the dark rooms with no electricity or running water, often without doors, and in the fields as a series of cold waves brought freezing drizzle and dropped the temperature to 32 degrees. The Amber Motel had no functioning toilets. A corner room chosen as the communal bathroom filled up a foot deep with excrement and refuse. Conjunctivitis spread among the children, whose parents couldn't afford medicine. Refugees killed ducks from the *resaca* behind the Amber Motel and roasted them over open fires to feed their families.[19]

Twenty-six miles north in Harlingen, another 200 to 300 people slept on the concrete sidewalk and the asphalt parking lot outside the INS building in order to hold places in line to submit their asylum applications. Private citizens and churches took in hundreds more. Lázaro Ernesto Flores, a Cuban who had come to the United States in 1960, housed twenty-one Nicaraguans and a Guatemalan in his seventeen-foot trailer in Brownsville.[20]

Sharks of the Fields

While refugees suffered from the weather, illness, mosquitoes, lack of food and water, and worried about their asylum applications, con men as young as sixteen stole thousands of dollars from them. High school kids pawned themselves off as lawyers at Casa Romero, penciling in political asylum forms, often so sloppily that the INS refused to accept them.

"I don't get paid for this," eighteen-year-old Ricky Gonzalez said as he filled in an asylum application for a Nicaraguan under a makeshift shelter at Casa Romero. "I do it to help the people."[21] While Gonzalez and his sixteen-year-old friend José Rodriguez bilked refugees for their money, they put the refugees' children to work washing Rodriguez's Pontiac Fiero. The next day at Casa Romero, Gonzalez told me he did not prepare asylum applications and claimed he had not been there the day before. Rodriguez said, "We work together, helping the people fill in asylum forms for $2.50 each."

But Julio Viera, a Nicaraguan who slept in the bushes across the road, had paid Rodriguez $260 to fill in four asylum applications, for him and three nephews. "He took about ten minutes for each one," Viera said.

Rodriguez recalled, "it's possible" he had charged Viera $260 to fill in four asylum applications, claiming that the money was to cover the cost of photocopying the applications—a four-page document. Rodriguez and Gonzalez worked by themselves, without a lawyer. Neither of them had training in immigration law or in preparing immigration forms. "It's very easy, if you know English," Rodriguez said.

Amado Rivera, a Nicaraguan who slept at Casa Romero, had another opinion. "Bandits are what they are," he said. "*Cabrones.*"

Dozens of people in the fields confirmed that Gonzalez and Rodriguez regularly visited Casa Romero and charged $50 to $75 to prepare asylum forms. "Those lawyers there fill out the forms for $50," said Mariena, a Nicaraguan woman, pointing at Gonzalez and Rodriguez.

We put Gonzalez and Rodriguez on page 1 of the *Brownsville Herald,* and they disappeared; then Ovilio Cabrera showed up. Cabrera had already been fired by a Harlingen attorney, sued by the Texas attorney general for unauthorized practice of law, and put under court order to cease and desist, but there he was in the fields, taking $50 a head for penciled-in asylum applications.[22] Taxi drivers charged refugees $50 apiece for the five-mile drive from the river to Casa Romero, then charged more to fill in asylum forms.

As the new year began, at least eighty-four children younger than seventeen slept at Casa Romero or in the fields around it.[23] I counted forty-nine in the bushes; thirty-five inside Casa Romero were younger than ten, according to the house co-director, Sister Norma Pimentel. A cold wave had dropped temperatures into the thirties, and the children were getting sick.

"Many suffer from diarrhea, hunger, bronchitis," said Carlos Sanchez, twenty-nine, a medical student from Nicaragua who had arrived January 3 with his wife and two children—Carlos, twenty-one months old, and Herenia, ten months.

What's bad is that we can't get into Casa Romero, and we can't work. The conditions here are subhuman. The sanitary conditions are nonexistent. With no medical attention, the children suffer hunger. Rice and beans are not adequate for them. There is shit everywhere, and there are children everywhere. They live in the open air. The dust, and the temperature and the shit affect the babies' health. Whether it's an undocumented immigrant or not, I believe a baby deserves a little bit of milk.[24]

Refugees ate because the poor people of Brownsville fed them. Every day people arrived in beat-up station wagons and old pickup trucks to ladle out hot beans, rice, and tortillas. Although some taxi drivers gouged refugees for the ride from the river, other cabbies brought them food. No government body did a thing for them.

Next to the bush where the Sanchez family slept, in a tent made of sticks, old clothes, and plastic garbage bags, Lázaro Gonzalez waited with his wife and three children for an asylum interview. They had come to the United States to escape the Salvadoran civil war. Their oldest son was of draft age. "We came looking for peace," Lázaro said. "We live by the will of God. At times the children cry. They want to do something, but there is nothing to do. They are bitten by mosquitoes, eating perhaps two times a day from people who bring food."

Lázaro's seventeen-year-old son showed me a paper cup full of popcorn. "This is what I'm eating today."[25]

In the next tent, Dino Aron Sandoval, one year old, was ill with fever and diarrhea. He had been unconscious all day. A volunteer from a Brownsville church came to take him and his mother to a doctor. Dino's father, Francisco Carrera, twenty-seven, watched them pick their way through the refugee camp and enter a stranger's car. "At least here, we're not dying in war."

The Tale of the Good Samaritans

From December 5, 1988, until February 16, 1989, when the INS changed policy again, an emergency corps of fifteen INS employees interviewed asylum applicants in Harlingen on a "last in, first out" basis. New applicants were interviewed, told to return in thirty days for a decision, and ordered to remain in the Rio Grande Valley. Because of the crushing workload, thousands of pending applications from people already confined to the valley were bumped into administrative limbo. The U.S. border had effectively been moved to the northern end of the INS Harlingen District, the four counties of southmost Texas. Brownsville looked like a war zone.

Neighbors of Casa Romero were either sympathetic to the refugees or dead set against them; as in Central America, there was no middle ground.

"It's no problem for us, 'cause they never bother us at all," said José Nieto, manager of The Fix-It Center, an auto repair shop across the street from Casa Romero. "Some of them come and ask for water, but they're real polite."

The Casa's next-door neighbors were not so tolerant. "We hate it, we hate it, we hate it," said an elderly Anglo woman who would not give her name.

"They throw all their garbage on my place," her husband said. "I picked up nearly thirty beer bottles yesterday, and a whiskey bottle. We can't cut the grass and make hay because it's full of junk."[26]

Permanent residents of Brownsville, most of whom speak Spanish, were more sympathetic than the winter tourists, retirees from the Midwest who generally do not speak Spanish. None of the residents of Paul's Trailer Park, across the road from Casa Romero, had a kind word to say.

"It bothers me," admitted Bill Hughes, of Independence, Missouri, who had been a winter resident for eleven years. "They come in the park. Usually they're asking for something, and I don't know what 'cause I don't speak their language and they don't speak mine. They come here as late as seven or eight at night and jabber at us and we don't know what they want."

"I can't say they've bothered us," said an elderly man playing pool in the trailer park's recreation room. "It just don't look right."

The refugees had two friends and protectors in the neighborhood, Debra and Joe Ubach, managers of U&U Mart, a little wooden grocery store two blocks north of Casa Romero on Minnesota Avenue. The Ubachs chased *coyotes* away from the store and helped refugees fill out asylum forms for free. "They don't speak the language and they need somebody to translate for them," Debra said.

They come here for political asylum. By the time they get here they've been ripped off; some of the women have been raped; the men have been beaten. They come in here and get taken advantage of by the community. This so-called nun that runs [Casa Romero] ... allows the taxi drivers to go in and fill out forms and they charge seventy or eighty dollars for it. We help them here for free, for nothing. ... Can you imagine being treated like they're being treated, without a cent to your name?[27]

After I put Debra's words in the *Brownsville Herald,* the Ubachs lost the lease on their store. "The whole issue is that we allowed them in here and we were trying to help them," Debra said after she was evicted. "We've never been late with our rent."[28]

Their landlord, who had run the store when it was called JC's Market, had posted signs stating, "Central Americans are not allowed on these premises." Joe Ubach had removed the signs. When I called the landlord for a comment, he told me to go to hell.

I went back to the store as the Ubachs tried to sell the last few cans on the shelves. They lost $4,000 they had invested in the business. It was my fault, but they didn't hold it against me. "Just yesterday we ran off a *coyote*" who was trying to extort $1,800 from three Guatemalans staying at Casa Romero, Debra told me. No sooner had she spoken than the three young men entered the store. Edwin, twenty-two, said it was true the Ubachs had run off the *coyote*. The *coyote* wanted $600 from each of them to take them to New York. They had paid the coyote $1,500 to bring them from Guatemala.

"I said, 'Listen, no one needs $1,800 to travel out of Brownsville,'" Debra added. "I told him point blank, 'You're a *coyote* and you know it.' It's kind of heartbreaking, because people know us now and trust us. They come to us and ask us, 'Now what are we going to do?'"

Death Squad Deserters

Not everyone in the fields was an innocent refugee. Death squad members were there too, sharing cups of popcorn and rice and beans with young draft dodgers they might have had to kill in El Salvador. Proyecto Libertad helped one death squad member leave South Texas and get to Minnesota, where he won political asylum. He was a Salvadoran air force sergeant who had tortured people as part of his job. When he refused to reenlist, his commanding officer had him whipped and threatened to kill him. The sergeant fled to the United States, where he made a videotape in which he testified that the Salvadoran military systematically tortured and killed prisoners of war and hid the evidence from U.S. military advisers.[29]

In the hour-long videotape, the sergeant, who was a member of the *Grupo de Operaciones Especiales* (Special Forces Group), stated he was whipped with a radio antenna for refusing to torture people. When he told his U.S. military advisers about the torture sessions, his Salvadoran captain threatened to kill him. The torture sessions continued, hidden from the U.S. advisers. In support of his claim to asylum, the sergeant presented his Salvadoran air force identification card with his name, photo, and serial number, a military credit card with his name and picture, two military cloth patches from special forces units, photos of him in uniform with other soldiers, and other documents.[30]

The sergeant was not proud that he had tortured people. "You could conclude from the fact that he was granted asylum that the judge felt it was a credible claim, and that he feared reprisals from the military," said Louis Smith, the Minneapolis attorney who represented the sergeant at his asylum trial. "The key to the case was using expert witnesses."[31] Dr. Rosa Garcia, a psychologist at the Center for Victims of Torture in Minneapolis, had testified that the sergeant "showed the signs and symptoms of suffering a severe trauma like torture," Smith recounted. The Center for Victims of Torture is a nonprofit clinic founded in 1986 by the Minnesota Lawyers' International Human Rights Committee. It is one of four such clinics in the world and the only clinic for torture victims in the United States. Dr. Garcia declined to comment on any of her patients' cases.

In the videotape, the sergeant described the tortures the Salvadoran military inflicts on prisoners of war, including electric shock, suffocation, beatings, and rape. His descriptions are consistent with the Non-Governmental Human Rights Commission 1986 report on torture compiled inside Mariona prison.[32] "But whether they talk or not, they would always be killed," the sergeant said. "These are things I have seen."[33]

His U.S. advisers, whom he called Colonel Marcos (Mark), Major Bill, and Sergeant Mitchell, worked only during the day. The prisoners were interrogated and tortured at night, often by electric shock to the penis, administered with U.S.-supplied electric generators. "One day they forgot to hide the cables, the wires, the pliers. The American adviser came and said, 'Well, Sergeant, what is all this?' And I said, 'Well, Captain, I can't lie. What happens is, when you go home they torture people here.'"[34]

The U.S. adviser reprimanded a Salvadoran captain, who then threatened the sergeant with death. "It stopped for a few days, but then it went on the same," the sergeant said. "No one talks about this because, well, if you talk, your head falls."

Jonathan Moore, a paralegal at Proyecto Libertad, helped prepare the sergeant's asylum application. Moore spoke with him often over four months and conducted the videotaped interview in Spanish. "He's a tough little soldier," Moore said.

> He's not a leftist at all. He thinks the U.S. is great, and the military advisers are the best guys in the world. He didn't like the torture, and he didn't like the officers that were doing it, and that he was threatened and called a guerrilla because he would not do it himself. He was into the military macho culture, but in a sense he was more chivalrous. He had a different concept of military honor.[35]

Willful Ignorance in Washington

The INS, the Pentagon, the State Department, my congressman and senators, the U.S. embassy in El Salvador, and the Salvadoran embassy in Washington had no comment on the sergeant's case.[36] They refused to read documents I offered to send and refused to comment about why immigration judges ruled that the torturers' stories were true but their victims' stories were not—why military torturers were granted asylum but their victims were rejected.[37]

Salvadorans detained in immigration prisons still could not win asylum, but after the Iran-Contra hearings had discredited U.S. policy in Central America, immigration judges began to grant asylum to a few deserters from army death squads after they had bonded out of detention. Immigration judge Glenn MacPhaul granted asylum to a seventeen-year-old Salvadoran army deserter who testified that army recruits are made to torture and kill animals and humans as part of their basic military training. Antonio testified that while at the Army Center for Military Training, or CEMFA, in La Union Department, he and other recruits who were forcibly conscripted in the summer of 1989 were made to kill dogs and vultures by biting their throats and twisting their heads off. The army training center was built with U.S. tax dollars as part of the Reagan administration's drive to "professionalize" the Salvadoran army.[38]

After killing the animals, Antonio said, he was made to watch soldiers torture and kill suspected dissidents and was told that he would have to torture people as part of his training. His drill instructors told him that torturing people would "make you more of a man, give you more courage."[39]

While on guard duty in a tower, Antonio witnessed other recruits torturing a suspected "subversive" in the plaza below: "They were tearing out his fingers and his fingernails. Then they killed him and cut off his head. After they did that, they cut his body into pieces as though it were a toy and they played with the arms for entertainment."[40]

Antonio saw soldiers kill other suspects at the army base by drowning or decapitating them. Men were held in an underground prison at the CEMFA, crowded so tightly into cells there was no room to sit; water in the cells came up to the prisoners' knees. They were starved or tortured to death: "They took them out to torture them, to kill them, cutting off parts of their body, and then they cut off their heads after they were dead."[41]

Antonio testified that after witnessing the torture, "I couldn't sleep. My nerves were shot. ... They told me that I'd have to do the same thing, and that way I'd become more of a man."

After he deserted, the army came to his house "seven or ten times" the next month, looking for him. He hid in a sewer near the house and slept in the woods at night. Two of his neighbors had also deserted, and the army killed both of them. One of the corpses turned up at a body dump called El Mirador, a canyon where "there are a lot of skeletons everywhere. When all this happened, I couldn't stand it anymore," Antonio told Judge MacPhaul. He fled to the United States.

The INS attorney, Agnelis Reese, told the judge Antonio didn't deserve asylum. "He was never ordered to torture or kill any human being," Reese said. "It is the government's position that [Antonio's] position is no different from that of any other deserter. He did not wish to fight ... so he fled his country."[42]

MacPhaul told Antonio to return to his court in a week, when he would render a decision. Antonio went home to a shelter for unaccompanied minors, drank rubbing alcohol that night, and became violently ill. One week later he returned to court to hear MacPhaul read his decision. MacPhaul said he found Antonio to be a credible witness, who had testified in a "flat monotone," like one who has witnessed things "beyond his years. ... The world is too much with him," MacPhaul said. The judge said he gave "no weight to the State Department letter ... as it appears to be a form letter" that did not address any details of Antonio's case. He said Antonio would have been forced to commit "gross abuses of human rights" had he failed to desert. However, he said, Antonio's case "failed to show that human rights violations by the army are the policy of the Salvadoran government." He granted Antonio political asylum.[43]

Antonio, a short, round-faced boy with no beard, showed no emotion when MacPhaul's decision was translated. I congratulated him in the hallway after the hearing. He didn't want to talk. "I feel pretty bad today," he said. "I don't know why." He walked slowly out of the INS building in Harlingen accompanied by his attorney, Anne Marie Gibbons, and the Proyecto Libertad paralegal who had helped him in his case. Now that he had won asylum, he needed a place to live.

The Joya Martinez Case

The only deserter from the death squads who spoke in the United States under his own name was not so fortunate as Antonio. Cesar Vielman Joya Martinez is a self-confessed murderer and death squad member. After bonding out of INS detention in January 1990, he went to Washington and testified to members of Congress that he had been a member of Department 2—the intelligence section of the Salvadoran army's First Infantry Brigade. He told Congress and reporters that he had operated under the supervision of U.S. military advisers, who had given his intelligence unit unmarked vans they used to abduct, torture, and assassinate suspected leftists in El Salvador. The U.S. advisers also provided $3,000 a month, some of which was used to rent a "safe house" where he and others tortured suspected dissidents. His U.S. advisers had an office next to his commanding officer, Major Diaz Hernandez, who directed the death squad operations.[44]

Joya Martinez said he had participated in the torture and murder of at least eight people and that his death squad worked "in connection with North American advisers that had a private office inside Department 2 of the First Infantry Brigade." He called the intelligence division of the First Infantry Brigade "the principal mechanism for promoting death squads in El Salvador."[45] Joya said his U.S. advisers were a major and a captain whose names he did not know. Everyone in the death squad operated under a code name. His code name was Alex.

The First Infantry Brigade murdered six Jesuit priests and their two housekeepers at the University of Central America in San Salvador on November 16, 1989. The next day, soldiers drove a car past the office of the Catholic Archdiocese of El Salvador, announcing by loudspeaker: "Ignacio Ellacuria and Martín Baró are now dead. We'll continue killing communists. We are the First Brigade."[46]

Eduardo Torres, a spokesman for the Salvadoran embassy in Washington, acknowledged that Joya "was a member of the armed forces ... in the First Infantry Brigade and a member of an intelligence unit," and that "in about June 1989 he participated in a counterinsurgency action" in which Joya and two other soldiers beat two civilians to death.[47]

Torres described Joya's actions, like the actions of the nine Salvadoran soldiers who murdered the Jesuit priests, as "individual abuses of authority." He compared Joya's actions with those of Colonel Guillermo Benavides, director of the Salvadoran Military College, who met with other high-ranking officers in the hours before and after the assassination of the Jesuits. Benavides's actions "do not prove government involvement in the death squads. He was head of the military college, but he was an individual."[48]

Joya Martinez said otherwise. He fled El Salvador in July 1989 after the bungled operation in which he and the Salvadoran embassy admit he helped beat two people to death. He fled to Honduras, then Belize, where the Commission for the Defense of Human Rights in Central America obtained for him a safe-conduct pass to Mexico City. There he dictated a nine-page, single-spaced statement to the Mexican Academy of Human Rights. The statement asserted that assassinations by his group intensified immediately after the May 1989 election of Salvadoran President Alfredo Cristiani of the ARENA party and that the assassinations were approved by Salvadoran intelligence chief Major Diaz Hernandez and battalion commander Colonel Francisco Elena Fuentes. Joya confirmed that suspected leftists were killed by torture during interrogations, after which the death squad disposed of their bodies by throwing them into the sea. He further stated that the army planned "a final offensive in late 1989 that would entail more clandestine captures in the metropolitan area, keep a constant watch, and carry out pursuits of members of humanitarian institutions."[49]

Joya Martinez spoke to the Mexican Academy of Human Rights on August 28, 1989—more than two months before the guerrilla offensive of November 1989, launched by the FMLN after the bombing of the FENASTRAS (National Federation of Trade Unions) office, which had killed ten people and injured thirty-six, and the October 31 bombing of the office of the Committee of Mothers of the Disappeared.[50]

In the June 1989 counterinsurgency operation confirmed by the Salvadoran embassy, Joya Martinez reported that he joined the U.S.-trained Atlacatl Battalion and helped capture seven suspected guerrillas in Apopa, north of San Salvador.

> The battalion commander ... informed us that an order had been received that there were specific orders to assassinate both the principal commanders that had been captured. The commander of the terrorists, Edwin N., a youth of 21 years, white, thin, dark hair, was assassinated or died as a consequence of the torturing and was buried in a haphazard manner in Tres Ceibas [near Apopa], his body covered with dirt and stones.[51]

After torturing the other suspects, "orders arrived that we were to leave the zone, since it was risky that humanitarian sources had discovered that a member of the special forces from the First Infantry Brigade had been infiltrated into the Atlacatl Battalion."[52]

When family members of the detained and assassinated suspects came looking for their relatives, Joya "told [them] that the detainees were [being held] in the [First] Infantry Brigade, and that one had been killed at ... Tres Ceibas." For that, Major Diaz Hernandez reprimanded him, "since people and relatives of the detainees were sure that the deceased terrorist had been captured by the Atlacatl Battalion." He admonished Joya that he "needed to be hidden by the department's personal security." Through another member of the death squad, Joya learned he was to be "hidden" by being assassinated in a U.S.-supplied van. He deserted.[53]

Spokesmen for the U.S. State Department, the Salvadoran embassy, and the INS told me that Joya Martinez was not a credible witness. They said he was wanted in El Salvador as a suspect in the murder of two people—Lucio Parada and Joaquin Miranda Marroquin. The State Department added that Joya's unit was suspected of killing "at least seventy" people.[54]

After Joya Martinez told his story to U.S. newspapers, the INS rearrested him. Joya Martinez is the only Salvadoran ever arrested while out on bond and charged with criminal reentry to seek asylum. Entry without inspection is not a crime—it is a civil violation. The Border Patrol arrested more than 100,000 undocumented Salvadorans between 1981 and 1990. Those who commit a crime while out on bond or who fail to appear for a hearing after bonding out can be rearrested and placed under a higher bond, usually $10,000. Of those 100,000 cases, only once did the INS rearrest a Salvadoran asylum applicant and charge him with criminal reentry, though he had committed no crime and had not missed a hearing. He was simply waiting for his asylum trial. It is difficult to avoid the conclusion that Joya Martinez's mistake was to get his name in the papers. The INS locked him up, raised his bond to $10,000, kept him away from the press, and put him on a plane to El Salvador, where he was sent to Mariona prison.[55]

By then, another member of Joya Martinez's death squad had confirmed his story. The woman, whose code name was Blanca, named her supervisor as Cesar Joya Martinez. Blanca, who also spoke to the Mexican Human Rights Commission, said she was paid $100 a month, plus "bonuses." She had given the First Infantry Brigade the names of six people they later arrested, interrogated, and killed. She also worked for two American advisers in the First Infantry Brigade, and in the towns of Tres Ceibas, Apopa, and Aguilares. After her victims were killed, "I sometimes went to their funerals and reported on who was there and what was said," Blanca told the *Boston Globe*. She reported that Joya Martinez showed her orders for the arrest and interrogation of suspects and that the orders were "usually signed by Maj. Diaz Hernandez."[56]

All these statements are consistent with what death squad deserters had told me since 1984: that they had injected "suspected terrorists" with LSD, tortured them with electroshock, and subjected them to mock executions—lining them up against a wall and firing at them with blanks; the "preferred methods" of assassination were strangulation, cutting the throat, and decapitation, which left no telltale bullets that could be traced to army-issued weapons.[57]

Most death squad members, understandably, had little interest in talking about what they did. Neither did the Justice Department. Except for Joya Martinez, whom the INS denounced as unreliable and whom the State Department accused of participating in "at least seventy" murders, the INS and State Department had a standard response to questions about death squads: They refused to discuss any cases, "in order to protect the applicant."[58]

The Exodus Begins

By the winter of 1988–1989, most Central Americans in Brownsville probably did not meet the statutory definition for political asylum. Most were Nicaraguans. Few of the hundreds of Nicaraguans I spoke with claimed they would be singled out for persecution because of their "race, religion, nationality, political opinion, or social group." They came because they knew Nicaraguans would be welcome in the United States. The Salvadorans and Guatemalans kept coming even though they knew they would not.

In a cold, dark suite of rooms on the second floor of the Amber Motel lived four women, all of them eight months pregnant. More women lived in nearby rooms with babies, many of whom were sick. Cándida Echavarría from Nicaragua had been arrested with her husband David and their three children, ages six, seven, and eight. "The Mexican immigration arrested us at San Fernando [near Matamoros]," David said. "They took all our money from us, $2,500."[59]

The U.S. Border Patrol arrested the Echavarrías before they found out where to apply for asylum. They could leave South Texas if they paid the $3,000 travel bond, but that money was gone. Cándida planned to have her baby at the Amber Motel.

With her was Wendy Raquel Sanchez, who had been living at the Amber Motel for more than a month when I met her in January 1989. Her thirteen-month-old son was sick. "He has an eye infection. They are stuck together," she told me. The baby's eyes were red with conjunctivitis. There was no money for medicine.

Carolina Lamuza from Nicaragua also planned to have her baby at the Amber Motel. "We can do nothing because we do not know how to defend ourselves from the Immigration. If they would let us work, so we could defend ourselves ..." Her voice trailed off.

The Amber Motel was in bankruptcy proceedings, and the city of Brownsville was the trustee. To evict the refugees, Brownsville would have had to sue itself. On January 6, as another cold front approached, city health inspectors nailed a notice to the door frames and windowsills of the Amber Motel that the city would demolish the building if the health hazards were not removed. That day, the U.S. Housing and Urban Development agency approved $41,000 in emergency funding to house Brownsville refugees—somewhere.[60]

Also that day, a Friday, refugee advocates sued U.S. Attorney General Richard Thornburgh and INS Commissioner Alan Nelson in Brownsville federal court. The class action lawsuit claimed that INS had no legal right to confine asylum applicants to the Harlingen INS District; that INS policies implemented under the December 5 memo denied asylum seekers the right to counsel by restricting their travel, denying them work permits, and speeding up INS decisions on their asylum claims; and that the new policies violated the Administrative Procedures Act, which requires that new laws and regulations that will significantly affect the public be printed in the Federal Register and that a thirty-day period of public comment be offered before the new regulations take effect. "The substance of the policy is debatable, the procedures are not," Proyecto Libertad attorney Mark Schneider said. "What's clear is they have violated the Administrative Procedures Act."[61]

"I'm not sure that there is legal authority to restrict [the movement of] people that aren't even in [deportation] proceedings," commented Robert Rubin, attorney for the Lawyers' Committee on Urban Affairs in San Francisco, co-counsel in the suit.[62] The lawsuit requested a temporary restraining order to rescind the new INS policies, at least until the requirements of the Administrative Procedures Act could be satisfied.

The INS denied there had been any real policy change at all. "We have a right to require them to stay within a geographical boundary," INS spokesman Duke Austin asserted. "To be in detention doesn't mean that you have to be behind a fence."[63] Judge Filemon Vela scheduled a hearing for Monday, January 9.

On Sunday, Cameron County sheriff's deputies posted No Trespassing signs on the field by Casa Romero and gave about 300 refugees twenty-four hours' notice to leave the property. Sheriff Alex Perez said the field was private property and that the owner had requested he do it.[64]

After hearing arguments Monday, Judge Vela restrained the INS from requiring refugees to post a travel bond, ordered the INS to let asylum seekers leave the INS Harlingen District, and prohibited the agency from enforcing the travel ban and detention policy until February 20.[65] Vela's order set off a massive exodus of refugees from Brownsville.

Trailways added five bus runs a day to Miami. The manager of the Trailways bus station said more than 750 Central Americans per day bought bus tickets from Brownsville to Miami during the week of January 9 to 13.[66] Miami city officials opened Bobby Maduro Stadium to refugees, then closed it within a day when more than 250 Nicaraguans showed up.[67] The Nicaraguans had to leave the stadium by January 25, when the Baltimore Orioles would begin spring training.

The exodus from Brownsville gained impetus when U.S. Representative Solomon Ortiz announced on the afternoon of Judge Vela's court hearing that just two of the first 272 asylum applications filed under the new expedited procedures had been granted. Overnight, the approval rate for Nicaraguan asylum applicants had dropped from 53 percent to 1 percent.[68]

The Amber Motel

On Tuesday, January 10, the Brownsville City Commission voted to close the Amber Motel for health code violations. City workers rousted the refugees and cleaned and sealed shut the Amber Motel Wednesday afternoon. The workers carried garbage and burned-out television sets from the rooms and threw everything into the empty swimming pool. Police officers were a polite presence. City buses took about 120 refugees to five Brownsville churches that opened their doors as temporary shelters.[69]

Refugees who thought Brownsville was the coldest place they had ever been set out without a cent or a change of clothes to hitchhike to Chicago. Oscar David, twenty, from El Salvador, slung a homemade knapsack over his shoulder. "I'm going to Houston, however God takes me, on foot, a ride," he said. David had fought in the Salvadoran army for three years. He left El Salvador January 2 because "there are guerrilla everywhere."[70]

I went to St. Mary's Church as the evacuation continued. Refugees lay on cots and blankets on the floor of the parish hall and talked about how to get out of Brownsville. Father Gilbert Borja, the church deacon, reported that there had been no problems, but he didn't know how long people would be allowed to stay. On the floor, the word was that they would have to leave by Saturday. An elderly Honduran woman, Zoila Noemi Ventura, wanted to go to Miami, but she didn't know how to get to Harlingen to file her papers. "I'm just like *el chonte* [a Honduran bird]. He opens his mouth to sing, '*Pío, pío, pío.*' They give him a little something in his beak, and that's it."

The Crisis Spreads

On Friday the thirteenth, Miami City Manager Cesar Odio and Dade County Assistant Manager Tony Ojeda came to Brownsville to warn Central Americans to expect no help in Miami. "I think the refugees here need to know the refugee services in Miami are exhausted," Ojeda said. "There seems to be this feeling that if you get to Miami, you can get everything. You can't. We don't have anything. ... Miami INS is not issuing work permits. We just want everyone to understand that we won't be able to cope if they come. We just don't have the resources. They could end up in the streets. It's going to be the same in Miami as it is here, maybe worse."

"The inn is full," Odio said.[71]

It was no use. The word had gone out in 1986, when Miami INS District Director Perry Rivkind stopped deporting Nicaraguans from Miami, and again in 1987 when Meese approved the issuance of work permits.[72] The lawsuits, restraining orders, temporary injunctions, and constantly changing detention policies in the winter of 1988–1989 had no immediate effect on the refugee flow. Refugees arrived and left Brownsville by the thousands. More than 8,000 people requested political asylum at the Harlingen INS office in January.[73]

On Saturday, January 14, about 100 refugees moved into the TRICO building on Iowa Avenue, an abandoned windshield-wiper factory a mile from Casa Romero. The American Red Cross announced it would take responsibility for housing the refugees. Texas's Republican Governor Bill Clements said he would not spend a penny to help South Texas deal with refugee housing or health problems. "It is a local problem and it should be addressed by Cameron County," Clements said. Cameron was the only county in the United States that was supposed to have its own foreign policy.[74]

By January 16, 290 refugees were sleeping on army cots and on the concrete floor of the TRICO building. The next day in Miami, a black motorcyclist was shot to death by a city policeman; riots erupted in which two people died.[75] Black community leaders pointed to Bobby Maduro Stadium, complaining that the U.S. government was helping refugees but mistreating and killing its own citizens.[76] Miami's Nicaraguan community of 100,000 clamored for public assistance for the new immigrants, and their ideological soul mates, the politically powerful Cubans, supported them. The refugee problem had become a national issue.

Harlingen Gets Washington's Attention

As the ashes cooled in Miami on Friday, the owner of the TRICO building in Brownsville gave the refugees four days to vacate. The Red Cross looked for a new shelter and found some abandoned, red-brick U.S. Department of Agriculture buildings by the Rio Grande that had once stored pesticides. The buildings are a block south of the Fort Brown Hotel & Resort, one of Brownsville's major tourist centers. The refugees moved into the buildings by Fort Brown, where Red Cross volunteers would house them for more than a year and face the same abuses and uncertainties as the refugees: midnight wake-ups and searches by the Border Patrol and conflicting statements from INS officials about the legality of the Red Cross services.[77]

On January 31, Judge Vela held a hearing on his restraining order against the INS and decided to let it stand for twenty more days. Vela was inclined to let the INS begin its detention policy on February 20. On the night of January 31, the Brownsville City Commission passed a resolution asking the federal and state governments for help in housing the refugees and safeguarding the health of immigrants and citizens in the lower Rio Grande Valley.

Governor Clements had refused to help, and the federal government did not respond to the city resolution, so the mayors of Brownsville, Harlingen, and San Benito met with the county's top official, Cameron County Judge Tony Garza Jr., on February 3. Garza emerged from the meeting calling for a response from the federal government "by Friday [February 10]." Failing this, Garza said, he and the mayors had "formulated a more aggressive plan to elicit some sort of federal response ... something that will get the attention of the federal government."[78]

The only federal official to address the problem was Texas Senator Lloyd Bentsen, who wrote a letter to U.S. Attorney General Richard Thornburgh, asking that he allow refugees to leave South Texas. "It is clear that the current INS policy will turn South Texas into a massive detention camp,". Bentsen wrote. "Operating costs will be paid not by the federal government but by citizens, churches, charitable organizations and local governments in one of the poorest regions of the nation."[79] He recalled the federal government had provided emergency impact aid to South Florida during the

Cuban refugee crisis in 1980 and felt it should provide emergency aid to South Texas now.

Neither Bentsen nor Tony Garza got a reply. The streets were still in chaos. Border Patrol officers in the McAllen Sector had arrested 7,055 people in January, of whom 1,933 were "other than Mexican." OTMs arrested in South Texas are overwhelmingly Central Americans. The INS reported that 755 people had been released on their own recognizance in January and ordered to stay in the lower Rio Grande Valley, 319 were imprisoned at the INS detention center at Bayview, and the Red Cross was housing more than 300 near Fort Brown. Arrests of OTMs increased in early February. There was no sign that the refugee crisis was ending.[80]

On February 10, the South Texas mayors got the attention of the U.S. government. The city of Harlingen evicted the INS from its offices on Teege Boulevard for health code violations. More than 300 people had been camping outside the building to hold their places in the asylum line. There were no restroom facilities outdoors. Business owners in a shopping plaza across the street had complained that the chaos frightened away customers. Harlingen officials chained and locked the doors to the INS buildings Friday morning. The INS had to send its employees home.[81]

The INS refused to accept asylum applications that day. Every time the agency refused to accept an asylum application from a Salvadoran, the INS and the city of Harlingen violated the federal court orders in *Orantes-Hernandez v. Thornburgh* and *Nuñez v. Boldin*. Yet what was Harlingen to do? It was the first haven for Central Americans in the United States. Refugees were sleeping on concrete in the rain; they roamed the streets from Brownsville to Donna. Thousands more were packing their bags in Central America and heading north.

"You ought to see the lines at the immigration office," Patrick Hughes telephoned from San Salvador. "The lines are half a block long. They are issuing 600 passports a day." Hughes had gotten the number from the Salvadoran passport office. Three thousand Salvadorans a week were seeking passports to escape the war legally.[82]

Hughes was working with the Non-Governmental Human Rights Commission, accompanying Salvadoran human rights workers on the theory that the presence of a U.S. citizen might protect them from persecution from the Salvadoran government. "A whole combination of things is making people think this is the time to get out," Hughes said. The Lutheran church in San Salvador had been bombed on December 28. The homes of the dean and vice dean of the College of Humanities of the University of Central America were bombed two weeks later. A medical student was killed January 16. Two other medical students were abducted that day; two headless corpses appeared in the street two days later. "A good friend of mine disappeared Sunday [January 15]," Hughes said. Pablo Martinez, a

member of the Non-Governmental Human Rights Commission, was captured by heavily armed civilians and driven off in a van with tinted windows, the trademark vehicle of death squads. He had not been seen since.

Hughes said the flow of Salvadorans returning from the United States
had increased support for the right-wing ARENA party, which controlled
the country's legislative assembly. "ARENA slashed by two-thirds the fees
people have to pay for license plates for their vehicles [brought back from
the United States]," Hughes noted. Many Salvadorans residing legally in
the United States purchase used cars and pickup trucks for resale in El Salvador at three or four times the purchase price. ARENA also passed legislation allowing Salvadorans to bring in up to $400 worth of audio and video
equipment, which can be quickly resold. "ARENA is facilitating profit-
making on the whole refugee experience," Hughes explained, "and it's un-
derstandable. It turns people's eyes away from what's happening here.
They're all going to the U.S., they think."

A study from the University of Central America in San Salvador—written
by one of the Jesuit priests who would be murdered one year later—estimated that money orders sent to El Salvador from the United States provided more national income than the coffee crop. People had replaced coffee as El Salvador's most valuable export.[83] "Here in this country these
people are called patriots," Hughes said, "because they make money and
send it back, and that keeps the country afloat."

> In my neighborhood last week the FMLN said you'd better start storing beans,
> sugar, and water because there are going to be hard battles in the neighbor-
> hood. In my apartment building you see people bringing in big plastic tanks
> that store an extra twenty or thirty gallons of water. People take it very seri-
> ously. There's no question there's going to be an increased flow of Salvadorans.
> There are big numbers heading to the States.[84]

Hondurans Join the Exodus

The INS does not keep track of the number of Hondurans it arrests, but
Hondurans were coming in increasing numbers—hungry farmers, refugees
from Contra territory by the Nicaraguan border, and deserters from the
Honduran army, the guerrilla, and the Contras. I interviewed eight Hondurans at the Red Cross shelter on January 31, 1989. Esteban, twenty-
three, lamented that crime and instability had increased in Honduras since
the Contra army began disintegrating. "You can buy a machine gun for
twenty lempiras [$7.15] at the border" from Contra deserters.[85]

Hunger and poverty had driven two farmers, Álvaro and Deras, from
Honduras. They each earned five lempiras a day as farmworkers [2.80 lempiras equal $1.00]. A liter of milk cost .50 lempiras; a pound of sugar .80

lempiras. They each had paid 1,500 Guatemalan quetzales to a Guatemalan *coyote* who took them to Matamoros with fifty other Central Americans: five Hondurans, eight Salvadorans, and thirty-nine Guatemalans.[86] "He does two trips a month," Deras said, "on the first and the fifteenth."

The *coyote* had promised them life would be grand in the United States, that they could work. "What he promised us was marvelous," Álvaro said. "Then he dumped us in Matamoros and we came here and found we cannot work." They never would have left Honduras had they not heard the INS was issuing work permits. Many of the Hondurans had borrowed the money from relatives for their journey, so their unsuccessful trip north had the effect of further impoverishing entire families.

Two men named Hector, twenty-three and nineteen, came together from Atlántida Province. Mexican soldiers robbed them of all their money and their extra clothes in Tapachula. They came the rest of the way "walking, asking for rides and food, fleeing the soldiers."

Régulo, forty-six, also from Atlántida, fled because he had collaborated with the Honduran army in spying on two guerrilla groups that live in the mountains, the Morazan Front and the Cinchoneros. He received anonymous threatening letters from the guerrilla. "I couldn't go to another country in Central America because there is war in El Salvador, and in Nicaragua it's the same, and in Guatemala there are guerrilla too."

Annual per capita income in Honduras was $640—$12 a week. Sixty percent of the people were illiterate. Life expectancy was forty-nine years, and half of the children in rural areas died before they reached age five.[87]

"We in Honduras like Americans," Francisco said. "A lot of them go to the ruins [of Copán], and we're glad to see them. There are Americans all over Honduras. The United States protects our country. But if you try to talk to an American here, he turns you over to the *migra*."

None of the Hondurans planned to come back to the United States. "It's a sad journey through Mexico," Francisco said. "I would not come back. I've suffered enough on this voyage. If they deport me, I hope they do it by plane, so I won't have to go through Mexico again."

The Plan for the Southern Border

Judge Vela ordered Harlingen to let the INS back into its offices on Monday, February 13.[88] Three days later, in another unpublished memo, the INS outlined the massive detention project that would begin February 21. The "INS Enhancement Plan for the Southern Border" noted that "asylum claims in Harlingen, Texas have risen from 400 per month in spring of 1988 to over 400 a day since January 15."

The high number of requests at the Harlingen District Office is expected to continue. ... The flow has strained INS resources in south Texas to its limits and adversely impacted operations in major cities like Los Angeles and Miami. The influx has raised serious public health and economic concerns in the areas of the U.S. which have been affected. Citizen discontent at the affected locations has visibly grown, particularly in Harlingen and Miami. The response to the situation so far has done little to discourage additional migration.[89]

The plan called for the INS to increase the capacity of Los Fresnos prison from 425 to 5,000 by erecting huge tents. Asylum applicants were to be interviewed and given a decision within three hours; those denied asylum would immediately be incarcerated. The agency would send more than 500 immigration officers from around the country to South Texas, including 269 Border Patrolmen, 30 prison guards, 215 asylum adjudicators, and 15 anti-smuggling agents. The INS would "mount an aggressive ... campaign for the media, general public, and Congress ... [to] make a clear case against entry without inspection, even when followed by a claim for asylum."[90]

INS officers at the *corralón* would use the "quick profile of apprehended Central Americans" that was ordered in the December 5 memo and share the information with the CIA, the Defense Intelligence Agency, and the State Department; they would set up at the immigration prison "mechanisms for ... communicating with foreign governments," though INS and State Department officials have always said that information in political asylum applications is confidential.[91]

The February 16 "Enhancement Plan" shows that the INS planned to interview 400 applicants a day and decide 96 percent of their cases "within three hours of completion of the interview."

This includes initial review of the complete application (I-589, G-325, and FD-258), entry into the Central Index System and file creation, interview, preparation of interview summary and request for an advisory opinion, review of asylum application by BHRHA [the State Department's Bureau of Human Rights and Humanitarian Affairs] and preparation of an advisory opinion, completion of adjudication by a second examiner, review and signature of final decision by supervisor, and presentation of decision to the alien.[92]

To "maintain high level quality control of asylum adjudication process, all detailed officers will receive one day of specialized asylum training."[93] A videotape of a State Department employee training INS employees in how to adjudicate asylum applications shows how the *corralón* was turned into a deportation mill. The tape was made at an INS training session in Los Angeles.[94] On the tape, Mark McCleggen of the State Department's Bureau of Human Rights told INS "special adjudicators" who were about to be assigned to Los Fresnos to "go with" State Department policy rather than consider asylum claims on their merits. McCleggen added that there was "a running joke" about Salvadorans killed in the civil war. He said the most "popular" claim Salvadorans make for asylum is "'My cousin was killed by the guerrillas in 1982.' We have a running joke back at the Bureau that there are no cousins left in El Salvador."[95]

An INS employee asked McCleggen what to do if refugees described credible incidents of persecution by a government friendly to the United States. McCleggen's videotaped reply was, "Stick with the State Department response."

The State Department representative told INS examiners they "have to assume" refugees will "adjust the truth or exaggerate" their claims of persecution. He even gave refugees a time limit within which to die. One asylum applicant, for example, reported that his mother, brother, and sister had been killed in successive months. In the videotape, McCleggen dismissed his testimony: "This person was denied. People are taken away by death squads, but it wouldn't happen within a matter of months. They would kill your mother on Monday and shoot your brother on Wednesday and come for you on Thursday."

The State Department acknowledged that McCleggen went to Los Angeles in late 1988 to train an INS group. "We don't know what he said because he never returned to our office," said David Burgess, a spokesman for the Bureau of Human Rights.[96]

The "special adjudicators" who were trained during the videotaped session were put to work during the detention project at Los Fresnos.

The Detention Policy Begins

The INS announced on Tuesday, February 14, that the agency would no longer accept asylum applications in Harlingen. Beginning the next day, refugees would have to go to the *corralón* to seek asylum.[97] There is no public transportation to the prison, which is twenty-six miles from Brownsville and twenty-five miles from Harlingen.

Two hours after the new policy started, at 2 A.M. on February 15, Border Patrol agents arrested Santos Lejía, a church volunteer, as he drove twelve Central Americans to the new asylum processing station—enormous khaki army tents set up inside the fences past the checkpoint on the long driveway to the prison. The twelve Central Americans were put in the *corralón*. Lejía was told that further attempts to transport undocumented people would result in confiscation of his Chevrolet van.[98]

Proyecto Libertad attorney Mark Schneider called Lejía's arrest "insane."

This is a very blatant example of how INS is now systematically discouraging refugees from applying for asylum. When they set up the detention center, they knew it was thirty miles from Brownsville and Harlingen. They knew there was no public transportation out there. They knew the refugees would have to walk the thirty miles out there. They knew the citizens of Brownsville and Cameron County were helping the refugees, and now they are harassing and intimidating the good Samaritans for helping refugees.[99]

The U.S. Court of Appeals for the Fifth Circuit had ruled in 1985 that it is not illegal to drive undocumented people to an INS office. In overturning Stacey Merkt's conviction for driving Salvadorans to the INS office in San Antonio, the three-judge panel wrote, "Just incidental transportation [of] an illegal alien will not make you guilty of that offense [transportation]. It has to be something that furthers that person's illegal presence in the United States."[100] Still, McAllen Sector Border Patrol chief agent Silvestre Reyes insisted that he "cannot and will not ... say it's all right for people to transport illegal aliens to the asylum station," and that people who did so ran the risk of having their vehicles impounded. INS press spokesman Mario Ortiz concurred that driving refugees to the prison to apply for asylum is "a risky thing and you probably shouldn't do it." Eleazar Tovar, attorney for the Border Patrol in McAllen, was immovable: People who drive refugees to the prison "can be charged, detained, indicted, and prosecuted. Once they go before a jury, the jury may find that they were taking them to apply for political asylum; then that's a defense."[101]

Proyecto Libertad paralegal Jonathan Moore, whose job required him to drive refugees to and from the *corralón,* called the Border Patrol statements "a working definition of intimidation. They're saying, 'We can arrest you, but you can get off.' What are they arresting you for? 'We know that you're not doing anything illegal, but make sure you're not doing anything wrong next time either'?"

Lisa Brodyaga called the Border Patrol's threat to impound citizens' cars "pure harassment. I'd be happy to sue the pants off anybody for that."

Refugees didn't know what the law was. U.S. citizens didn't know what the law was, and the Border Patrol didn't care what the law was. Thousands of people were in the same murky legal situation as Cándida and David Echavarría and their three children, the Nicaraguans who had been evicted from the Amber Motel. The Border Patrol had arrested and released them under a $3,000 "travel bond." Then Judge Vela ordered the INS to let refugees travel. Yet the only INS document the Echavarrías possessed that would keep the Border Patrol from rearresting them ordered them to stay in South Texas. What would happen to them if they left Texas? Nobody knew.

Brownsville churches mounted a last-minute effort to get refugees out of South Texas before the detention policy went into effect. Gene Nunley, the director of the Red Cross shelter at Fort Brown, said on February 20, "The biggest thing for us is we fed 700 people last night, and only about 500 slept here. A couple hundred people left here."[102]

Mervyn Mosbacker Sr., a retiree and volunteer worker for Church World Service, helped collect donations to get refugees bus fare out of South Texas. His son, Mervyn Mosbacker Jr., was an assistant U.S. attorney in Brownsville: He prosecuted alien-smugglers. "We're not doing anything illegal and we're not about to," Mosbacker said. "The sad thing is that we have to make decisions on who can and who can't go because we can't serve all the people that are here. The most we can do is help the people with small children to get out of here."[103]

The miserable conditions in which refugees lived spurred church congregations who had stayed away from refugee issues to help now. "In the face of sick babies and pregnant women and people that have been so horribly abused coming through Mexico, I think it is terribly inappropriate to talk politics before you reach out a helping hand," remarked Jim Folts, rector of the Episcopal Church of the Advent, which had helped about forty asylum applicants buy bus tickets out of the Rio Grande Valley. "At first we limited ourselves to pregnant women and people that were sick, and families struggling with young children," Folts said the morning before the detention policy started. "In the past twenty-four hours we've changed our focus to people that don't have any money and want to get out. There is no benefit for the people of Central America or for the Valley for the people to stay here."[104]

Even conservative Texans who wanted to keep immigrants out of the United States understood that INS policy was hurting South Texas. The federal government had achieved the impossible: It had united the left-wing Sanctuary Movement with right-wing Protestant superpatriots—against itself. Taxi drivers and others who spoke Spanish and were willing to risk their cars charged refugees $50 a head to drive them to the *corralón,* where they were allowed to apply for asylum and travel—until Monday night, February 20.

On Tuesday morning the INS began to interview asylum applicants immediately, deny their claims, and put them in prison. The first day of the detention policy, Lázaro Ernesto Flores led the seventeen refugees staying in his trailer in a march to protest the new policy. All the refugees were arrested and put in detention at the *corralón.* Flores went home to an empty trailer. That day, 633 people were interviewed for political asylum at the *corralón.* Nearly all of them were denied, arrested, and detained. Few of them knew the INS policy had changed. Two days later, on Thursday, only ten people turned up to apply for asylum.[105]

The detention project swept Central Americans from the streets of South Texas, and as the refugees' presence became less evident, the national and international press went away.[106] Yet despite the INS press releases, Central

American immigration continued to increase. Border Patrol arrests of Central Americans in the McAllen Sector rose from 1,934 in January to 2,351 in February and 3,786 in March.[107]

Cross-Border Dragnet

As U.S.-funded warfare in Central America exacerbated the flow of immigrants, the increased Border Patrol pressure on the U.S.-Mexican border played into the hands of corrupt Mexican officials who preyed upon Central American refugees. Washington was aware that Mexican Judicial Police and immigration and customs officials stole millions of dollars from Central American refugees in the 1980s and committed innumerable acts of violence.[108] Even Central Americans traveling legally in Mexico were held up by bandits with badges.[109] The U.S. response was to provide INS officers to train Mexican police so they could arrest more of them.

On the second day of the detention policy, February 22, 1989—the day Mexican police kidnapped, robbed, and sold Veronica Coronado and her friend Wendell to the alien smuggler Raul Torres—INS Mexico City District Director E. Michael Trominski sent the first of three cables to the INS Office of Foreign Relations in Washington, D.C., describing the operations of ten INS agents working in ten cities in Mexico, Guatemala, and El Salvador.[110]

Major smugglers are chartering buses. ... A number of family-size groups, apparent Central Americans, were seen being escorted by apparent police or security guards. ... The buses reportedly stay away from the federal highways because of fear of "ripoffs" from the Federales. They use the back roads instead of the main highways. ... The smuggling operations seem to be very well coordinated. One group of aliens (38 Guatemalans and 1 El Sal) were reported to have stopped at a very small roadside stand and meals were ready for all of them. ... The group of 39 noted above was reportedly ripped off in the amount of 5M [million] pesos [U.S. $2,100] by the Federal Highway police who then called the municipal police."[111]

One of Trominski's agents was working across the river from Brownsville, in Matamoros.

The bus depot is being worked by Mexican Customs and other agencies, all on the take. The bribe situation has caused the smugglers to off-load groups outside of Matamoros and to get them downtown by other means, avoiding the bus station. ... Our FSN Investigator was approached yesterday on the streets four times by smugglers offering their services.[112]

The trail of corruption ran all the way to El Salvador.

[An] intelligence item ... from San Salvador, had specific information regarding alien smuggling by air from San Salvador to Tapachula. The information was specific, including names of pilots and aircraft tail numbers. I gave my personal observation that, if true, such an operation could not take place without some sort of "official" help.[113]

The Mexican Immigration regional delegate in Veracruz told one of Trominski's investigators that "police corruption outside of his organization was a major problem. ... He is aware of the purpose of this project and has promised to cooperate."[114] Trominski shared his agents' reports with Mexican Immigration Director General Susana Torres Hernandez.

Press reports about Trominski's memos caused a furor in Mexico. Opposition parties from the left and right blasted the ruling PRI party's acquiescence in the INS violation of Mexican sovereignty. It didn't help that Trominski's operation was revealed just days after the Mexican Immigration Service had conducted a joint operation with the U.S. Border Patrol in California. Agents from both countries swept across both sides of the border between Tijuana and San Diego on February 23. Mexican immigration agents arrested nearly 500 Mexicans in Mexico, yet had nothing to charge them with. It's not illegal for a Mexican to be near the U.S. border.[115] In trying to stop the flow of Central American refugees without stopping the wars in Central America, the U.S. government had embarrassed an important ally—the friendly administration of Mexican President Carlos Salinas de Gortari.

No End in Sight

Illegal immigration from Mexico had decreased after the 1986 Immigration Reform and Control Act, which discouraged Mexican immigration by making it illegal for undocumented people to work in the United States. Border Patrol arrests of undocumented Mexicans in each of the nine border sectors decreased by an average of 28 percent in the five-month period from January to May 1988 compared to January–May 1989. But arrests of Central Americans (OTMs) increased in every sector by an average of 72 percent. In April–May 1989, well after the South Texas detention policy had taken effect, Border Patrol arrests of OTMs in the McAllen Sector were up 85 percent from 1988, from 1,776 to 3,287.[116]

By March 1989, more than 2,000 refugees were sleeping under the tents at the *corralón*. The Brownsville Red Cross shelter held more than 1,000. For health reasons, the City Commission had restricted occupancy of the Red Cross shelter to 800, so the Red Cross opened up another shelter for 500 in San Benito, close to the original Casa Romero. Private and public agencies opened shelters for unaccompanied refugee children in Raymondville, Los Fresnos, and Mission.[117]

On March 30, Red Cross Director Gene Nunley estimated that 200 to 300 of the two Red Cross shelters' 1,078 occupants were children of school age. Many were traumatized by war. Nine-year-old Enrique Luna from Guatemala and ten-year-old James Bismark of Nicaragua argued about whose country was worse as they picked up trash in the yard and stacked it in a wheelbarrow. Luna said a cocaine dealer had just killed a lot of children in Guatemala. "Yes, but in Nicaragua it's worse than Guatemala," Bismark said. "The Contras and the Guardia kill people and then go up to the mountains. They have food and clothes, but they come and kill you and steal your clothes and shoes and leave you naked, and then go back to the mountains."[118]

Family unity was a "high priority" for the INS, and families would not be separated, INS Commissioner Alan Nelson assured in an appearance in Brownsville.[119] But the INS began dropping off children and babies at the Red Cross shelter and locking up their parents at the *corralón* on the day the detention policy began. Blanca Nubia Lagos, twenty, from Nicaragua, was sent to prison while her twenty-month-old baby was left at the Red Cross shelter in the care of friends. Otilia Sarmiento, sixty-seven, from Honduras, was separated from her daughters and six-month-old grandchild and sent to the *corralón*. Marco Antonio Zeledon, forty-five, a high school principal from Nicaragua, was arrested and detained, yet his wife and children were turned over to the Red Cross.[120]

Lady Dinorah Borjas, twenty, was ordered deported with her four-month-old son, Luis, a U.S. citizen. The INS cannot legally deport a U.S. citizen, but INS spokeswoman Virginia Kice said she expected Luis would "want to return" to Central America with his mother, even though the INS had no legal power to deport him. "That happens to Mexican children all the time," Kice said.[121]

Refugees who were denied asylum at their brief interviews had the right to request a hearing before an immigration judge, but they didn't know that, and the INS didn't tell them. Borjas showed me a form letter that denied her request for asylum. "There is no appeal from this decision," the letter stated, in English. "You may renew your request for asylum or apply for benefit of section 243(h) of the Immigration and Nationality Act in subsequent proceedings before an immigration judge."[122] Borjas and three women with identical letters said they had no idea what the letters meant. "It means deportation," Borjas said. "I don't know what it means. They just said to sign it and that was it."[123]

Otilia Sarmiento, Borjas's mother-in-law, said their family had fled from Choluteca, Honduras, a town near the Nicaraguan border used as a refuge by the Contras. The family went through the asylum interview without a lawyer and had no idea what had happened. Sarmiento said the INS officers told her, "The asylum they were giving me was the roof and the bed and the food they were giving me in the *corralón*. They explained nothing to me."

The System Breaks Down

More than 200 refugees stood in line for hours at the Brownsville Red Cross shelter on February 28. The INS had sent "processing officers" to "explain asylum procedures" to them.[124] I talked to more than 100 people in line. None of them knew what they were waiting for. I wormed my way into the interview room as the INS official in charge shouted an order in English: "Tell those people to wait for the bus and to get on the bus when it comes. Don't tell them anything more." The bus took them to detention at the *corralón*.

Inside the camp, confusion reigned. A Guatemalan woman died in the camp that day under circumstances that were never made clear.[125] Deportations began March 5 from the airstrip by the *corralón*. Two hundred seventy-eight Central Americans were deported that month, mostly Salvadorans, none Nicaraguan. The INS cut off media access to the prison when deportations began because of "an increase of tension within the camp," INS spokeswoman Virginia Kice said. The prison population was 2,002 on March 9; Kice said new arrivals averaged 200 a day.[126]

More than 500 deportation hearings a day were scheduled at seven courts in the prison and in Harlingen.[127] There were six de facto detention centers in the lower Rio Grande Valley; some detainees had been sent to Laredo or El Paso. A Border Patrol officer assigned to bring thirty-eight unaccompanied children to the Harlingen immigration court on March 22 could find only eight of them. "They've got people everywhere. They don't know where people are," the officer in charge of scheduling court hearings said in frustration. Refugees were ordered deported for "failing to appear" at a hearing because the INS couldn't find them in order to bring them to court.[128]

In the crowded hallway of the INS building in Harlingen I met Bert Bosnans, an attorney for the South Texas Immigration Council. An immigration judge had just told Bosnans that he would not advise anyone of his right to free legal services unless Bosnans "was willing to represent all of them. He said he didn't want any impediment to these people going back home. He said it would be an impediment if they had free legal services."[129]

Immigration judges speaking on the record in court hearings tried to dissuade Salvadorans from seeking asylum and misrepresented U.S. law to them. I sat through three asylum hearings in Harlingen on March 22. In two of them the immigration judge ordered Salvadorans deported without telling them they had the right to request asylum—a violation of the *Orantes-Hernandez* injunction. In the third hearing, José, twenty-five, from the guerrilla stronghold of Morazan, told the judge that if he was deported, he'd prefer to be deported to Belize, because of the war in El Salvador. (Political asylum applicants who are denied asylum have the right to request deportation to a third country so long as it is not contiguous to the United States.)

The judge said if the man wanted asylum he would have to submit an application in English and wait for a court date. "I'm not sure when that would be, but the last hearing I scheduled was two months in the future. You might be able to get to Belize faster by getting deported to El Salvador and then getting yourself to Belize."

José said, "If it's a problem, then I'll return to my country."

The judge ruled the man "made a knowing, conscious decision not to apply for asylum." He was deported to El Salvador.[130]

As the deportations and the prison trials continued, attorneys from Texas and California sued the INS for contempt of court. The March 30 lawsuit cited wholesale violations of the *Orantes-Hernandez* order, including mass deportations of Salvadorans, denial of access to attorneys, and immigration judges' refusal to inform detained Salvadorans of their right to request political asylum.[131] Judge Kenyon scheduled a hearing on the contempt motion for April 4 in Los Angeles. On that day, the INS had 635 deportation hearings scheduled in Los Fresnos and Harlingen.[132]

As the *Orantes-Hernandez* hearing continued in Judge Kenyon's court on April 6, an INS attorney dragged a Guatemalan asylum applicant from a courtroom in the *corralón* and deported him in defiance of the immigration judge's order to close the man's case and release him. "I believe he wanted to apply for asylum," immigration judge Charles Auslander said. "He was certainly not under an order of deportation."[133]

The detainee, Efraín Martinez Cabrera, was taken to an asylum hearing in a prison courtroom on April 6. Auslander said the INS trial attorney, Mike Ochoa, could not find a case file or an order of arrest for Martinez, so the judge found no basis to detain him. He ordered Martinez released and told him to talk with a Proyecto Libertad paralegal in the courtroom.

Judge Auslander, the paralegal, and an attorney present in the courtroom said Ochoa physically prevented Martinez from talking with the paralegal, then dragged him from the courtroom back into prison with the help of a prison guard. Martinez was put on a bus to the Houston airport at 5 A.M. the next morning and deported to Guatemala.

"I don't know how that could have happened ... even though I said there was no order of deportation," Auslander said. After Ochoa and the guard forcibly removed Martinez, Auslander canceled court hearings for the rest of the day and reported Ochoa to Chief Immigration Judge William Robie in Washington, D.C.[134]

The INS was transferring judges and trial attorneys to Los Fresnos from all over the country. Even INS prosecutors were outraged by what was happening at the *corralón*. An INS prosecutor reported Ochoa's behavior to me calling it "unconstitutional."[135] Similar abuses occurred in other judges' courts. On the day Judge Auslander refused to hold any more deportation hearings, he and two other immigration judges at the *corralón* closed the cases of about sixty detainees and ordered the INS to release them either because the INS could not produce arrest orders for them or because the judges found the arrest orders illegal. The INS refused to release any.[136]

Mark Schneider, Martinez's attorney, described the events of April 6 as an indication of "the contempt of INS for the court system. [Martinez] turned himself in willingly, asked for asylum ... and got deported, even though he had a judge's order releasing him. This is the ultimate proof that INS is not willing to obey the law. Their intent is to deport people in spite of the law. This is a rogue operation down here. Why have judges if INS can ignore them and just do what they want?"[137]

On April 28, Judge Kenyon ordered the INS to stop deporting Salvadorans from the *corralón* unless they had been advised of their legal rights by an attorney not connected with the INS. Kenyon cited an April 20 deportation of 120 detainees carried out at 4 A.M. on a privately chartered jet to rule that a court order was necessary "to prevent irreparable harm."

> As an indication that detainees are not being advised of their rights in any meaningful manner, the Court has learned that out of a group of 67 Salvadorans deported on April 20, 1989, *none* were represented by counsel at their deportation hearings. The Court finds it difficult to believe that each of these individuals learned of and knowingly and effectively waived his or her right to asylum.[138]

Kenyon's order allowed Proyecto Libertad workers to enter the tent city at the prison and hold group meetings to tell detainees their legal rights. After they learned their rights, the detainees were given a hearing, denied asylum, and deported. The INS kept its perfect record of never granting asylum to a Salvadoran detained in the Harlingen District.

A Decade of Abuse

The South Texas detention project was the culmination of a decade of illegal policies and led directly to the final decision in *Orantes-Hernandez v. Thornburgh* and an even more sweeping decision in *American Baptist Churches v. Thornburgh*. A three-judge court of appeals unanimously upheld Kenyon's final order in *Orantes-Hernandez* on November 20, 1990. The appeals court found that Kenyon had ordered the INS on June 2, 1982, to refrain from its practice of "routinely coercing Salvadorans to 'voluntarily depart' the United States in lieu of exercising their rights to a deportation hearing and to seek political asylum." Kenyon had found in 1982 that the INS was "failing to advise Salvadorans of their right to seek political asylum within the United States and was interfering with, or preventing, Salvadorans from exercising their right to assistance of counsel ... and [placing] Salvadorans in solitary confinement without notice and a hearing." Nonetheless, "despite the existence of the preliminary injunction, the INS continued to engage in a pattern and practice of coercion and that the members of the plaintiff class continued to be prevented from exercising their rights both to apply for asylum and to obtain counsel."[139]

Judge Kenyon's final order, upheld by the appeals court, explicitly states the dangers faced by Salvadoran deportees, including "arbitrary arrest, short term detention, torture including the use of electric shock, *capucha,* beatings, rape, 'disappearance,' extra-judicial executions, abductions, threats against family members, intimidation, forced ingestion of food, false imprisonment, mock executions, sleep deprivation, mass killings, and forced relocations."[140] Kenyon's order describing abuses by Salvadoran and U.S. authorities continues for sixty-three pages.

The appeals court found the INS

> forced or tricked [Salvadorans] into signing for voluntary departure ... told [a Salvadoran] she had to sign and if she did not she would remain in jail for a long time ... told [another Salvadoran] that asylum was only for people who were fleeing their country because they were an enemy of the government or an assassin ... told [a Salvadoran woman] that political asylum "wasn't given" in the United States, and that if she did not sign for voluntary departure she was going to be in detention for a long time in a jail where there "were only men" ... that if she asked for asylum, the money she posted for her bail would be lost and she would be returned to El Salvador; another agent told her that the information she gave them would be sent to El Salvador. ... the INS agent grabbed [another Salvadoran woman's] hand and physically forced her to make an X as her signature on Form I-274 [requesting "voluntary repatriation"] ... the court found that INS agents were misrepresenting eligibility for asylum, telling class members that information on the applications would be sent to El Salvador, and threatening to transfer class members to remote locations if they exercised their right to request a hearing or to apply for asylum. ... It is significant that the government offered no contradictory evidence to suggest these events did not occur.[141]

The appeals court order continues in this vein for forty-five pages.

One month after the U.S. Court of Appeals for the Ninth Circuit upheld Kenyon's order in *Orantes-Hernandez,* the Justice Department settled the case of *American Baptist Churches v. Thornburgh.* The case overturned every denial of asylum to a Salvadoran or Guatemalan who had sought refuge in the United States under the Reagan administration and under the administration of George Bush until October 1, 1990.[142] *American Baptist Churches v. Thornburgh* overturned more than 100,000 decisions by U.S. immigration judges—more judicial decisions than any other case in U.S. history. As in *Orantes-Hernandez,* a federal judge wrote a stinging rebuke to Justice Department policies that originated in the office of the U.S. attorney general and the White House.

But the refugee crisis was not over yet. Civil war continued in El Salvador, and the United States continued to arm and train Salvadoran death squads. The court order in *American Baptist Churches v. Thornburgh* guaranteed safe haven only to Salvadorans and Guatemalans who had entered the United States by October 1, 1990. It guaranteed nothing to the refugees who continued to arrive. The decade of the 1980s ended, as it had begun, with the Salvadoran army murdering priests and the U.S. embassy and State Department trying to cover it up.

Notes

1. U.S. Attorney General Edwin Meese III created the Nicaraguan Asylum Review Unit on July 2, 1987, to prevent Nicaraguans from being deported. Political asylum applications from Nicaraguans whose claims were denied were sent to the office, which could overturn the denial and grant asylum, or in an absolutely meritless case, simply hold the application indefinitely, enabling the applicant to stay in the United States. Nicaraguans are the only nationality protected by such an agency.

2. Throughout President Reagan's two terms, officials in the State and Justice Departments defended the U.S. government's policy of deporting Salvadorans by arguing that Salvadorans were economic migrants who came to the United States in search of work rather than refugees who came to save their lives. Cecilio Ruiz, assistant director for detention and deportation in the Harlingen INS District, summarized their curious assessment: "Of course they come here to look for work. They look for work here because there's war there." Cecilio Ruiz, interview with the author, December 1988, Port Isabel Service and Processing Center, Bayview, Texas (the *corralón*).

3. For example, the Honduran National Investigatory Police, DIN, were implicated in the torture and assassination of numerous Honduran union organizers and members of the political opposition. More than eighty people disappeared after being abducted by security forces from 1981 to 1984, Americas Watch reported in "Honduras: On the Brink, A Report on Human Rights Based on a Mission of Inquiry," written in conjunction with the Lawyers Committee for International Human Rights and the Washington Office on Latin America, February 1984.

4. Commission for the Study of International Migration and Cooperative Economic Development, "Unauthorized Migration: An Economic Development Re-

sponse" (Washington, D.C.), xv, July 1990. Congress created the commission and ordered it to write the report as part of the 1986 Immigration Reform and Control Act.

5. Associated Press, "Immigration Rules Are Eased for Nicaraguan Exiles in U.S.," *New York Times,* July 9, 1987. The INS announced the new policy in a press release on July 8, 1987. The two-page press release states: "No Nicaraguan who has a well-founded fear of persecution will be deported in the absence of a finding by the Justice Department that the individual has either engaged in serious criminal activity or poses a danger to the national security;

"Every qualified Nicaraguan seeking a work authorization will be entitled to one, and all INS officials are directed to encourage and expedite Nicaraguan applications for work authorizations;

"INS officials will encourage Nicaraguans whose claims for asylum or withholding of deportation have been denied to reapply for reopening or rehearing of such claims ..."

In numerous interviews with the author, INS officials have denied there is a memo of July 7, 1987, ordering INS to grant Nicaraguan asylum applicants work permits and protection from deportation. However, a December 5, 1988, memo from the INS deputy commissioner states: "The Meese memorandum of July 7, 1987, does not require automatic granting of work authorization to asylum applicants whose claims are frivolous." "Nicaraguan Asylum/Harlingen Situation."

6. Statistics on arrests, deportations, and voluntary repatriations are from the U.S. Immigration and Naturalization Service Office of Statistics in Washington, D.C.

7. Ibid. Some were "voluntarily repatriated," which is a legal term that does not mean a person returns willingly to his or her homeland. Refugees who waive the right to an asylum hearing, or anyone who does not contest the deportation process, can accept voluntary repatriation instead of deportation. The difference is that a deportee who reenters the country within five years can be charged with criminal reentry; those who are voluntarily repatriated and reenter the country are subject to the civil, not criminal, charge of entry without inspection—the same charge they faced originally.

8. In fiscal year 1987, 84 percent of Nicaraguan political asylum applications were granted; 53 percent were granted in fiscal year 1988. The acceptance rate for Salvadorans in those years was 4.5 percent and 3.6 percent, respectively. But INS statistics are notoriously unreliable; in reality, the Nicaraguan acceptance rate was higher than reported, and the Salvadoran rate was lower. The INS reported 2,684 Salvadorans sought asylum in fiscal year 1987 and 27,048 in fiscal year 1988. But only 805 Salvadoran asylum applications were adjudicated in fiscal year 1987, of which 29 were granted, and 3,932 Salvadoran applications were adjudicated in fiscal year 1988, of which 110 were granted. The actual approval rate for Salvadorans was about 1 percent. Nicaraguans were protected from deportation by INS district directors' fiat and by the Nicaraguan Asylum Review Unit, raising the de facto asylum rate for Nicaraguans to nearly 100 percent.

9. *Guillermo Perez Fuentes et al. v. Omer G. Sewell et al.,* Civil Action no. B-88-101, U.S. District Court, Brownsville, Texas, August 15, 1988.

10. Ibid.

11. Lisa Brodyaga, interview with the author, October 1988.

12. The INS policy of releasing affirmative asylum applicants on their own recognizance and ordering them to stay in the Harlingen INS District began in September 1988. As was often the case with INS policies in South Texas, no formal announcement of the new policy was made. Attorneys found out about it when their clients returned to their offices in Harlingen or Brownsville rather than being detained at the *corralón*. INS spokesmen have told the author that no document exists by which the new policy can be dated. Attorney Lisa Brodyaga, Proyecto Libertad paralegal coordinator Jonathan T. Jones, INS press spokeswoman Virginia Kice, and INS press spokesman Art Moreno, interviews with the author, 1989.

13. INS Deputy Commissioner James L. Buck, "Nicaraguan Asylum/Harlingen Situation" (memorandum to INS Executive Staff, December 5, 1988), 3–5.

14. The "Nicaraguan media strategy" stated that "responses to press inquiries on the issue of enhanced asylum processing at Harlingen are to be coordinated with the INS press information office at the Central Office [in Washington]": "Nicaraguan Asylum/Harlingen Situation," 5. The INS Central Office also was to benefit from a "local computerized databank on PCs to hold and disseminate information on all walk-in processed asylum applicants at Harlingen ..." The media strategy was further detailed on page 9 of a succeeding INS memo, "Enhancement Plan for the Southern Border" (memorandum, February 16, 1989): "Mount an aggressive, proactive information campaign for the media, general public, and Congress, both before and during enhanced operations in South Texas. Make a clear case against entry without inspection, even when followed by a claim for asylum." Page 2 of the "Enhancement Plan" suggests "a media campaign aimed toward public understanding and acceptance of the distinction between claims made from a third country and those made after entry without inspection." In other words, Salvadorans were supposed to seek asylum at the U.S. embassy in San Salvador rather than in Texas.

15. "Nicaraguan Asylum/Harlingen Situation," 5.

16. Ibid., 6.

17. Ibid., 3.

18. The four counties of southmost Texas—Cameron, Hidalgo, Starr, and Willacy—perennially have the highest unemployment rate in Texas, according to statistics released monthly by the Texas Employment Commission. Unemployment in September 1995 was 24.7 percent in Starr County, 18.6 percent in Hidalgo County, 17.4 percent in Willacy County, and 11.5 percent in Cameron County. Per capita income in 1993 in Starr County was $6,306, $10,085 in Hidalgo County, $10,092 in Willacy County, and $11,042 in Cameron County.

19. A *resaca* is a horseshoe-shaped lake, a former bed of the Rio Grande before the river's frequent floods were controlled by dams upstream. The tale of the disappearing ducks was related to the author by several refugees at the Amber Motel in January 1989.

20. Lázaro Ernesto Flores, telephone interview with the author, December 1988. Flores was discovered by *Brownsville Herald* reporter Rebecca Thatcher.

21. Ricky Gonzalez, José Rodriguez, and dozens of refugees at Casa Romero and the field north of it, interviews with the author, December 29, 1988. Robert Kahn, "Refugees Easy Marks for 'Bandits,'" *Brownsville Herald,* December 30, 1988.

22. Ibid.

23. Dozens of refugees in and around Casa Romero, and Sister Norma Pimentel, interviews with the author, January 5, 1989. Robert Kahn, "Law Requires Young Aliens Attend School," *Brownsville Herald,* January 6, 1989.

24. Ibid.; Carlos Sanchez, interview with the author, January 5, 1989. The author visited Casa Romero and the adjoining fields several times a week throughout the winter of 1988–1989. Conditions the refugees suffered are described in "Brownsville Refugees," *Z Magazine,* November 1990.

25. Lázaro Gonzalez, his wife and three children, and their neighbors in the field north of Casa Romero, interviews with the author, January 5, 1989. Kahn, "Law Requires Young Aliens Attend School."

26. More than a dozen neighbors of Casa Romero on Minnesota Avenue, Brownsville, interviews with the author, January 3, 1989. Robert Kahn, "Casa Romero's Neighbors Divided over Aliens Influx," *Brownsville Herald,* January 4, 1989.

27. Ibid.

28. Joe and Debra Ubach and three Guatemalan immigrants, interviews with the author, January 24, 1989. Robert Kahn, "Refugee Benefactors Losing Lease on Store," *Brownsville Herald,* January 25, 1989.

29. The author watched the sergeant's videotape on November 28, 1988, in the offices of Proyecto Libertad in Harlingen and interviewed Jonathan Moore, the paralegal who prepared the sergeant's case. Robert Kahn, "Salvadoran Tells About Torture by the Military," *Brownsville Herald,* November 29, 1988.

30. The author examined photocopies of the documents included in the sergeant's petition for political asylum.

31. Attorney Louis Smith, telephone interview with the author, November 29, 1988. Kahn, "Salvadoran Tells About Torture by the Military."

32. Salvadoran Non-Governmental Human Rights Commission, "Torture in El Salvador" (Ayutuxtepeque, El Salvador, September 24, 1986). Translated by Lisa Brodyaga.

33. Salvadoran sergeant, videotape interview conducted by Jonathan Moore, Harlingen, Texas.

34. Ibid.

35. Jonathan Moore, interview with the author, November 28, 1988.

36. As a reporter for the *Brownsville Herald,* the author called the offices of Texas Senators Lloyd Bentsen and Phil Gramm, U.S. Representative Solomon Ortiz, and spokesmen for the State Department, Pentagon, INS, and U.S. and Salvadoran embassies to request comments on the case of the sergeant and other death squad members and torture victims. The politicians' responses are described in the author's columns, "Killing Children Is Part of the Game Plan," *Brownsville Herald,* February 15, 1990, and "Rep. Ortiz Feels Sorry for One Person a Day," *Brownsville Herald,* March 7, 1990.

37. The author asked Texas Senator Phil Gramm and U.S. Representative Solomon Ortiz to comment on statements by death squad deserters and documents showing U.S. complicity in the murder of Salvadoran civilians. Gramm's office said not to bother sending the documents, and Ortiz refused to comment. Senator Bentsen's office requested the documents and made no public comment, though Bentsen took quiet steps to help some refugees.

38. The author attended Antonio's asylum trial in Harlingen on July 2, 1990, and also the July 9 hearing at which Judge Glenn MacPhaul rendered his decision. Robert Kahn, "17-Year-Old Salvadoran Says Army Teaches Torture," *Brownsville Herald,* July 3, 1990; and "Salvadoran Deserter Gains Asylum," *Brownsville Herald,* July 10, 1990.

39. Testimony of "Antonio," July 2, 1990, at political asylum trial in immigration judge Glenn MacPhaul's courtroom, Harlingen, Texas. Antonio was represented by Anne Marie Gibbons of Pro-Bar, a project of the Texas Bar Association.

40. Ibid.

41. Ibid.

42. Statement of INS trial attorney Agnelis Reese, July 2, 1990, in political asylum trial of Antonio, Harlingen.

43. The author was present when Judge MacPhaul rendered his decision granting Antonio political asylum on July 9, 1990, Harlingen.

44. Joya Martinez dictated a nine-page, single-spaced statement to the Mexican Academy of Human Rights in El Salvador on August 29, 1989, in Mexico City, hereafter referred to as "Joya Statement." U.S. news reports drawing on his declaration include Robert Kahn, "Salvadoran Death Squad Member Describes Operations," *Brownsville Herald,* January 23, 1990; Joe Feuerhead, "Trained to Kill in El Salvador," *National Catholic Reporter,* November 10, 1989; and Larry Bensky, "A Soldier's Story: Unanswered Questions About the Jesuit Killings," *Texas Observer,* November 9, 1990.

45. Joya Statement, 8.

46. "U.S. Official Links Salvadoran Right to Priests' Death," *New York Times,* November 18, 1989. Ellacuria and Martín Baró were rector and vice rector of the University of Central America.

47. Salvadoran embassy spokesman Eduardo Torres, telephone interview with the author, January 22, 1990.

48. Colonel Guillermos Benavides ordered the November 16, 1989, assassinations of six Jesuit priests, according to a U.S. Congressional Research Service translation of a January 18, 1990, indictment filed in the Fourth Criminal Court of El Salvador. The seventeen-page indictment, translated by Deanna Hammond of the Congressional Research Service, is attached to a letter from Carl Ford, acting assistant secretary of defense for international security affairs, to U.S. Representative Joseph Moakley, chairman of a congressional task force investigating the murders of the Jesuits. The letter bears the date-stamp April 10, 1990. The April 30, 1990, "Interim Report of the Speaker's Task Force on El Salvador" also accuses Benavides of direct complicity in the murders.

49. Joya Statement, 7.

50. Attacks on Salvadoran unions and human rights organizations in the days before the FMLN offensive were reported in the *New York Times:* "Bombings at Salvadoran Leftists' Office Kills Eight," November 1, 1989; "Salvador Rebels Quit Peace Talks (-) They Accuse the Government in the Bombing of Union Office Fatal to Nine," November 3, 1989; "Leftist Salvador Party Accuses Army of 3 Killings," November 9, 1989; and "Relief Group in Salvador Reports Repression," November 12, 1989. Joya's statement, and the increased attacks on Salvadoran unions and the

political opposition, indicate that the FMLN offensive of November 1989 was launched in retaliation for the "final offensive" of the army.

51. Joya Statement, 4.

52. Ibid.

53. Ibid., 5.

54. Salvadoran embassy spokesman Eduardo Torres and State Department and INS spokesmen, telephone interviews with the author, January 22, 1989.

55. Americas Watch, "Extradition Sought for Alleged Death Squad Participant" (Washington, D.C., August 14, 1991). U.S. Magistrate John Primomo in San Antonio ruled on November 18, 1991, that Joya Martinez could be extradited to El Salvador. Joya's subsequent deportation was reported by the Associated Press.

56. Andrew Blake, *Boston Globe* dispatch, March 15, 1990, reprinted in "Second Salvadoran Death Squad Member Corroborates Story," *Brownsville Herald,* March 16, 1990.

57. The author interviewed deserters from death squads in Los Fresnos, Oakdale, and Tucson.

58. Between 1984 and 1993, the author regularly asked INS spokesman Duke Austin for comments on Salvadorans seeking asylum in the United States.

59. Cándida and David Echavarría, interviews with the author at the Amber Motel, Brownsville, Texas, January 7, 1989. Robert Kahn, "Mothers Face Tough Road," *Brownsville Herald,* January 8, 1989.

60. Veronica Flores, "HUD OKs Money," *Brownsville Herald,* January 6, 1989. The *Herald* was an afternoon paper in 1989. Announcements made in Washington in the morning could be reported the same day in Brownsville.

61. *Morazan, Vasquez et al. v. Richard Thornburgh and Alan Nelson,* U.S. District Court, Southern District of Texas, January 6, 1989. Robert Kahn, "Suit Questions INS Policy," *Brownsville Herald,* January 8, 1989.

62. Ibid. Robert Rubin, interview with the author, January 6, 1989.

63. INS spokesman Duke Austin, telephone interview with the author, January 6, 1989. Robert Kahn, "South Texas Refugee Situation Is Near Chaos," *National Catholic Reporter,* January 20, 1989.

64. Cameron County Sheriff Alex F. Perez, interview with the author, January 9, 1989; and author's personal observations.

65. *Morazan, Vasquez et al. v. Richard Thornburgh and Alan Nelson.* Kahn, "South Texas Refugee Situation Is Near Chaos."

66. Trailways bus station manager, Carl Guelker, interview with the author, January 13, 1989. "Brownsville Refugees"; and "Miami, Saying It's Overburdened, Tells Nicaraguans to Stay Away."

67. Miami City Manager Cesar Odio and Dade County Assistant Manager Tony Ojeda, interviews with the author, January 13, 1989. Robert Kahn, "Florida Officials Try to Head Off Flood of Refugees," *Brownsville Herald,* January 13, 1989; and "Miami, Saying It's Overburdened, Tells Nicaraguans to Stay Away."

68. U.S. Representative Solomon Ortiz, interview with the author, January 9, 1989. Robert Kahn, "Ortiz Wants Peace with Nicaragua," and "Low Asylum Rate Brings Bad News to Nicaraguans," *Brownsville Herald,* January 10, 1989.

69. The author witnessed the evacuation of the Amber Motel on January 11, 1989, and visited the churches to which refugees were evacuated.

70. Oscar David, interview with the author, January 11, 1989. Robert Kahn, "Refugees Ousted from Amber," *Brownsville Herald,* January 12, 1989.

71. Kahn, "Florida Officials Try to Head Off Flood of Refugees"; and "Miami, Saying It's Overburdened, Tells Nicaraguans to Stay Away."

72. INS Miami District Director Perry Rivkind announced on April 16, 1986, that he would not deport Nicaraguans from his district: "Key Federal Aide Refuses to Deport Any Nicaraguans," *New York Times,* April 17, 1986. Attorney General Edwin Meese's special protection for Nicaraguans was reported in "Immigration Rules Are Eased for Nicaraguan Exiles in U.S.," a July 8, 1987, Associated Press dispatch from Washington printed in the July 9, 1987, *New York Times.*

73. "Asylum claims in Harlingen, Texas have risen from 400 per month in spring of 1988 to over 400 a day since January 15," the INS reported in its February 16, 1989, internal memo, "Enhancement Plan for the Southern Border," Executive Summary, 1.

74. Rickey Dailey, "Clements Says Valley Should Expect No Help for Refugees," *Brownsville Herald,* January 18, 1989.

75. "Fatal Shooting by Miami Police Sets off a Melee," *New York Times,* January 17, 1989; and "More Than 200 Arrested in Miami After Night of Racial Disturbances," *New York Times,* January 18, 1989.

76. In its January 17 article, the *New York Times* reported, "The disturbance came on the official observance of the birth of the Rev. Dr. Martin Luther King Jr. and after allegations by blacks in recent months of police brutality and a loss of jobs among blacks because of a large influx of Hispanic immigrants." On January 18 the *New York Times* reported, "Throughout the day—on the street, at news conferences and in interviews—blacks complained that Miami treated blacks unfairly and gave favorable treatment to Hispanic immigrants. They complained that little was done to help poor blacks, many of them lifetime residents here, to find housing and jobs, but that much was done to help Hispanic immigrants. ... One black teen-ager among the hundreds milling in the streets of Overtown Monday night referred to Nicaraguans when he shouted to a reporter: 'They get everything! Nothing for us!'"

77. After the South Texas detention policy began, Border Patrol and INS officials threatened to arrest U.S. citizens and impound their vehicles if they drove refugees to the asylum processing station, though the officials acknowledged that the citizens would not be violating any law by doing so.

78. Basilio Hernandez, "County Officials Want Answers from Washington," *Brownsville Herald,* February 3, 1989; and Robert Kahn, "INS Restraining Order Extended," *National Catholic Reporter,* February 10, 1989.

79. Paul Rodriguez, "Bentsen Asks Attorney General to Review Refugee Policy," States News Service dispatch printed in *Brownsville Herald,* January 12, 1989.

80. INS spokeswoman Virginia Kice in Harlingen, an intelligence officer at the McAllen Sector Border Patrol headquarters, and Red Cross shelter director Gene Nunley, interviews with the author, February 1–7, 1989.

81. Robert Kahn, "Harlingen, Texas, Evicts INS," *National Catholic Reporter,* February 24, 1989.

82. Patrick Hughes, telephone interview with the author, January 18, 1989. Robert Kahn, "Salvadorans Likely to Flood Brownsville," *Brownsville Herald,* January 19, 1989.

83. Segundo Montes, "Salvadoreños refugiados en los Estados Unidos," Instituto de Investigaciones y Instituto de Derechos Humanos, Universidad de Centroamerica José Simeon Cañas, San Salvador, El Salvador, 1987; and "El Salvador 1989: Las remesas que envian los salvadoreños de Estados Unidos; Consecuencias sociales y económicos," Universidad de Centroamerica José Simeon Cañas, 1990. Dollars sent from refugees in the United States continue to be a major portion of the Salvadoran economy today. In 1994, two years after the Salvadoran civil war ended, Salvadoran refugees in the United States "sent almost $1 billion to relatives in El Salvador, according to academics and Government officials, a sum that nearly rivals the nation's export earnings": Doreen Carvajal, "In U.S., El Salvador Helps Own Refugees Get Asylum," *New York Times,* October 26, 1995.

84. After the Salvadoran guerrilla's offensive began on the evening of November 11, 1989, Salvadoran immigration to the United States through south Texas more than quadrupled. Border Patrol officers in the McAllen Sector arrested 179 Salvadorans in November 1989 and 775 in January 1990. Statistics from Border Patrol intelligence office, McAllen, Texas, February–March 1990.

85. Eight Hondurans at Brownsville Red Cross shelter, interviews with the author, January 30, 1989. Robert Kahn, "Hondurans Coming to U.S. in Increasing Numbers," *Brownsville Herald,* January 31, 1989.

86. The value of the Guatemalan quetzal declined from one to the dollar to about four to the dollar during the 1980s.

87. Walter LaFeber, *Inevitable Revolutions* (New York: W. W. Norton, 1983), 9.

88. "Miami, Saying It's Overburdened, Tells Nicaraguans to Stay Away."

89. U.S. Immigration and Naturalization Service, "Enhancement Plan for the Southern Border," Executive Summary, 1.

90. U.S. Immigration and Naturalization Service, "Enhancement Plan for the Southern Border," 9–10.

91. Ibid., 12, 18.

92. Ibid., 14.

93. Ibid.

94. Undated INS videotape of State Department Bureau of Human Rights and Humanitarian Affairs employee Mark McCleggen training INS employees in Los Angeles to become special adjudicators at Los Fresnos. The INS logo is prominently displayed on the dais from which McCleggen delivered his training session. The authenticity of the videotape was confirmed by INS and State Department officials. Robert Kahn, "INS Video Suggests Policy Contradiction," *Brownsville Herald,* May 17, 1990, and "INS Training Video Faulted for Its Political Edge," *Boston Globe,* May 23, 1990.

95. All McCleggen quotations are from the INS videotape.

96. David Burgess, spokesman for the U.S. State Department Bureau of Human Rights and Humanitarian Affairs, telephone interview with the author, May 16, 1990. Refugee advocates did not discover the INS training videotape until after the South Texas detention project ended. Its discovery helped convince the Justice Department to settle the *American Baptist Churches v. Thornburgh* case, which overturned every denial of asylum to a Salvadoran or Guatemalan in the 1980s.

97. INS spokeswoman Virginia Kice, telephone interview with the author, February 14, 1989.

98. The Border Patrol arrests were witnessed by *Brownsville Herald* reporter Greg Beals. Greg Beals and Robert Kahn, "Transporting Central Americans to Processing Center Can Be Risky," *Brownsville Herald,* February 15, 1989.

99. Attorney Mark Schneider, interview with the author, February 15, 1989. Robert Kahn, "Attorneys, Border Patrol Wrangle over Alien Transport," *Brownsville Herald,* February 17, 1989.

100. *United States of America v. Stacey Lynn Merkt,* 764 F2d 266 (1985). Conviction reversed and remanded.

101. McAllen Sector Border Patrol chief agent Silvestre Reyes, INS spokesman Mario Ortiz, Border Patrol attorney Eleazar Tovar, Proyecto Libertad paralegal Jonathan Moore, and attorney Lisa Brodyaga, telephone interviews with the author, February 15, 1989. Kahn, "Attorneys, Border Patrol Wrangle over Alien Transport."

102. Gene Nunley, director of Brownsville Red Cross shelter, interview with the author, February 20, 1989. Robert Kahn, "Church Groups Help Get Refugees out of Valley," *Brownsville Herald,* February 21, 1989.

103. Mervyn Mosbacker Sr., volunteer worker for Church World Service, interview with the author, February 20, 1989.

104. Jim Folts, rector of Episcopal Church of the Advent, interview with the author, February 20, 1989.

105. Statistics on numbers of asylum applicants were provided by INS spokeswoman Virginia Kice and the Border Patrol intelligence office in McAllen, Texas.

106. The author was a reporter for the *Brownsville Herald* throughout the INS detention project. As a courtesy, the *Herald* opened its newsroom to correspondents from other newspapers, who often outnumbered *Herald* reporters in the first days of the detention project. By the end of the first week of the detention project, the visiting correspondents had gone.

107. The Border Patrol intelligence unit in McAllen provided the author with daily reports of arrests of Mexicans and "other than Mexicans."

108. INS Mexico City director E. M. Trominski, "SITREP #1—Project 091," "SITREP #2—Project 091," "SITREP #2.1—Project 091," and "Notes from briefing by INS intelligence-gathering teams operating out of Mexico" (memoranda to office of Foreign Relations and INS in Washington, February 22 and 23, 1989).

109. Mexican police corruption is documented in Bill Frelick's report, "Running the Gauntlet: The Central American Journey Through Mexico" (U.S. Committee for Refugees, Washington, D.C., January 1991); and Americas Watch, "Human Rights in Mexico: A Policy of Impunity" (New York, June 1990). On one night in June 1991, Mexican police took the author's Salvadoran wife off a bus four times and demanded bribes to let her pass with our three children. They were traveling legally, with Salvadoran passports and Mexican visas. The police threatened to hold her alone on the highway and let the children go on without her: The children were six, seven, and twelve years old.

110. Trominski, "SITREP #1—Project 091," February 22, 1989; "SITREP #2—Project 091," "SITREP #2.1—Project 091," February 23, 1989, and "Notes from briefing by INS intelligence-gathering teams operating out of Mexico." The intelligence briefing was conducted by INS officers Sam Martin and Manuel Cornejo—the former head of the immigration prison at Florence, Arizona.

111. Trominski, "SITREP #1" and "Notes from briefing by INS intelligence-gathering teams operating out of Mexico."

112. Trominski, "SITREP #2.1," summarizing an INS agent's report from Matamoros.

113. Trominski, "SITREP #2."

114. Trominski, "SITREP #1." Situation reports 1 and 2 both mention sharing information with Mexican Immigration Director General Susana Torres Hernandez.

115. The arrests of hundreds of Mexicans on their own national soil were widely reported in Mexico and in Spanish-language newspapers in the United States. "*La policia mexicana no es auxiliar de la Patrulla Fronteriza de EU*" [The Mexican Police are not an auxiliary of the U.S. Border Patrol], *La Jornada* [Mexico City daily newspaper], March 11, 1989; "*México seguirá colaborando con Patrulla Fronteriza de EU*" [Mexico will continue collaborating with the U.S. Border Patrol], *La Opinion* [Los Angeles daily newspaper], March 9, 1989. Mexican government cooperation with the U.S. Border Patrol was denounced on the floor of the Mexican Congress.

Though publication of Trominski's memos briefly complicated U.S.-Mexican relations, it helped free a few refugees from the clutches of the alien smuggler Raul Torres. The author's March 14 story in the *Brownsville Herald,* "Matamoros Police 'Selling' Refugees, Who Say Coyotes Held Them Hostage," included Torres's name, a description of his blue van, his address at 12 El Carmen Street, and selections from Trominski's memos. A Matamoros newspaper translated the story and published it the next day with no byline. Torres freed all his hostages that night, took them across the river, and disappeared.

116. Statistics are from interviews with Border Patrol intelligence agents in all nine sectors on the U.S.-Mexican border, July 1990. Border Patrol sectors are named for the city of the sector headquarters: McAllen, Laredo, Del Rio, Marfa, and El Paso, Texas; Tucson and Yuma, Arizona; and El Centro and San Diego, California.

117. The population of the INS detention center at Los Fresnos was provided by INS spokeswoman Virginia Kice: Robert Kahn, "70 Are Deported; INS Camp Tense," *Brownsville Herald,* March 10, 1989. The population of the Brownsville Red Cross center was provided by shelter director Gene Nunley: Robert Kahn, "Refugee Children Want to Go to School," *Brownsville Herald,* March 30, 1989.

118. Brownsville Red Cross shelter director Gene Nunley and children detained at the shelter, interviews with the author, March 30, 1989. Kahn, "Refugee Children Want to Go to School."

119. INS Commissioner Alan Nelson spoke at a press conference in Brownsville on February 20, 1989: Robert Kahn, "Plans Unclear for Refugee Women, Children," *Brownsville Herald,* February 21, 1989. The author interviewed dozens of refugees at the Brownsville Red Cross shelter and Los Fresnos immigration prison between February 23 and 28, 1989: Robert Kahn, "Immigration Service Has Family Problems," *Brownsville Herald,* February 24, 1989, and "Four-Month-Old U.S. Citizen Faces Deportation," *Brownsville Herald,* March 1, 1989.

120. Kahn, "Immigration Service Has Family Problems."

121. Kahn, "Four-Month-Old U.S. Citizen Faces Deportation."

122. Refugees can request political asylum directly from an INS district director or from an immigration judge. If the district director denies asylum, the application can be "renewed" by going through the usual process—an asylum trial before an

immigration judge. The judge's decision can be appealed to the Board of Immigration Appeals, then to a federal court. Thus, the INS letter stating, "There is no appeal from this decision [of the Harlingen district director]," is technically correct, though misleading. The application *can* be resubmitted.

123. Lady Dinorah Borjas and Otilia Sarmiento, interviews with the author, February 28, 1989. Kahn, "Four-Month-Old U.S. Citizen Faces Deportation."

124. INS officer in charge, Brownsville Red Cross shelter, interview with the author, February 28, 1989. Robert Kahn, "Asylum Seekers Find INS' Procedures Confusing," *Brownsville Herald*, March 2, 1989.

125. Virginia Kice, spokeswoman for the INS in South Texas, confirmed in early March 1989 that the Guatemalan woman had died in the *corralón* February 28. Kahn, "70 Are Deported, INS Camp Tense." Sixty-one people were deported on Sunday, March 5, and nine more were deported on Thursday, March 9, Kice said. Of those seventy deportees, fifty-one were Salvadorans, fourteen were Guatemalans, and five were Hondurans.

126. Kahn, "70 Are Deported, INS Camp Tense."

127. The author counted the cases on posted court dockets in Harlingen and at the *corralón*.

128. Border Patrol officer and the official with the Executive Office of Immigration Review who was in charge of scheduling political asylum trials in Harlingen, interviews with the author, March 22, 1989. Robert Kahn, "INS Breaking the Rules, Attorneys for Aliens Say," *Brownsville Herald*, March 23, 1989.

129. Attorney Bert Bosnans, interview with the author, March 22, 1989. Kahn, "INS Breaking the Rules, Attorneys for Aliens Say."

130. Deportation hearing of José F., March 22, 1989, Harlingen immigration court, witnessed by author.

131. Robert Kahn, "INS Being Sued over Bayview Conditions," *Brownsville Herald*, March 31, 1989.

132. The author counted the cases on posted court dockets in Harlingen and at the *corralón*.

133. Immigration judge Charles Auslander, interview with the author, April 6, 1989. Robert Kahn, "INS Defies Judge to Deport Alien," *Brownsville Herald*, April 7, 1989; "INS Defies Judge's Order in Texas," *National Catholic Reporter*, April 21, 1989; and "Complaints About INS Attorney Referred to Ethics Committee," *Brownsville Herald*, June 16, 1989.

134. Proyecto Libertad sued the INS for Martinez Cabrera, and a federal judge ordered the INS to send an agent to Guatemala to find Martinez, bring him back to the United States, and allow him to apply for political asylum. Proyecto Libertad attorney Mark Schneider, personal communication with the author, 1990.

135. INS prosecuting attorney on special assignment to Los Fresnos, interview with the author, April 6, 1989.

136. Robert Kahn, "Attorneys Seek INS Release of Detainees," *Brownsville Herald*, April 14, 1989.

137. Kahn, "INS Defies Judge to Deport Alien," and "Complaints About INS Attorney Referred to Ethics Committee."

138. "Order and Preliminary Injunction," *Crosby Wilfredo Orantes-Hernandez et al. v. Richard Thornburgh, Attorney General of the United States*, U.S. District

Court, Central District of California, April 28, 1989, Judge David V. Kenyon. Emphasis in original.

139. *Crosby-Wilfredo Orantes-Hernandez et al. v. Richard Thornburgh*, U.S. Court of Appeals for the Ninth Circuit, November 20, 1990.

140. *Crosby-Wilfredo Orantes-Hernandez et al. v. Edwin Meese III*, U.S. District Court, Central District of California, April 29, 1988. *Capucha*, or "the hood," is a torture in which a prisoner is hooded and suffocated. When the hood is released and the prisoner gasps for air, caustic lime powder is thrown into the hood, then it is tightened again.

141. *Crosby-Wilfredo Orantes-Hernandez et al. v. Richard Thornburgh*, U.S. Court of Appeals for the Ninth Circuit, November 20, 1990, 22–31.

142. *American Baptist Churches et al. v. Richard L. Thornburgh, Gene McNary, and James A. Baker III*, U.S. District Court, Northern District of California, December 19, 1990, U.S. District Judge Robert Peckham.

Other People's Blood

We are a nation of immigrants.

—President Jimmy Carter, on signing the 1980
Refugee Act

THE FMLN OFFENSIVE LAUNCHED in November 1989 failed to capture one major objective—the air force base at Ilopango airfield. The Salvadoran air force was therefore able to bomb and strafe residential neighborhoods occupied by the guerrilla throughout the two-week offensive. Air force helicopters strafed Mejicanos, an enormous working-class neighborhood, on Sunday, November 12, the first full day of battles.[1] Heavy fighting was reported in eight of the fourteen departments of El Salvador. The government banned radio broadcasts nationwide and announced a state of siege. The U.S. embassy confirmed at least 339 dead.[2]

On Tuesday, November 14, the embassy estimated that 1,500 guerrillas were involved in the offensive. U.S. Ambassador William Walker told the *New York Times* that the guerrillas controlled one-third of the capital, San Salvador, a city of more than 1 million. The army reported 309 guerrillas killed, 160 wounded, and 60 captured. The guerrillas had suffered a casualty rate of 35 percent by the second day of the offensive, according to the Salvadoran army and the U.S. embassy. Fierce fighting continued for two more weeks.[3]

The *New York Times* first reported on Wednesday, November 15, that civilians were burning dead bodies in the streets. But residents of Mejicanos who fled to the United States arrived with stories of troops and death squads who had strangled with barbed wire and burned alive young men found out of uniform.[4]

Early Thursday morning, about thirty Salvadoran troops from the army's First Infantry Brigade dragged the rector and vice rector of the University of Central America from their bedrooms and shot them to death, along with four faculty members. Rector Ignacio Ellacuria, Vice Rector Ignacio Martín Baró, and their colleagues Joaquin Lopez y Lopez, Juan Ramon Moreno Pardo, Segundo Montes Mozo, and Amando Lopez Quintanilla were Jesuit priests. The death squad also killed Julia Elba Ramos, who kept house for the priests, and her teenage daughter, Celina.[5] All members of the death squad had received military training from the United States, at U.S. taxpayer expense.[6] Later that day, the army arrested ten Lutheran church workers, including Medardo Gomez, the Lutheran bishop of San Salvador.[7]

As the fighting intensified, Salvadoran Attorney General Mauricio Eduardo Colorado advised all Catholic priests to leave El Salvador because "large parts of the Salvadoran population" believed priests and bishops were responsible for the "recent unrest" in the country.[8]

At 5:30 A.M. on Monday, November 20, the ninth day of the offensive, about thirty Salvadoran National Guard troops arrested seventeen church workers at St. John the Evangelist Church in San Salvador. The Salvadoran government announced it had killed 1,050 guerrillas, wounded 564, and captured 164—119 percent of the guerrilla troops estimated to be involved in the offensive by the U.S. embassy. That was just in the capital. Reporters were forbidden to leave San Salvador to investigate the situation in the seven other departments where battles continued.[9]

On Tuesday, the FMLN took control of Escalón, the wealthiest neighborhood in the country. Army planes and helicopters buzzed the area but did not bomb or strafe the opulent houses. The FMLN also seized the Hotel El Salvador, formerly the Sheraton, on the edge of Escalón. Trapped in the Sheraton was a contingent of U.S. Marines—military advisers and trainers of the Salvadoran armed forces. Neither the Marines nor the FMLN attacked their enemies in the hotel.[10]

President Bush announced on Wednesday that he had sent specially trained Delta Force commandos to El Salvador to rescue twelve Green Berets in the Sheraton. But this was a political gaffe for Bush because he had neglected to confer first with Salvadoran President Alfredo Cristiani.[11] The Green Berets were released before the commandos arrived.[12]

On Thursday in Washington, D.C., U.S. Attorney General Richard Thornburgh refused to release information to a federal judge for the trial of CIA agent Joe Fernandez, a key player in the Iran-Contra scandal. As CIA station chief in Costa Rica, Fernandez had helped send military supplies to Nicaraguan Contra troops, an activity forbidden by Congress. Many of the illegal arms had gone through the Ilopango airfield.[13]

That same day, Lucia Barrera, the only eyewitness to the murder of the Jesuits, arrived in Miami with her husband under the "protection" of the FBI and the U.S. State Department. At FBI headquarters in Miami on Friday, the Barreras were interrogated by Salvadoran army Lieutenant Colonel Manuel Antonio Rivas Mejía in the presence of two FBI agents and a witness from the State Department. The Barreras did not know that Rivas was Salvadoran or that he was an army officer. The FBI agents had introduced him to Lucia Barrera as a doctor.[14] While the Barreras were being interrogated, charges against CIA agent Fernandez were dismissed because Thornburgh had refused to release information that would indicate whether Fernandez's actions had been approved by superiors.[15]

Lucia Barrera and her husband were interrogated for four days. The FBI agents and Lieutenant Colonel Rivas repeatedly accused them of lying and threatened to deport them to El Salvador. One FBI agent repeated intimidating questions: "Who told you to say this? Which one of the priests put you up to this?" Another tried to convince Jorge Barrera, a baker, that one of the murdered priests was a guerrilla. "You have family among the guerrilla. Tell us who they are." The FBI agents taunted Jorge whether he was sure his wife had earned her living with the priests as a housekeeper—intimating that she was a prostitute or a guerrilla.[16] By the end, Lucia Barrera later recalled to the Lawyers Committee for Human Rights, "I couldn't stand it anymore and wanted to be left in peace. I finally told them what they wanted to hear. I said I had seen nothing that morning the priests were killed."[17] The FBI gave the Barreras three lie detector tests each, based on Lucia Barrera's altered testimony that she had seen nothing. They failed all of them.[18]

On Sunday, December 10, Salvadoran President Alfredo Cristiani held a press conference to announce that the Barreras had failed six lie detector tests.[19] Where his information came from—the FBI, the State Department, or Lieutenant Colonel Rivas Mejía—he didn't say. Salvadoran Archbishop Arturo Rivera y Damas defended the Barreras in his Sunday homily that day, arguing that they had been subjected to "psychological torment ... subjected to an authentic brainwashing and blackmailed with the threat of deportation."[20] Six days later, the *New York Times* printed the first account of the Barreras' interrogation, an opinion piece by Paul Tipton, president of the Association of Jesuit Colleges and Universities.[21]

At the same time, the director of Salvadoran Immigration Services reported that more than 1,500 Salvadorans per day were seeking passports in San Salvador in order to be able to leave the country legally. According to the Guatemalan government, 5,000 Salvadorans had sought shelter there legally since the offensive began. Thousands more were hiding in Guatemala without proper documents.[22]

Despite the threats of deportation and four days of interrogation by the FBI, the U.S. government treated the Barreras better than it had treated most Salvadoran refugees in the 1980s. After their FBI interrogators, Lieutenant Colonel Rivas, and the State Department had impugned the Barreras' testimony so thoroughly that nothing they said would be credible in U.S. courts, the INS granted them "humanitarian parole" for one year and permits that allowed them to work in the United States.[23] Two days later, the fate of the Barreras disappeared from U.S. press reports, when the United States invaded Panama.

Another Salvadoran Exodus

As the U.S. Army pursued Manuel Noriega, the latest wave of Salvadoran refugees arrived in the United States. U.S. Border Patrol arrests of Salvadorans quadrupled in the McAllen District, where officers arrested 179 Salvadorans in November, 396 in December, and 775 in January 1990.[24]

In response, INS Commissioner Gene McNary called a press conference in Brownsville on February 7, 1990, to announce an $11 million detention project.[25] The INS again set up large circus-style tents at Los Fresnos prison at a cost to taxpayers of $15,000 a week.[26] Overnight, McNary increased the official capacity of the detention center from about 600 to 10,000. It was the same "solution" to immigration problems the INS had invented the year before.

No one ever slept under the tents. The INS spent more than $150,000 on a show of force at Los Fresnos while 200 miles upriver in Laredo, the Border Patrol was releasing Salvadorans on their own recognizance, asking them to leave the country within thirty days. As two Laredo attorneys put it, "Realistically, this lets the person get to where he's going" without becoming an INS arrest statistic.[27]

The Refugee Problem in Perspective

Throughout the 1980s, the Reagan and Bush administrations defended their treatment of Salvadoran refugees by invoking the enormity of the immigration pressure on the southern U.S. border. They rebuked critics of U.S. policy, especially in European democracies, which they argued did not face the refugee problems the United States did. But when the Soviet Union collapsed in 1991 and civil war consumed Yugoslavia, Western Europe did face similar refugee problems. More than 2.5 million people had been forced from their homes in Yugoslavia by the summer of 1992, and 10,000 more were fleeing every day, according to the U.N. High Commissioner for Refugees.[28] Refugees from ethnic conflicts in the former Soviet Union and refugees from political violence and starvation in Somalia, Ethiopia, and Sudan numbered millions more.

Germany accepted 694,303 political asylum applicants in 1991–1992, many of them from the former Iron Curtain republics of Romania, Poland, and the former Czechoslovakia. The level of civilian violence against refugees in Germany reached levels unapproached in the United States: Seventeen refugees and Germans died in anti-immigrant violence in 1992 in more than 2,000 attacks, often by neo-Nazis.[29] Germany tightened its asylum policies in 1993, allowing the country to refuse entrance to refugees. Yet Germany did not deny that the immigrants were refugees, and German police forces battled neo-Nazis in the streets to protect refugees. German police and intelligence agencies—so far as we know—did not infiltrate refugee communities in Germany to sow terror and disinformation, as the FBI did among Salvadoran refugees and their sympathizers in the United States.[30]

More than 5 million refugees fled civil war in Afghanistan in the 1980s, mostly to Pakistan. Despite the burden of caring for them—a much greater burden for a poor country than Central Americans were for the United States—Pakistan did not forcibly return refugees to the war in Afghanistan. By 1993, Afghanistan itself had accepted more than 60,000 Tajiks who had fled conflict between communists and Islamic fundamentalists in Tajikistan.[31]

Mexico, a poor country whose police forces have an abysmal human rights record, accepted more than 200,000 Salvadoran and Guatemalan refugees in camps in Chiapas and Campeche States in the 1980s.[32] Though conditions in the camps were miserable, Mexico did not forcibly deport the refugees. Nor did Zaire deport the hundreds of thousands of Rwandans fleeing civil war in 1994.[33]

Despite the greater problems Europe faced in the 1990s, most European countries took seriously their human and legal responsibilities to refugees. Though refugee policies became increasingly restrictive as the Yugoslavian civil war, the African famines and warfare, and Soviet unrest continued, refugee policies in Europe were discussed openly, and changes in them were announced to the public. Danish Justice Minister Erik Ninn-Hansen resigned in 1989 when it was revealed he had blocked visas for relatives of Sri Lankan refugees. Danish Prime Minister Poul Schleuter resigned in January 1993 when an inquiry found he had covered up an illegal policy that refused visas for relatives of Sri Lankan refugees.[34]

Refugees and International Law

As violence drove refugees from a region far bigger than Central America, Western Europe faced a refugee crisis much greater than the United States in the 1980s. Yet the nations of Western Europe could not look to the United States for guidance; the U.S. Justice Department had systematically ignored its own refugee laws for a decade. The illegally funded Contra war against Nicaragua had created tens of thousands of refugees, yet President Bush pardoned high-ranking CIA and State and Defense Department officials who were indicted for their roles in the Iran-Contra scandal. No one ever suggested an inquiry, much less indictment, of U.S. officials for their roles in the illegal deportations of Salvadorans.[35]

The refugee policies of most Western nations, including Europe and the United States, are based on definitions and protocols established after World War II in the Geneva Conventions. Article 44 of Geneva Convention 4 states that "refugees may not be forcibly repatriated until after the cessation of hostilities" in their home country and that "refugees may not be sent to any state that has not satisfactorily demonstrated a willingness or ability to comply with humanitarian norms." The principle that refugees shall not be deported to a country at war is known in international law as *non-refoulement*. Article 147 of Geneva Convention 4 defines violation of the principle of *non-refoulement* as a "grave breach" of the Geneva Conventions. Protocol Additional 1, article 85.5, states that grave breaches of the Geneva Conventions are considered war crimes.[36]

The Reagan administration not only violated the Geneva Conventions by its summary deportation of Salvadoran and Guatemalan refugees, but it criticized its ideological enemies for *not* doing the same.

The General Accounting Office (GAO) reported in 1984 that Nicaragua was the only Central American "country of first asylum" that integrated refugees into the general population rather than isolating them in camps. "The Nicaraguan government provides refugees with basic assistance and residency status. It also allows refugees to work and treats them like Nicaraguan citizens."[37] State Department comments appended as notes to the GAO report state that Nicaragua "may be too quick to offer the settlement option, when it would be preferable to wait a decent interval to test the possibility of voluntary repatriation."[38]

"Voluntary repatriation" does not mean that a refugee willingly returns home. In U.S. immigration law, it means the arrestee does not challenge the deportation process and waives his or her right to a trial.[39] Thus the State Department, in the GAO report, criticized Nicaragua for *failing to violate* the Geneva Conventions.

One Simple Lesson

It is far from clear whether peace will hold in El Salvador or Nicaragua. What is clear is that peace for Central America became possible only when the United States acknowledged that the poor people of the region do not threaten U.S. interests. With the Cold War over and the Salvadoran military disgraced again by its murder of the Jesuits, El Salvador's government had to face the reality that it had outlived its usefulness to the Pentagon and to the White House ideologues. Only then did the Salvadoran government enter serious negotiations with the FMLN. As the RAND Corporation reported in 1991, "American leverage has vastly increased because the Salvadoran regime realizes that Washington no longer has pressing reasons to continue supporting it."[40]

A decade of warfare that left hundreds of thousands dead throughout Central America also encouraged the creation of emigration routes refugees used to escape from the wars. By now many of these routes have become well established. Salvadorans from Chalatenango know they stand the best chance of finding fellow townspeople in the San Francisco Bay area; refugees from La Union head to Washington, D.C. Guatemalans from the Quiché highlands take the west coast route through Tucson, and Hondurans who cannot find friends or family in Miami will likely find an acquaintance in New Orleans. Through his policy of war, the president who warned that the border was out of control unwittingly supplied the human traffic that filled these emigration routes.

With the end of the Cold War, the United States no longer faces a monolithic, faceless evil against which to stand in unity. U.S. politicians must look elsewhere for an organizing principle by which to rally the voters. All signs indicate that the "illegal alien" is becoming that faceless wraith against whom U.S. citizens will be asked to take a stand. There is virtually no shortcoming in U.S. society—declining schools, gang violence, increasing crime, eroding wage standards, social conflict, overpopulation—that is not being blamed on immigrants.

The subject of immigration has always been resonant with emotion: the abandoned homeland, the fear and excitement of the journey, the new life in a strange land. But the subject has now become so laden with emotion that the voice of reason can scarcely be heard in the United States. Whether we should close our doors to refugees and immigrants in the future is the subject for another book. Beyond dispute, however, is that the United States failed to live up to its own standards and obey its own laws in the 1980s. After abusing immigrants for a decade in our "processing centers," we are now making them scapegoats for a host of social ills from which immigrants also suffer. Because their Central American homelands are no longer geopolitically important and are so far away, the United States government and its citizens have been able to avoid confronting the immense tragedy we have wrought in Central America.

It was peace—not U.S. immigration policy—that ultimately reduced Central American immigration to the United States. This country was able to stop making war in Central America only after the White House and the Pentagon acknowledged, in reports that are still being suppressed, that the entire decade of lies, atrocities, and cover-ups had been just an experiment, with other people's blood.

Notes

1. "Salvador Rebels Mount Attacks Across the Capital," Associated Press dispatch of November 11, 1989, printed in *New York Times,* November 12, 1989; and "Salvador Rebels Launch Offensive; Fighting Is Fierce (-) Hundreds Feared Killed (-) President's House Is Among the Guerrillas' Targets—U.S. Teacher Is Slain," *New York Times,* November 13, 1989.

2. "Salvadoran Army Counterattacks in Capital City (-) Hundreds Dead or Hurt (-) Heavy Combat Also Reported in Other Parts of Country—Long Fight Possible," *New York Times,* November 14, 1989. Los Angeles legal and human rights organi-

zation El Rescate prepared an hour-by-hour account of the offensive: "El Salvador Chronology," vol. IV, no. 11, November 1989. Six victims of the Salvadoran army offensive in Mejicanos spoke to the author in the Brownsville area from April to December 1990.

3. "Salvador Army Steps up Raids on Strongholds of Rebel Forces (-) 24-Hour Curfew Placed on 6 Big Communities on Capital Outskirts," and "U.S. Sees 'No Threat' to Salvador Government," *New York Times,* November 15, 1989.

4. "Salvador Army Is Said to Seize Rebel Positions (-) Guerrillas Are Reported on the Brink of Defeat"; and "Salvadorans Ask U.S. for Arms Aid," *New York Times,* November 16, 1989; Salvadorans in Brownsville, Harlingen, San Benito, and Los Fresnos, Texas, interviews with the author, April–December 1990. At least one of the Salvadorans who witnessed strangulation and burning of civilians received political asylum in the United States.

5. The murders of the Jesuits are described by the soldiers who carried out the killings in a U.S. Congressional Research Service translation of an indictment filed in the Fourth Criminal Court of San Salvador on January 18, 1990. The seventeen-page indictment is attached to a letter from Carl W. Ford Jr., acting assistant secretary of defense for international security affairs, to U.S. Representative Joseph Moakley, letter date-stamped as received April 10, 1990.

6. The Salvadoran army murder of the Jesuits was investigated by a special committee of the U.S. Congress Central American Task Force, led by Representative Joseph Moakley. "Interim Report of the Speaker's Task Force on El Salvador," April 30, 1990. Moakley's investigation revealed that the death squad that killed the Jesuits had broken off a U.S. Army training session to go to San Salvador to commit the murders: "All of the soldiers charged with murdering the Jesuits, except Colonel Benavides, received at least some U.S. training, including four who received training in the United States. Sadly, the entire unit that allegedly carried out the crimes was participating in a U.S. training exercise during the two days immediately prior to the murders" (11). Moakley's report revealed the names of the members of the army death squad and the names of the U.S. military advisers who trained them. These names are listed in an April 10, 1990, letter to Moakley from Carl W. Ford. More details of the Salvadoran government and military cover-up of the murders are contained in a January 7, 1991, letter to Moakley from staff members Jim McGovern and Bill Woodward, entitled "Staff Trip to El Salvador." Photocopy in author's possession.

7. "Embassy in Salvador Offers to Protect Witnesses," *New York Times,* November 18, 1989.

8. "Salvadoran Asks Pope to Remove 'Some Bishops,'" *New York Times,* November 19, 1989.

9. "Salvadoran Security Forces Raid Episcopal Church, Arresting 17," *New York Times,* November 21, 1989.

10. "Salvador Rebels Take Over Parts of Luxury Hotel (-) Daylong Siege In Capital (-) Release of the Civilian Guests and Retreat by Some of the Rebels Reported," *New York Times,* November 22, 1989.

11. "Bush Claims Role in Hostage Rescue in Salvador Hotel (-) Commandos Dispatched (-) Officials Backtrack Later—Say Troops Arrived After Rebel Standoff Ended," *New York Times,* November 23, 1989.

12. "The Green Berets at the Barricades: 28 Hours at the Besieged Salvador Hotel," *New York Times,* November 23, 1989.

13. "Case Dismissed in Contra Affair, Clearing Agent (-) Judge Cites the Blocking of Secret Information," *New York Times,* November 25, 1989; and "The C.I.A. Role in Salvador: Air Base Described as the Key," *New York Times,* October 15, 1986.

14. Paul Tipton, "Witness to Murder in El Salvador," *New York Times,* December 17, 1989; "Witnesses in Jesuit Slayings Charge Harassment in U.S.," *New York Times,* December 18, 1989; "The Jesuit Trial, An Observer's Report," *News from Americas Watch,* December 13, 1991.

15. "Case Dismissed in Contra Affair, Clearing Agent."

16. Tipton, "Witness to Murder in El Salvador"; "Witnesses in Jesuit Slayings Charge Harassment in U.S."; Moakley, "Interim Report."

17. Tipton, "Witness to Murder in El Salvador"; and Moakley, "Interim Report," 22–26.

18. *New York Times,* December 17 and 18, 1989; and "Interim Report," pp. 22–26. The FBI refused to let Moakley's committee interview the agents who had interrogated the Barreras: "Interim Report," 24.

19. "Dispute in Salvador on Witness in Jesuit Case," *New York Times,* December 11, 1989.

20. "Dispute in Salvador on Witness in Jesuit Case"; and Moakley, "Interim Report," 22–26.

21. Tipton, "Witness to Murder in El Salvador."

22. "Fighting in Salvador Prompts a New Exodus," *New York Times,* December 17, 1989.

23. "Witnesses in Jesuit Slayings Charge Harassment in U.S."

24. Border Patrol arrest statistics provided by McAllen Border Patrol Sector intelligence office, McAllen, Texas, March 1990.

25. Rebecca Thatcher, "INS Cracks Down, Bayview Center Capacity Raised to 10,000," *Brownsville Herald,* February 8, 1990.

26. INS spokeswoman Virginia Kice estimated the cost of the tents as $15,000 to $16,000 a week: Robert Kahn, "Bayview Tents Devoid of Tenants," *Brownsville Herald,* March 6, 1990.

27. Immigration attorneys José Tellez and Patrick Hughes, telephone interviews with the author, March 5, 1990; Kahn, "Bayview Tents Devoid of Tenants."

28. Statistics on Yugoslavian refugees are from Clare Nullis's Associated Press dispatch from Geneva, Switzerland, July 29, 1992, quoting U.N. High Commissioner for Refugees Sadako Ogata.

29. U.S. Committee for Refugees, "World Refugee Survey 1992" (Washington, D.C.), 70–72; Juan O. Tamayo, Knight-Ridder news dispatch from Berlin, October 14, 1991; and Terrence Petty, Associated Press dispatch from Bonn, October 10, 1991.

30. Ross Gelbspan, *Break-ins, Death Threats and the FBI* (Boston: South End Press, 1991).

31. In Afghanistan, "the proxy war of the superpowers thus became in 1991 more of a civil war, with regional powers—in this case, Pakistan, Iran, and Saudi Arabia—competing for influence among the warring parties. Although no longer a

Cold War battlefield, the civil war, which has cost an estimated 1.5 million dead, 2 million injured, more than 6 million refugees, and 2 million internally displaced out of a total pre-war population of 15 million, continued in 1991." U.S. Committee for Refugees, "World Refugee Survey 1992," 94.

In Pakistan, "the [Afghan] refugees' fate was largely in the hands of the *mujahedin* leaders who could not agree among themselves about their goals or on preconditions for repatriation of 3,185,265 registered, and an estimated 406,000 unregistered, Afghan refugees in Pakistan. Unregistered refugees continued to arrive throughout 1991" (105).

The dissolution of the Soviet Union produced immense numbers of refugees. At least 300,000 Armenians fled from Azerbaijan; more than 100,000 Ossetians fled to Russia; at least 18,000 Georgians were driven from their homes, most from Tbilisi. "Hundreds of thousands have left other republics such as Uzbekistan, the Baltics, and even areas of Russia itself, such as the Autonomous Republic of Tuva on the Mongolian border. ... With more than 65 million people forcibly or voluntarily outside their 'ethnic homelands,' including perhaps 25 million Russians, the potential for mass migration is staggering, though republic leaders well recognize the danger" (78–79).

32. Mexico had accepted more than 150,000 Guatemalan refugees by 1984, Americas Watch reported in the September 1984 report "Guatemalan Refugees in Mexico 1980–1984," 5. By 1991, Mexico's Central American refugee population had grown to 400,000 according to Tom Barry, ed., *Mexico: A Country Guide* (Albuquerque, N.Mex.: The Inter-Hemispheric Education Resource Center, 1992), 230. Barry estimates that 45 percent were Guatemalan, 34 percent Salvadoran, 13.7 percent Honduran, and 6 percent Nicaraguan.

33. The Rwandan civil war began on April 6, 1994, when a plane crash killed President Juvenal Habyarimana and Cyprian Ntayamira, president of Burundi. By August more than 1 million Rwandans had fled to the Zairian border, including 500,000 who fled the country in just two days in mid-July. The *New York Times* and *Los Angeles Times* carried reports on the plight of the refugees almost daily through the summer of 1994. The *Los Angeles Times* reported that 1.2 million Rwandan refugees were living along the border of Zaire in mid-August.

34. Jan M. Olsen, Associated Press dispatch from Copenhagen, January 14, 1993. Danish Speaker of Parliament Hans Peter Clausen, who replaced Ninn-Hansen as justice minister, also resigned.

35. President George Bush pardoned six Iran-Contra conspirators on Christmas Eve 1992, four of whom had been convicted of or pleaded guilty to felonies and two of whom were awaiting trial. Former Secretary of Defense Caspar W. Weinberger was awaiting trial on charges of perjury and making false statements about a 1985 secret missile shipment to Iran; Clair E. George, head of CIA covert operations, was awaiting sentencing for two felony counts of lying to Congress; Duane R. "Dewey" Clarridge, a senior CIA official, was awaiting trial on seven counts of perjury and making false statements about a 1985 shipment of missiles to Iran; Assistant Secretary of State Elliott Abrams pleaded guilty in 1991 to withholding information from Congress and was sentenced to two years' probation and 100 hours of community service; Alan G. Fiers Jr., head of the CIA Central American Task Force, pleaded guilty to withholding information from Congress and was sentenced to one

year probation and 100 hours of community service; former National Security Adviser Robert C. McFarlane pleaded guilty in 1988 to withholding information from Congress and was fined $20,000 and sentenced to two years' probation and 200 hours of community service.

The controversial pardons came twelve days before Weinberger was to go to trial in "a case that was expected to focus on Mr. Weinberger's private notes that contain references to Mr. Bush's endorsement of the secret shipments to Iran," the New York Times reported. Iran-Contra special prosecutor Lawrence E. Walsh told the Times, "The Iran-Contra cover-up, which has continued for more than six years, has now been completed." "Bush Pardons 6 in Iran Affair, Averting a Weinberger Trial; Prosecutor Assails 'Cover Up' (-) Bush Diary at Issue (-) 6-Year Inquiry into Deal of Arms for Hostages All but Swept Away," New York Times, December 25, 1992.

36. Karen Parker, "Geneva Convention Protections of Salvadoran Refugees." This undated 1984 legal argument of twenty pages with ninety-two footnotes was submitted to immigration judge Michael Horn in the first Salvadoran political asylum case ever won by an attorney with Proyecto Libertad. The case involved a fisherman who had been tortured by his company's private death squad for trying to organize a union. Horn granted asylum in 1986, more than two years after hearing the case. Parker is a San Francisco attorney specializing in international law.

37. General Accounting Office, "Central American Refugees: Regional Conditions and Prospects and Potential Impact on the United States" (Washington, D.C., July 20, 1984), 10. A "country of first asylum" is the first country to which a refugee flees after leaving his or her homeland.

38. Ibid., 47.

39. See "Brownsville," note 7.

40. Benjamin C. Schwartz, "American Counterinsurgency Doctrine and El Salvador: The Frustrations of Reform and the Illusions of Nation Building" (report prepared for the undersecretary of defense for policy, RAND Corporation, Santa Monica, California, 1991), xiii.

Suggested Readings

Alegría, Claribel, and D. J. Flakoll. *Para Romper el Silencio—Resistencia y Lucha en las Cárceles Salvadoreñas,* Mexico City: Ediciones Era, 1984.

American Baptist Churches et al. v. Richard L. Thornburgh, Gene McNary, and James A. Baker III, U.S. District Court, Northern District of California, December 19, 1990, U.S. District Judge Robert Peckham.

Americas Watch Committee and the American Civil Liberties Union. *Report on Human Rights in El Salvador.* New York: Vintage Books, 1982.

———. *Second Supplement to the Report on Human Rights in El Salvador.* Washington, D.C.: Center for National Security Studies, 1983.

———. *Third Supplement to the Report on Human Rights in El Salvador.* Washington, D.C., July 19, 1983.

Analysis of the New Salvadoran Government and Its International Context. Frente Farabundo Martí para la Liberación Nacional–Frente Democrático Revolucionario, Political-Diplomatic Commission, El Salvador, June 1984.

Anderson, Scott, and Jon Lee Anderson. *Inside the League.* New York: Dodd, Mead, 1986.

Anderson, Thomas. *Matanza,* New York: Curbstone Press, 1992.

Arendt, Hannah. *Eichmann in Jerusalem: A Report on the Banality of Evil.* New York: Viking Penguin, 1994.

Bacevich, A. J., James D. Hallums, Richard H. White, and Thomas F. Young. *American Military Policy in Small Wars: The Case of El Salvador.* Washington, D.C.: Pergamon-Brassey's International Defense Publishers, Institute for Foreign Policy Analysis, 1988.

Barnet, Richard J. *Global Reach: The Power of the Multinational Corporations.* New York: Simon & Schuster, 1974.

Barriers to Reform: A Profile of El Salvador's Military Leaders. Report to the Arms Control and Foreign Policy Caucus, sponsored by Rep. Howard Berman, Sen. Mark Hatfield, and Rep. George Miller. Prepared by the staff of the Arms Control and Foreign Policy Caucus, Washington, D.C., May 21, 1990.

Barry, Tom, Beth Wood, and Deb Preusch. *Dollars and Dictators: A Guide to Central America.* New York: Grove Press, 1983.

Bolaños Hernandez v. INS, 767 F2d 1277, 1282 (9th Cir., 1984).

Bonner, Raymond. *Weakness and Deceit: U.S. Policy and El Salvador.* New York: Times Books, 1984.

Bricker, Victoria Reifler. *The Indian Christ, The Indian King: The Historical Substrate of Maya Myth and Ritual.* Austin: University of Texas Press, 1981.

Buendía, Manuel. *La CIA en México.* Océano, Fundación Manuel Buendía, Coyoacan, Mexico City, 1986.

Cardoza-Fonseca v. INS, 767 F2d 1448 (9th Cir., 1985).

Castillo, Otto René. *Informe de una injustícia,* San José, Costa Rica: Editorial Universitaria Centroamericana, 1982.

Clements, Charles. *Witness to War: An American Doctor in El Salvador.* New York: Bantam Books, 1984.

Conover, Ted. *Coyotes: A Journey. Through the Secret World, of America's Illegal Aliens.* New York: Vintage Books, 1987.

Crewdson, John. *The Tarnished Door.* New York: Times Books, 1983.

Dalton, Roque. *Miguel Marmol.* New York: Curbstone Press, 1987.

———. *Poesía escogida.* San José, Costa Rica: Editorial Universitaria Centroamericana, Colección Séptimo Día, 1983.

Danner, Mark. *The Massacre at El Mozote: A Parable of the Cold War.* New York: Vintage Books, 1994.

Decree 507, Salvadoran National Assembly, December 3, 1980.

Decree 50, Salvadoran National Assembly, February 24, 1984.

Despite a Generous Spirit: Denying Asylum in the United States. U.S. Committee for Refugees, American Council for Nationalities Service, Washington, D.C., 1986.

Dickey, Christopher. *With the Contras.* New York: Simon & Schuster, 1985.

Diederich, Bernard. *Somoza.* New York: Dutton, 1981.

Dillon, Sam. *Comandos: The CIA and Nicaragua's Contra Rebels.* New York: Henry Holt, 1991.

Durham, William. *Scarcity and Survival in Central America: Ecological Origins of the Soccer War.* Palo Alto, Calif.: Stanford University Press, 1979.

El Salvador and Human Rights: The Challenge of Reform. Washington, D.C.: Americas Watch, 1991.

El Salvador's Decade of Terror: Human Rights Since the Assassination of Archbishop Romero. New York: Human Rights Watch and Americas Watch, 1991.

Failure: The Reagan Administration's Human Rights Policy in 1983. New York: Americas Watch, Helsinki Watch, and Lawyers Committee for International Human Rights, January 1984.

Jenny Lisette Flores et al. v. Edwin Meese III et al., "Opinion." U.S. Circuit Judge J. Clifford Wallace, U.S. Court of Appeals for the Ninth Circuit, June 20, 1990.

Free Fire: A Report on Human Rights in El Salvador. New York: Americas Watch, August 1984.

Frelick, Bill. *The Back of the Hand: Bias and Restrictionism Towards Central American Asylum Seekers in North America.* Washington, D.C.: U.S. Committee for Refugees Issue Brief, October 1988.

Fried, Jonathan, Marvin Gettleman, Deborah Levenson, and Nancy Peckenham, eds. *Guatemala in Rebellion.* New York: Grove Press, 1983.

García Márquez, Gabriel. "Los Sandinistas se toman el Palacio Nacional de Managua." Introduction to *La Batalla de Nicaragua,* by Gabriel García Márquez, Gregorio Selser, and Daniel Waksman Schinca. Mexico City: Bruguera Mexicana de Ediciones, 1979.

Garcia-Mir v. Smith, 766 F2d 1478 (11th Cir., 1985); *cert denied sub nom Marques-Melding,* 106 Sup. Ct. 1213 (1986).

Gelbspan, Ross. *Break-ins, Death Threats and the FBI: The Covert War Against the Central America Movement.* Boston: South End Press, 1991.

Guatemala: A Nation of Prisoners. New York: Americas Watch, January 1984.

Guatemalan Refugees in Mexico 1980–1984. New York: Americas Watch, September 1984.

Guevara, Che. *Guerrilla Warfare.* New York: Monthly Review Press, 1961.

Gutman, Roy. *Banana Diplomacy: The Making of American Policy in Nicaragua 1981–1987.* New York: Simon & Schuster, 1988.

Haggerty, Richard A., ed. *El Salvador: A Country Study,* Area Handbook Series. Washington, D.C.: GPO, 1990.

Haitian Refugee Center v. Meese, 791 F2d 1489-99 (11th Cir., 1986).

Harbury, Jennifer. *Bridge of Courage.* Monroe, Me.: Common Courage Press, 1993.

Herman, Judith Lewis. *Trauma and Recovery: The Aftermath of Violence—From Domestic Abuse to Political Terror.* New York: Basic Books, 1992.

Herrera-Bonilla v. Alan Nelson, U.S. District Court, Eastern District of New York, 86-2353, July 15, 1986.

Holguin, Carlos. *Children in INS Prisons: An Educational Assessment.* Prepared by the National Center for Immigrants' Rights in Los Angeles for the National Coalition of Advocates for Students, Boston, 1985.

Honduras: On the Brink, A Report on Human Rights Based on a Mission of Inquiry. Americas Watch, Lawyers Committee for International Human Rights, and the Washington Office on Latin America, February 1984.

Human Rights in Guatemala: No Neutrals Allowed. New York: Americas Watch, 1982.

Human Rights in Mexico: A Policy of Impunity. New York: Americas Watch, June 1990.

Human Rights in Nicaragua. New York: Americas Watch, April 1984.

Human Rights in Nicaragua, 1985–86. New York: Americas Watch, March 1986.

Immigration Act of 1990, 101st Cong., 2d sess. Report 101-955, October 26, 1990.

Immigration and Nationality Act. U.S. Congress, 1952.

The Immigration and Naturalization Service: Overwhelmed and Unprepared for the Future. Second report by the Committee on Government Operations, August 4, 1993.

Immigration and Naturalization Service v. Stevic, 104 Sup. Ct. 2489 (1984).

Immigration and Naturalization Service v. Elias-Zacarias, U.S. Supreme Court, Certiorari to the U.S. Court of Appeals for the Ninth Circuit, January 22, 1992.

Immigration Reform and Control Act. U.S. Congress, November 6, 1986.

"... in the face of cruelty": The Reagan Administration's Human Rights Record in 1984. Americas Watch, Helsinki Watch, and Lawyers Committee for International Human Rights, January 1985.

Interim Report of the Speaker's Task Force on El Salvador, April 30, 1990. U.S. Congress Central American Task Force, U.S. Rep. Joseph Moakley, chairman; and January 7, 1991, letter to Moakley from staff members Jim McGovern and Bill Woodward, "Staff trip to El Salvador."

Japanese Relocation Act. U.S. Congress, February 18, 1942.

Jean v. Nelson, 472 U.S. 846, 105 S.Ct. 2992, 86 L.Ed.2d 664 (1985).

Jungle Operations. Department of the Army Field Manual no. 31–35. Washington, D.C., September 1969.

LaFeber, Walter. *Inevitable Revolutions: The United States in Central America.* New York: W. W. Norton, 1983.

La Palma: A Hope for Peace. The Recognition of the Existence of Dual Power in El Salvador. Frente Farabundo Martí para la Liberación Nacional–Frente Democrático Revolucionario, Political-Diplomatic Commission, El Salvador, November 1984.

Lernoux, Penny. *Cry of the People.* Garden City, N.Y.: Doubleday, 1980.

———. *In Banks We Trust.* Garden City, N.Y.: Anchor Press/Doubleday, 1984.

———. *Fear and Hope: Toward Political Democracy in Central America.* New York: The Field Foundation, 1984.

———. *People of God: The Struggle for World Catholicism.* New York: Viking, 1989.

Little, Cheryl. *Conditions at Krome North Service Processing Center.* Miami: Haitian Refugee Center, June 1991.

Malan, Rian. *My Traitor's Heart.* New York: Atlantic Monthly Press, 1990.

McClintock, Michael. *The American Connection.* vol. 1: *State Terror and Popular Resistance in El Salvador.* vol. 2: *State Terror and Popular Resistance in Guatemala.* Avon, England: Zed Books, 1985.

Menchu, Rigoberta. *I, Rigoberta Menchu.* New York: Verso, 1984.

Methodology at Odds with Knowledge. New York: Americas Watch, 1982.

The Miskitos in Nicaragua, 1981–84. New York: Americas Watch, November 1984.

Montes, Segundo. *Salvadoreños refugiados en los Estados Unidos.* San Salvador, El Salvador: Instituto de Investigaciones y Instituto de Derechos Humanos, Universidad de Centroamerica José Simeon Cañas, 1987.

———. *El Salvador 1989: Las remesas que envian los salvadoreños de Estados Unidos; consecuencias sociales y económicos.* San Salvador, El Salvador: Universidad de Centroamerica José Simeon Cañas, 1990.

Montgomery, Tommie Sue. *Revolution in El Salvador.* Boulder, Colo.: Westview Press, 1994.

Morazan, Vasquez, et al. v. Richard Thornburgh and Alan Nelson, U.S. District Court, Southern District of Texas, January 6, 1989.

Nelson, Alan. Letter to Sharon House, Congressional Research Service, Education and Public Welfare Division, Library of Congress. Letter date-stamped June 26, 1984, from INS Commissioner in response to congressional inquiries about immigration prisons.

Neruda, Pablo. *Canto General.* Barcelona: Bruguera, 1980.

New Voices: Immigrant Students in U.S. Public Schools. Boston: National Coalition of Advocates for Students, 1988.

North, Oliver, with William Novak. *Under Fire.* New York: HarperCollins, 1991.

Noe Castillo Nuñez et al. v. Hal Boldin et al., "Memorandum and Order." U.S. District Judge Filemon B. Vela, U.S. District Court for the Southern District of Texas, Brownsville Decision, April 6, 1982.

Nyrop, Richard F., ed. *Guatemala: A Country Study.* Area Handbook Series. Washington, D.C.: U.S. Department of the Army, May 1983.

Oakdale Legal Assistance et al. v. Steven Schwalb et al., U.S. District Court, Lake Charles, La., August 27, 1986.

Crosby Wilfredo Orantes-Hernandez et al. v. Edwin Meese, Attorney General of the United States. "Deposition of Robert Kahn," July 24, 1985, Phoenix, Az.

Orantes-Hernandez v. Meese, "Affidavit of Steve Schwalb," July 8, 1986.

Orantes-Hernandez v. William French Smith, "Affidavit of Jules Bassin," September 28, 1983.

Crosby Wilfredo Orantes-Hernandez et al. v. Richard Thornburgh, Attorney General of the United States, "Order and Preliminary Injunction." U.S. District Court, Central District of California, April 28, 1989, Judge David V. Kenyon.

Orantes-Hernandez v. Thornburgh, U.S. Court of Appeals for the Ninth Circuit, November 20, 1990.

Parker, Karen. *Geneva Convention Protections of Salvadoran Refugees*. Unpublished, 1984.

Payeras, Mario. *Los Días de la Selva*. Mexico City: Editorial Nuestro Tiempo, 1983.

Guillermo Perez Fuentes et al. v. Omer G. Sewell et al., Civil Action no. B-88-101, U.S. District Court, Brownsville, Texas, August 15, 1988.

José Antonio Perez-Funez v. INS, "Opinion." U.S. District Judge Edward Rafeedie, U.S. District Court, Central District of California, January 24, 1984.

Plyler v. Doe, U.S. Supreme Court, 1982.

Popol Vuh. Translated from Mayan to Spanish by Adrián Recinos. Colección Popular. Mexico City: Fondo de Cultura Económica, 1981.

Refugee Problems in Central America. Staff report prepared for the use of the Subcommittee on Immigration and Refugee Policy, Committee on the Judiciary, U.S. Senate, September 1983.

El Rescate Legal Services et al. v. Executive Office for Immigration Review et al., "Memorandum of Decision." U.S. District Judge William P. Gray, U.S. District Court, Central District of California, December 14, 1989.

Rudolph, James D., ed. *Nicaragua: A Country Study*. Area Handbook Series. U.S. Department of the Army, Washington, D.C., 1982.

Salvadorans in the United States: The Case for Extended Voluntary Departure. Report no. 1. Washington, D.C.: ACLU National Immigration and Alien Rights Project, April 1984.

Scholes, France V., and Ralph L. Roys. *The Maya Chontal Indians of Acalan-Tixchel: A Contribution to the History and Ethnography of the Yucatan Peninsula*. Norman: University of Oklahoma Press, 1968.

Schwartz, Benjamin. *American Counterinsurgency Doctrine and El Salvador*. Prepared for the Undersecretary of Defense for Policy. Santa Monica, Calif.: RAND Corporation, 1991.

Solzhenitsyn, Aleksandr I. *The Gulag Archipelago*. 3 vols. New York: Harper & Row, 1974.

State of Texas v. Bruce A. Shirley, Lawrence N. Shea and Fernando Luna, Sr. d/b/a Oficina de Relaciones Latinas y Servicios para Inmigrantes and Servicios para Inmigrantes, Inc., "Plaintiff's Original Petition." June 16, 1987, and "Final Judgment and Agreed Permanent Injunction." January 28, 1988. Harris County District Court.

"Statement by Principal Deputy Press Secretary Speaks on Economic Sanctions Against Nicaragua," *Presidential Papers: Administration of Ronald Reagan, 1985*, May 1.

"Text of State Department Report on Communist Support of Salvadoran Rebels." *New York Times*, February 24, 1981.

Timerman, Jacobo. *Prisoner Without a Name, Cell Without a Number*. New York: Vintage Books, 1981.

Torture in El Salvador. Compiled in Mariona prison, Ayutuxtepeque, El Salvador, by members of the Salvadoran Non-Governmental Human Rights Commission (*Comisión de Derechos Humanos de El Salvador*). Trans. by Lisa Brodyaga. September 24, 1986.

Tower, John, Edmund Muskie, and Brent Scowcroft. *The Tower Commission Report.* New York: Times Books, 1987.

Unauthorized Migration: An Economic Development Response. Commission for the Study of International Migration and Cooperative Economic Development. Washington, D.C., July 1990.

United States of America v. Stacey Lynn Merkt, Fifth U.S. Circuit Court of Appeals, June 18, 1985. Conviction reversed and remanded, 764 F2d 266.

U.S. Code of Regulations. vol. 8: *Immigration.*

U.S. Congressional Research Service. Translation of indictment and arrest order for Guillermo Alfredo Benavides Moreno, Yusshi René Mendoza Vallecillos, José Ricardo Espinoza Guerra, Gonzalo Guevara Cerritos, Antonio Ramiro Avalos Vargas, Tomás Zarpate Castillo, Angel Pérez Vásquez, and Jorge Alberto Cierra Ascencio for the murders of Ignacio Ellacuría, Segundo Montes, Ignacio Martín Baró, Juan Ramón Moreno, Amando López, Joaquín López y López, Elba Julia Ramos, and Celina Ramos. Filed in the Fourth Criminal Court of San Salvador, 3:45 P.M., January 18, 1990. Attached to a letter date-stamped April 10, 1990, from Carl W. Ford Jr., Acting Assistant Secretary of Defense for International Security Affairs, to U.S. Rep. Joseph Moakley.

U.S. General Accounting Office. *Central American Refugees: Regional Conditions and Prospects and Potential Impact on the United States.* Publication no. NSIAD-84-106. July 20, 1984.

———. *Financial Management: INS Lacks Accountability and Controls over Its Resources.* Draft report. Washington, D.C., November 1990.

U.S. Department of State. *Country Reports on Human Rights Practices for 1984.* Report submitted to the Committee on Foreign Relations, U.S. Senate, and Committee on Foreign Affairs, U.S. House of Representatives, February 1985.

U.S. House Committee on Foreign Affairs. Subcommittee on Human Rights and International Relations and on Western Hemisphere Affairs. *Human Rights in El Salvador: Hearings.* 98th Cong., 1st sess., July 26, 1983.

U.S. House Committee on Rules. Subcommittee on Rules. *Extended Voluntary Departure for Salvadorans: Hearings on H.R. 4447,* June 20, 1984.

U.S. Immigration and Naturalization Service. *Asylum Adjudications: An Evolving Concept and Responsibility for the Immigration and Naturalization Service.* INS report. Washington, D.C., June and December 1982.

———. *Nicaraguan Asylum/Harlingen Situation.* From INS Deputy Commissioner James L. Buck to INS Executive Staff, December 5, 1988.

———. *Enhancement Plan for the Southern Border.* February 16, 1989.

U.S. Senate. Committee on the Judiciary. Subcommittee on Security and Terrorism. *Marxism and Christianity in Revolutionary Central America: Hearings.* 98th Cong., 1st sess., October 18 and 19, 1983.

Velasquez v. Nelson, U.S. District Court, Southern District of Florida, 86-1262, June 13, 1986.

Waghelstein, John D. *El Salvador: Observations and Experiences in Counterinsurgency.* Carlisle, Pa.: U.S. Army War College, January 1, 1985.

Weisman, Alan. *La Frontera: The United States Border with Mexico*. Tucson: University of Arizona Press, 1991.

Weschler, Lawrence. *A Miracle a Universe: Settling Accounts with Torturers*. New York: Pantheon, 1990.

Wolf, Eric. *Sons of the Shaking Earth*. Chicago: University of Chicago Press, 1959.

World Refugee Survey, 1992. U.S. Committee for Refugees, Washington, D.C. 1992.

World Refugee Survey, 1995. U.S. Committee for Refugees, Washington, D.C. 1995.

About the Book

During the 1980s hundreds of thousands of refugees fled civil wars and death squads in Central America, seeking safe haven in the United States. Instead, thousands found themselves incarcerated in immigration prisons— abused by their jailors and deprived of the most basic legal and human rights. Drawing on declassified government documents and interviews with prison officials, INS staff, and more than 3,000 Central American refugees, Robert S. Kahn reveals how the Department of Justice and its dependent agency, the Immigration and Naturalization Service, intentionally violated federal laws and regulations to deny protection to refugees from El Salvador and Guatemala who were fleeing wars financed by U.S. military aid.

Kahn portrays the chilling reality of daily life in immigration prisons in Texas, Arizona, and Louisiana. Behind the razor-topped prison walls, refugees were not simply denied political asylum; they were beaten, robbed, sexually assaulted, and sometimes tortured by prison guards.

Other People's Blood traces the ten-year legal struggle by volunteer prison workers and attorneys to stop the abuse of refugees and to force the Justice Department to concede in court that its treatment of immigrants had violated U.S. laws and the Geneva Conventions for over a decade. Yet the case of *American Baptist Churches v. Thornburgh*, which overturned more judicial decisions than any other case in U.S. history, is still virtually unknown in the United States, and today the debate over illegal immigration is being carried on with little awareness of the government policies that contributed so shamefully to this country's immigration problems.

Robert S. Kahn is a newspaper editor and freelance writer in California. His investigations of INS abuses in immigration prisons have appeared in the *Boston Globe,* the *Baltimore Sun,* and the *National Catholic Reporter.*

INDEX